teach® yourself

the internet and email for the over 50s

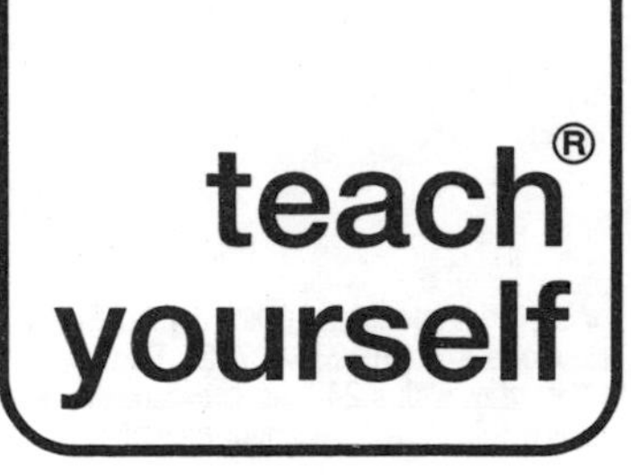

the internet and email for the over 50s

bob reeves

Launched in 1938, the **teach yourself** series grew rapidly in response to the world's wartime needs. Loved and trusted by over 50 million readers, the series has continued to respond to society's changing interests and passions and now, 70 years on, includes over 500 titles, from Arabic and Beekeeping to Yoga and Zulu. What would you like to learn?

be where you want to be with **teach yourself**

For UK order enquiries: please contact Bookpoint Ltd, 130 Milton Park, Abingdon, Oxon OX14 4SB. Telephone: +44 (0) 1235 827720. Fax: +44 (0) 1235 400454. Lines are open 09.00–17.00, Monday to Saturday, with a 24-hour message answering service. Details about our titles and how to order are available at www.teachyourself.co.uk

For USA order enquiries: please contact McGraw-Hill Customer Services, PO Box 545, Blacklick, OH 43004-0545, USA. Telephone: 1-800-722-4726. Fax: 1-614-755-5645.

For Canada order enquiries: please contact McGraw-Hill Ryerson Ltd, 300 Water St, Whitby, Ontario L1N 9B6, Canada. Telephone: 905 430 5000. Fax: 905 430 5020.

Long renowned as the authoritative source for self-guided learning – with more than 50 million copies sold worldwide – the **teach yourself** series includes over 500 titles in the fields of languages, crafts, hobbies, business, computing and education.

British Library Cataloguing in Publication Data: a catalogue record for this title is available from the British Library.

Library of Congress Catalog Card Number: on file.

First published in UK 2007 by Hodder Education, part of Hachette Livre UK, 338 Euston Road, London, NW1 3BH.

First published in US 2007 by The McGraw-Hill Companies, Inc.

The **teach yourself** name is a registered trade mark of Hodder Headline.

Typeset by Servis Filmsetting Ltd, Manchester.
Printed in Great Britain for Hodder Education, an Hachette Livre UK Company, 338 Euston Road, London NW1 3BH, by Cox & Wyman Ltd, Reading, Berkshire.

Hachette Livre UK's policy is to use papers that are natural, renewable and recyclable products and made from wood grown in sustainable forests. The logging and manufacturing processes are expected to conform to the environmental regulations of the country of origin.

Impression number 10 9 8 7 6 5 4 3 2

Year 2011 2010 2009 2008

contents

preface

This book is specifically designed for the more mature newcomer who wants to get to grips with the Internet and email. It assumes no prior knowledge of using a computer.

Jargon has been kept to a minimum and, where it has been used, it is clearly highlighted and referenced by a full 'jargon-busting' glossary with all glossary terms **highlighted in bold** in the text.

You can work your way through the chapters in order or you can dip in to the bits you are interested in. Before you dip in, if you are a complete novice user it is recommended that you first read through:

- Chapters 1–4, which cover general computing basics.
- Chapters 9–10, which cover the basics of using the Internet.

Some of the chapters share common themes so you may want to work through those in sequence:

- Chapters 5–8 cover all aspects of email.
- Chapters 11–14 are related to other ways of communicating with others using the Internet.
- Chapters 15 and 16 are about Internet safety.

Chapters 17–26 then cover using the Internet for everything from shopping to dating and pretty much anything else you can think of.

Once you have developed the basic skills for searching the Internet and finding your way around websites, you will soon be able to find your way to anything you want on the Internet even if the topic in which you are interested isn't covered specifically in this book. There are hints and tips throughout the chapters to help you on your way.

The book uses examples from the most common programs being used at present including Internet Explorer® 7 and Outlook Express®. It also uses other programs that are freely available to download from the Internet.

Finally, when you first start, computers can be a bit scary. One mature evening-class student commented that the computer screen is so cluttered it looks like a flight deck on an aeroplane with little buttons and signs all over the place. However, the big difference is that if you go wrong on the computer, it doesn't matter. Your computer is virtually impossible to break – so don't be scared of it, just click away and see what happens. Have fun.

Readers looking for a more general introduction to all aspects of computing may also be interested in *Teach Yourself Computing for the Over 50s*, also in the Teach Yourself series.

choosing a computer

In this chapter you will learn:

- **what the main parts of the computer are**
- **how to understand a computer specification**
- **what specification of computer you need to give you access to the Internet and to email**
- **how to choose an ISP and what connection speed to go for**
- **how to make your decision of what to buy and where to buy it**

Aims of this chapter

There is a bewildering choice when it comes to buying a computer. There are hundreds of different options, and you can end up spending a lot of money on things that you don't really need. This chapter will help you to work out what computer will be the most suitable for using the Internet, for using email, and for other things that you may want to do. Whether you are buying a computer for the first time, or perhaps upgrading to a new one, this chapter will help you decide what to get.

1.1 The computer system

When you buy a computer the manufacturer will publish the specification of the computer. A basic **computer system** is made up of the base unit, sometimes called a tower, a screen, **keyboard, mouse** and printer. Computer equipment such as this is called **hardware.**

You will also need what is called **software.** This refers to the programs that you will run on the computer. Programs are needed to let you do all the things you want to do like send emails and get onto the Internet.

A screen, tower, keyboard and mouse © iStockphoto.com/Clément Contet

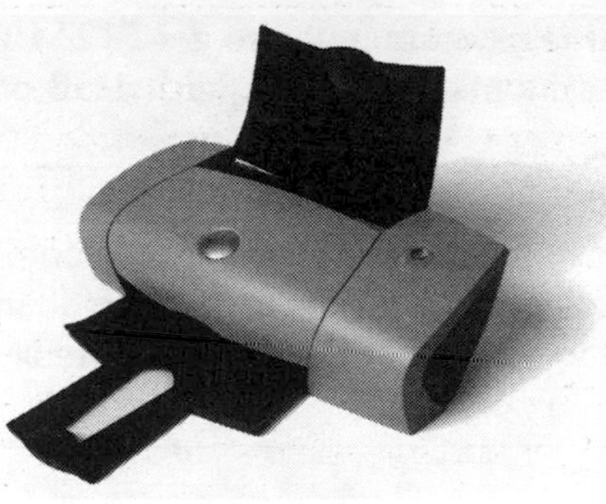

A printer © iStockphoto.com/Dennys Bisogno

The price of the computer is usually based on how fast it works and how much information you want to keep on it.

1.2 What you will need

The base unit or tower is where all the clever stuff goes on. The main features to look for when you are choosing your computer are:

Processor

The processor is the brains of the computer. Everything that is done on the computer goes through the processor. The speed is measured in **gigahertz (GHz)**. The simple rule is the higher the number of GHz, the faster your computer will work. Anything over 2GHz is perfectly adequate for most computer users.

Memory

This is sometimes called **RAM (random access memory)**. This is measured in megabytes (MB) or possibly gigabytes (GB). A gigabyte is 1000 times bigger than a megabyte. The simple rule here is the higher the number of MB (or GB), the faster your computer will run. Anything over 256MB is perfectly adequate for most computer users although it is recommended to get 512MB or more. Many computer systems now come with 1GB of memory.

Hints and tips
How important is speed? All modern computers are fast. Most things you do on the computer, such as surfing the Internet and emailing, do not require a really fast processor or lots of memory.

Hard disk (HDD)

This is the amount of information that the computer can store. Information is a very general term here and could mean words, numbers, pictures, movies or music. The size of the hard disk is measured in gigabtyes (GB) and, you guessed it – the bigger the number, the more information it will store. Anything over 80GB is more than adequate for most computer users, although it depends what you will be doing on the Internet. For example, if you plan to **download** lots of music and movies, you might choose to buy a bigger hard disk.

CD or DVD drive

These are the trays in the front of the tower that slide out so that you can put in a CD or DVD. CDs and DVDs have all sorts of information on them including computer programs, data and films. It is recommended that you get a DVD drive as these will cope with CDs and DVDs. A CD drive will only cope with CDs.

Sometimes the speed of the CD or DVD drive is shown. This is the speed at which it writes information onto the disk. Anything over 52× is perfectly adequate for most computer users.

Hints and tips
Computer manufacturers bring out new computers all the time, with faster processors and increased memory. This

means that your computer will start to become out-of-date quite quickly. This does not really matter for most users and a computer you buy now should be perfectly adequate for several years.

Monitor

This is the screen on which everything is displayed. As with the computer tower, there are thousands of variations to choose from. Most monitors now are flat, which means that they take up only a small amount of space on your desk. They also have less glare than earlier models, so it is recommended to get a flat screen. The main decision is about the size of the screen. The size is measured in good old-fashioned inches. Standard sizes are from 15 to 19 inches. Bigger screens are more expensive but are much easier to read. The best advice is to go to a shop and have a look at the different sizes.

Keyboard and mouse

You don't usually get much choice with these, as your computer will come with a standard keyboard and mouse. All keyboards are pretty much the same and you use them for typing in letters and numbers. The mouse is a pointing device. You point at things on the screen and click the buttons to make things happen. If you don't like wires everywhere, you can buy in a wireless mouse.

Hints and tips
Almost every keyboard is a QWERTY keyboard. This is due to the layout of the letters on the keyboard – the first six letters starting from the top left spell QWERTY. This layout is exactly the same as on typewriters.

Printer

This is for producing printed copies of anything you do on your computer. As with everything else to do with computers, there are thousands to choose from. The main decisions are whether you want an **inkjet** or a **laser** printer and whether you want colour or just black-and-white printouts. Inkjets are cheaper to buy, but the **ink cartridges** can run out quickly and are expensive to replace. Laser printers are more expensive to buy, produce slightly better quality and print more quickly. They use **toner** rather than ink. Toner cartridges are also expensive but do last quite a long time.

Colour printing is more expensive than black-and-white printing as you have to buy colour ink (or toner) cartridges as well as black cartridges. If you are unsure, the best bet is probably to buy a colour printer as this leaves your options open.

Hints and tips
Some printers can also be used as a **scanner** and a photocopier. If you think you will need to scan or copy documents, then it would be worth having a look at one of these.

1.3 The operating system

You will also need to choose what software you want. When you buy your hardware, you sometimes get some software with it. There is more on this in the next chapter, but at this stage you must make sure that the computer you buy comes with an **operating system**. This is a program that enables your computer to work and it is essential. The most common operating system is Microsoft Windows®, which normally comes 'bundled' with the computer (i.e. it is included in the price of the computer). Make sure any computer you choose has an operating system installed on it already.

Hints and tips
There are many different versions of Windows® and new versions come out all the time. Most new computers come

with Windows Vista™. The version before that was called Windows XP®. Either version is fine. Given the choice, you should go for Vista™ as it is the most recent.

1.4 Plugging in things using USB ports

In the next chapter, you will learn about a range of additional **devices** that can be plugged into your computer. Most of these devices attach using a **USB** connection. Make sure your computer has got at least six **USB ports.** A port is computer-speak for a socket where you can plug in something. This will allow up to six different devices to be plugged in at the same time.

USB ports

1.5 Connecting to the Internet

In order to connect to the Internet you will need a **modem**. This is a device that may be built into the desktop, or plugged into the back of the computer. You have to choose which company to get your Internet connection from, for example Tiscali, BT, AOL, etc. These are called **Internet Service Providers (ISPs)** and, as well as giving you access to the Internet, they will normally supply you with a modem to plug into one of the USB ports. The other end plugs into the telephone socket. You will also be supplied with **filters**, which you need to plug into any other phone sockets. These enable you to make phone calls while using the Internet at the same time.

If **broadband** Internet is available in your area then it is recommended that you get it. Broadband means that the access to all of the information on the Internet is quite quick. Without broadband, access is painfully slow.

You need to shop around for your ISP as there are several options. You can get access to the Internet through your normal phone line, or through cable if you are in area that has cable. With cable, you will be able to get a package that gives you TV channels, telephone calls and broadband Internet for a set monthly fee. In areas without cable, you can get a package that gives you telephone calls and broadband Internet for a set monthly fee. Alternatively, you can just pay for your phone and broadband separately.

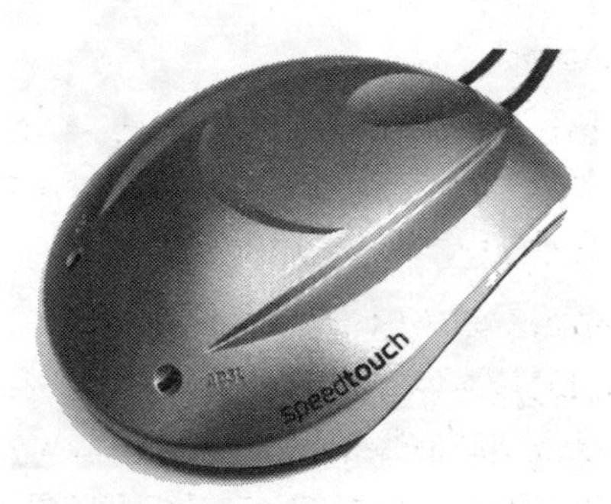

A modem

1.6 Internet connection speeds

When you are choosing your ISP you need to look at the 'connection speeds' that they offer. This refers to how quickly the information on the Internet will appear on your screen. Connection speeds are measured in **kilobits per second (kbps)** or **megabits per second (mbps)**. The higher the number, the faster you will be able to get information from the Internet. Typical connection speeds are anywhere between 512kbps (usually called 512K), all the way up to 10mbps. In some areas you will not be able to get very high-speed connections and you might not have any choice; 512K or 1MB is sufficient for most Internet users. If you think you will be downloading lots of music or movies, then you should see if you can get a faster connection speed.

Hints and tips
Ask your friends and relatives which ISP they use. Go on recommendation if you can.

1.7 Where to buy your computer

As you will discover when you try to buy a computer, there are several different manufacturers to choose from and you can buy from a range of places. Generally speaking, you get what you pay for and it pays to shop around.

High Street chains

These are quite competitive on price and have a good selection of computers. They are a safe bet if you don't have a good local specialist.

Specialist computer shops

The level of advice you get will probably be a lot better in a specialist computer shop, though they may not be able to be as competitive on price. They are usually very good at looking after you if you have any problems later. It's good if you can find one that comes recommended.

The Internet/mail order

You can get some real bargains from catalogues and the Internet (if you have access). Internet and mail order businesses don't have the overheads that the shops do and this is how they can do it cheaper. The disadvantage is that you won't get to see the computer 'in the flesh' before you buy it. Use a bigger company that you have heard of or that has been recommended. You could always find the one you want in a shop and then see if you can get the same thing cheaper on the Internet.

Warranties

Most new computers come with at least one year's warranty although this can be extended to three. Most warranties require the computer to be sent to the manufacturer, which means you will be without it for a week or so.

Summary

In this chapter we have discussed:

- What hardware (equipment) you need
- What 'specification' of computer you need
- How to choose an ISP
- What connection speed you need for the Internet
- Where to get a computer from

02 choosing other equipment you might need

In this chapter you will learn:

- **what other computer equipment you might need**
- **what specification of equipment is needed**

Aims of this chapter
Once you have chosen the basic computer system, you are now faced with another bewildering selection of equipment and devices that you can plug into your computer. These are sometimes referred to as computer peripherals. This chapter aims to explain the most common peripherals and advise on whether you need them or not, and what type to buy. This chapter looks at devices that you are most likely to need if you are using your computer mainly for Internet and email.

2.1 What peripherals do you need?

Many of the **peripherals** that you can buy have quite specific functions, so it is not worth investing in them unless you have good reason to do so. Most devices these days plug into your computer using a **USB** connection, which is why it is recommended that you get at least six **USB ports**.

Hints and tips
Most devices are now 'plug and play', which means that when you plug them in, the computer spots that they have been plugged in and they will work automatically.

Digital camera

You might choose to buy a digital camera if you want to be able to take and then send photographs to other people over the Internet. Any digital camera you buy can be plugged into any computer.

Digital cameras do not use film. Instead, they store the image electronically on a **card** that slots into the camera. You can store hundreds of images on a card and can transfer the images onto your computer where you can store and print them or send them to other people.

The main things to look for when buying a digital camera are:

Megapixels

This refers to the number of tiny dots used to make up the image. The larger the number of **megapixels**, the better clarity you get in your finished photographs. Anything over 3 megapixels is adequate for the average photographer.

Optical and digital zoom

This refers to the amount of magnification you can get, that is how far you can focus in on images that are far away. Optical zoom is better as it is achieved using the camera's lens: 3× optical zoom is usually sufficient. Digital zoom digitally zooms in on the image: 6× digital zoom is perfectly adequate.

LCD

This is the small screen that you use to preview the image. The size is measured in inches: 2.5 inches is adequate although larger screens are easier to see.

> **Hints and tips**
> You can also buy digital camcorders, which you can use to record moving images. Like a digital camera, you can transfer the images onto your computer where you can watch the film you have made, or send it to other people.

Web cam

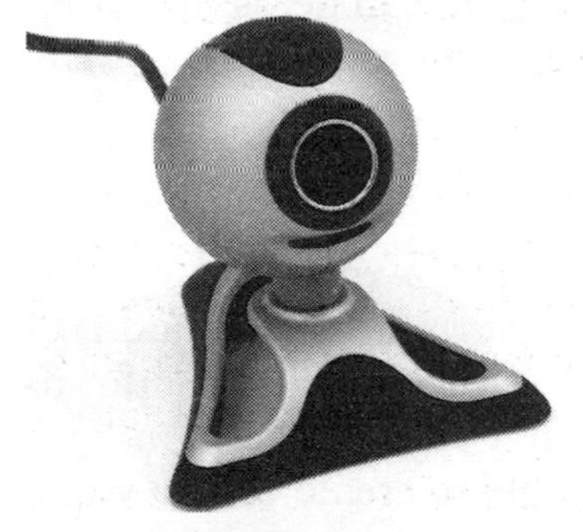

A web cam © iStockphoto.com/Mark Hayes

A **web cam** is a camera that you place on top of your monitor, which takes moving pictures of you! The idea of this is that you can contact people over the Internet and they can see and hear you while you are talking to them. If they have a web cam at their end, you can see them too. These are particularly useful if you have friends in other countries who you would like to see and hear, rather than just write to. Choose a web cam that has a **resolution** of 640×480 or higher. The higher the resolution, the clearer the images will be. If you want to be heard, you will need a web cam with a built-in microphone too.

Internet phone

These are special phones that plug into one of the USB ports. You can use them to make phone calls over the Internet. It is possible to buy phones that let you make 'normal' calls and Internet calls.

Speakers

These are just the same as the speakers in your Hi-Fi system or radio except you plug them into the back of your computer. You will need speakers if you want to play music or videos, or if you want to talk to other people over the Internet, for example, using a web cam. Make sure that you choose speakers that plug into the electricity supply otherwise they will not be loud enough. The amount of volume you can get is measured in watts (W). More watts means more volume.

CD/DVD rewriter

This allows you to make your own CDs or DVDs. There are many different formats of CD and DVD. A standard CD or DVD will allow you to read information from the disk, but not to put any information back onto it. You may want to be able to create (burn) your own CDs and DVDs. For example, if you download music or films from

A CD/DVD tray

the Internet, you may want to burn it onto a DVD. You can then listen to the music or watch the film straight from the DVD.

If you think you may want to do this, then you should make sure that you get a CD-R, CD-RW or DVD-R or DVD-RW. The R means recordable and the RW means rewritable. You can buy some that plug into a USB port or you can have one put into your base unit/tower.

Memory stick

This device is not specifically for Internet or email use but it can be a very useful and inexpensive item to have. A memory stick is a small storage device that lets you store information in a portable way. If you ever need to move information from one computer to another, then you will need one of these. It plugs into the USB port and you can

A memory stick

copy information onto it and then take it with you. For example, if you go to an evening class and want to take in some work that you did on your home computer, then you can use a memory stick. The amount that a memory stick can store is measured in **megabtyes** (**MB**) or **gigabytes** (**GB**). If you think you will be transferring lots of music or video, then you should buy a 1GB or 2GB memory stick. If not, 128MB or above will be adequate.

Summary

In this chapter we have discussed:

- What extra computer equipment (peripherals) you might need
- What 'specification' of peripheral to buy
- Digital cameras
- Web cams
- Speakers
- CD and DVD burners
- Memory sticks

03 choosing the programs (software) you might need

In this chapter you will learn:

- **what a computer program is**
- **which computer programs are essential**
- **what computer programs you might need**
- **about software versions**
- **about software that comes with devices**
- **about free software**
- **about licences**

Aims of this chapter

Once you have chosen your computer system and any other devices that you might need, you must then select which programs you want on your computer. Programs, or software allow you to use your computer to do all the things you want, such as emailing and surfing the Internet. This chapter will explain the most common types of software and look at all the software you may need.

3.1 What software do you need?

Software allows you to do the things you want to do. Without software, you can't do anything with your computer – it is just a pile of useless equipment. There are different types of software, each of which allows you to carry out different jobs on your computer. You may have heard of some already. For example: 'web browser' software is needed to access the Internet; 'email software' is needed to send and receive emails.

Some of the biggest businesses in the world are involved in making and selling software. It is a very competitive market, and these companies are always trying to get you to use their software. You may have heard of some of them, for example, Microsoft and Google.

This unit will look at some of the most common brand name software available.

Microsoft is the biggest name in standard software. Its owner, Bill Gates, is the richest man in the world. Microsoft is responsible for Internet Explorer®, Outlook® and Hotmail®, which are some of the most common software used for Internet and email. They also make Windows®. Now you can see why he's the richest man in the world!

Microsoft Outlook®/Outlook Express®

These are both email programs. You have to pay for Outlook®, which you can buy separately, or as part of

Microsoft® Office. You may have this on your computer already. You can get Outlook Express® for free as it comes with **Internet Explorer®**. We will use Outlook Express® as an example later in the book, though there are lots of other email programs you could use.

Hints and tips
Even if you do not plan to use email, you will probably still need an email address. This is because many websites ask you to register with them before you can use their website. The registration process is done using email.

Internet Explorer®

This is called a **browser** and is needed to view all of the information on the Internet. Internet Explorer® (IE) is usually found on any computer that has Windows® on it – so you have probably already got it. The latest version is called Internet Explorer® 7 and we will be using this throughout the book.

Web-based email

Most email software is **web-based**. This means that you do not need to buy it as you can use it for free on the Internet. An advantage of web-based software is that you can use it from anyone's computer – you do not have to use your own. Examples of free **web-based email** software are Gmail™, and Yahoo!® Mail. You will also get free email access from your **Internet Service Provider** (ISP).

Anti-virus

This software stops your computer getting infected with computer **viruses**. Viruses are small programs written by people with nothing better to do. They attack your computer and can damage it or the information that is on it. Anti-virus software searches your computer for viruses and kills them. If you buy anti-virus software you are entitled to **updates**, which means that you will get new versions of the software that will kill any new viruses. Two of the main providers of anti-virus software are Norton and McAfee.

Anti-spyware/adware software

Spyware and **adware** is software that installs itself on your computer without you knowing it, when you are using the Internet. It tracks what you do on the computer. The information is usually used for marketing purposes. So you may get lots of junk email (called **spam**), or lots of windows popping up trying to sell you something. These are called **pop-ups**. Anti-spyware/adware software gets rid of it. Make sure that your anti-virus software also gets rid of spyware and adware.

Media player

If you want to view videos and films, or listen to music you will need a **media player**. These are usually free and the most common ones are Windows Media® Player, or RealPlayer™. These will open up automatically whenever you try to play music or view a video or film.

Hints and tips
If you are buying a new computer, you should ask your computer shop to load all of the software onto the computer for you. This will save you a job.

3.2 Software versions

The businesses that make software are forever bringing out new versions. This means that they have added some new features to the software. Some of these new features are genuinely useful. You have to pay to **upgrade** to these new versions, and it is not always worth it.

When a new version is brought out, sometimes the screens look different and this can be very disconcerting or confusing. For example, Internet Explorer® 7 looks quite different from Internet Explorer® 6. However, you should find that the new version will do everything that the old version did, and some new stuff too.

It is not essential that you upgrade to the latest version of everything. If you are happy with the version you are using then you can stick with it.

3.3 Software supplied with devices

Whenever you buy a new **device** such as a digital camera or a **web cam,** it will come with a CD or DVD that contains the software for the device. All devices need software to make them work on your computer. The software also includes useful functions. For example, the software that comes with your digital camera will allow you to **browse** and edit your photographs onscreen. The problem with all this software is that every program is different. For example, the software supplied with a Canon camera will be different from that supplied with a Kodak camera.

Having said that, most software conforms to some standard rules, as you will see later. All software should also be supplied with a user manual to help you get started.

3.4 Free software

Generally speaking, you get what you pay for and this is also the case with free software! There is a lot of free software available on the Internet for you to **download**. If you buy a computer magazine, you often get a CD packed with free software. Some of this is genuinely good stuff. For example, software companies often give away older versions of their software to encourage you to buy the latest version. Some free software is free only for 30 days and then you have to buy it – so watch out for this. It will normally just run out after the 30 days without causing any problems. Some free software is free because it's rubbish.

As a rule, it is recommended that you put free software onto your computer only if you think you will be using it. The temptation is to clutter up your computer with all of this stuff because it is free. However, every time you add something to your computer, it does alter the settings, which might cause problems elsewhere. Also, you will end up with a long list of programs making it harder to find the ones you do want to use.

3.5 Licences

Finally, make sure that any free software you use is genuine. It is very easy to create copies of software and you may know people who offer you 'free' software. It is illegal to use software that you have not paid for. When you buy legitimate software you get a licence to use it on your computer. In theory, you can be heavily fined for using unlicensed software.

Make sure that you keep the original packaging of all software that you buy, as this is the licence. This also means making sure that you get a copy of Windows® from whomever you buy your computer from.

Summary

In this chapter we have discussed:

- The main items of software you will need
- Internet Explorer®
- Email
- Anti-virus software
- Software versions
- Software that comes with devices
- Free software
- Licences

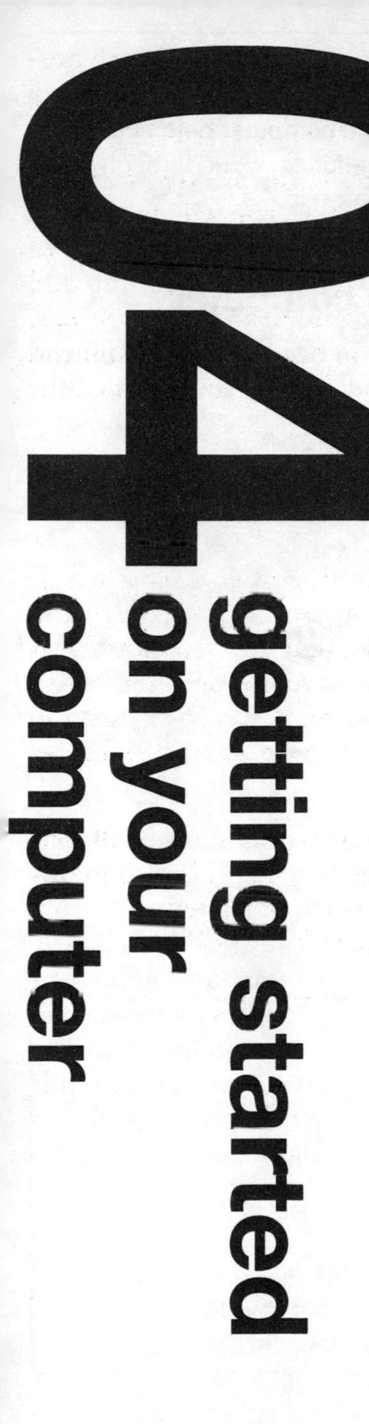

In this chapter you will learn:

- **how to switch your computer on and off**
- **how to use the mouse and keyboard**
- **about the Windows® desktop**
- **how to open and close programs**
- **how to open and close folders**
- **how to open and close Internet Explorer®**

Aims of this chapter
This chapter takes you from the very beginning assuming that you have never switched on a computer before. Even if you have, you might find it useful to work through this chapter on the basics of computer use.

4.1 Switching on the computer

To switch on your computer, you need to find the button that has this symbol on it.

This is the on/off button although you should actually use it only to switch on the computer.

1 Press the on/off button and release – and wait.

The computer will now go through a **start-up routine** that may take a few minutes. If nothing appears on the screen, it may be that the monitor is not switched on. The monitor also has an on/off switch, so make sure that this is on. You can tell that the computer and monitor are on as there is a small (usually green) light that will light up when they are on.

Hints and tips
The start-up routine is carried out by the Windows® **operating system** that we talked about in Chapter 1. It has to go through this routine every time you switch on.

Windows® will also switch off the computer when you tell it to, which is why you never need to use the on/off button to switch off your computer.

When it has finished its routine, you will see the **Windows® desktop**, which will look something like the image shown here. Note that this computer is using Windows XP®. If you are using a different version, for example Windows Vista™, then yours will look slightly different.

Think of the desktop to be like a normal desktop – a flat surface with lots of things on it. You will always start at the desktop and will use it a lot, so you need to get used to it. The small pictures you can see are called **icons**. You use the **mouse** to point and click on these so that you can open up programs and **folders**.

Also, note the 'Start' button in the bottom left-hand corner. This is often referred to as the 'Start menu' and will provide access to everything on your computer. This area at the bottom of the screen is called the **taskbar**. It shows which programs and folders are currently being used.

Hints and tips

The Windows® desktop can be customized. You can move the icons around and add your own background, called 'wallpaper'. This means that yours might not look exactly the same as the one shown here.

4.2 Using the mouse

To make things happen, you can either use the mouse or the **keyboard**. Your mouse will have at least two buttons called the left and right buttons. It may also have a scroll wheel between the two buttons.

As you move the mouse around on your mouse mat, it will move a small pointer on the screen. All programs work with a mouse – you simply point and then click on the icons and menus that you want to use.

Throughout this book, when you need to click on something on the screen, it will be shown in the text in single speech marks. For example, if you need to click on a menu on the screen called Save, the instruction will read: Click 'Save'.

To use the mouse:

1 Hold it lightly using the thumb on one side and your fourth and little finger on the other. This leaves your second and third fingers free for clicking and using the scroll wheel. You might want to practise moving the mouse around and watching as the pointer moves.

Hints and tips

Some mice are more sensitive than others, which means that the pointer will move by different amounts. If you use more than one computer, it might take a while to get used to a different mouse.

2 As well as pushing the mouse around, you will also need to lift it slightly from time to time. The mouse works only if it is flat on your mouse mat, but sometimes you simply run out of mouse mat! When this happens, you need to lift the mouse off the mat and reposition it in the centre of the mouse mat before you start moving it again. This might be a bit tricky when you first start, so have a play until you feel more comfortable with it.

Hints and tips
You can actually move the pointer all the way across the screen without having to move the mouse much at all using the lifting technique described here.

4.3 Clicking on things

There are three types of click:

- A left click (known as a click). This is used mainly when you want to select something from a list or menu.
- A double left click (known as a double click). This is another thing that might need a bit of practice when you start. A double click is when you click twice on the left button, quite quickly. You use this when you click on icons.
- A right click (known as a right click!). This provides access to hidden menus. Right clicks work only in certain places, as you will start to discover later.

Let's practise the clicks now.

1 First, from the desktop, click (that's a single left click) on 'Start' in the bottom left-hand corner.

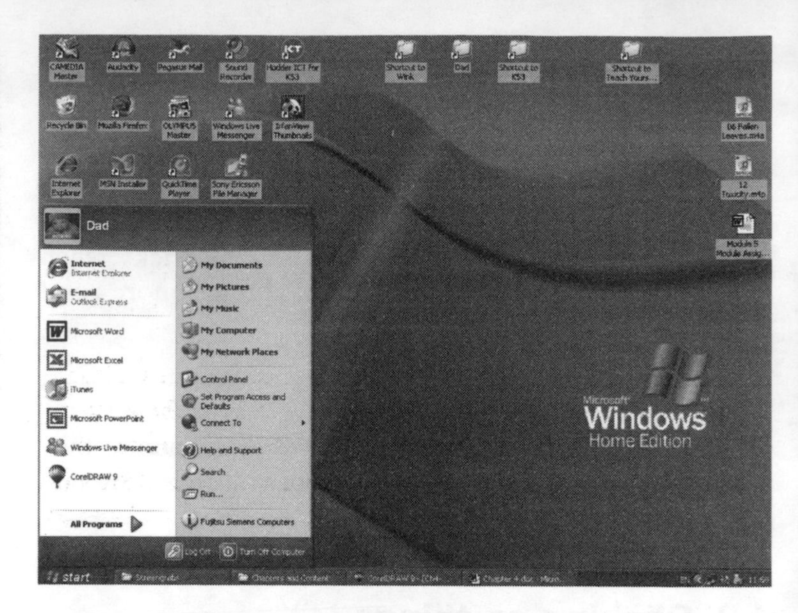

2 Click on 'My Documents'.
This will then show a window that looks a bit like this. It is called a window because it opens in a frame. Don't worry if yours does not have exactly the same number of little yellow folders in it, but it should look something like this:

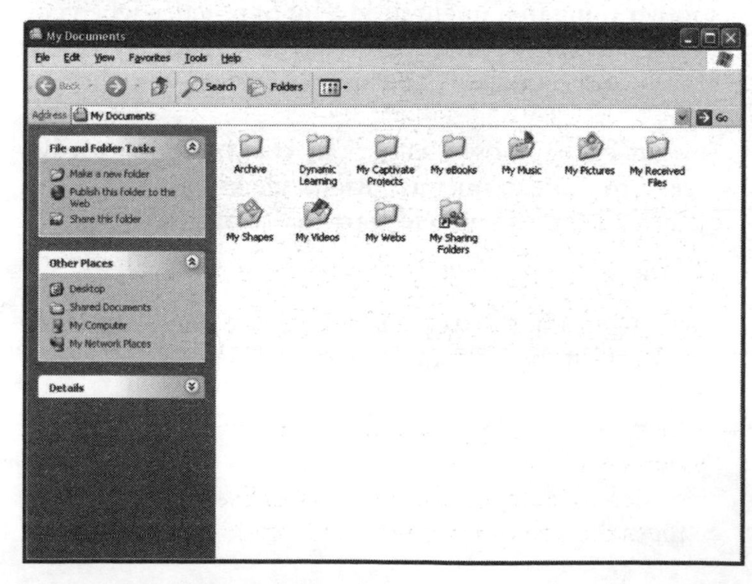

You will notice that there are three small icons in the top right-hand corner of the window. These are displayed in every window in every program that you ever use.

The first one is called **Minimize**. This closes the window but leaves it available in the taskbar so that you can get it back later.

3 Click on the 'Minimize' icon now. The window closes, but if you look at the taskbar (the bar across the bottom of the screen), you will see that it is still available here. This is useful as it means you can have lots of different things open at the same time, and can use the taskbar to get to them quickly.

4 To re-open the My Documents window, click on 'My Documents' now.

The second icon of the three is called **Restore**. This changes the size of the windows from full screen (where it fills the screen) to a smaller size. The advantage of this is that you can have several smaller windows all open at the same time.

5 Click on the 'Restore' icon now to see what happens.

6 Click on it again to restore the window to its original size. This is also known as **maximizing** the window. A window is maximized when it fills the whole screen.

The final icon is the cross. This closes the window. You will use this a lot as this is the main way of closing things down when you have finished with them.

To close this window:

7 Click on the little cross in the very top right-hand corner of the window as shown.

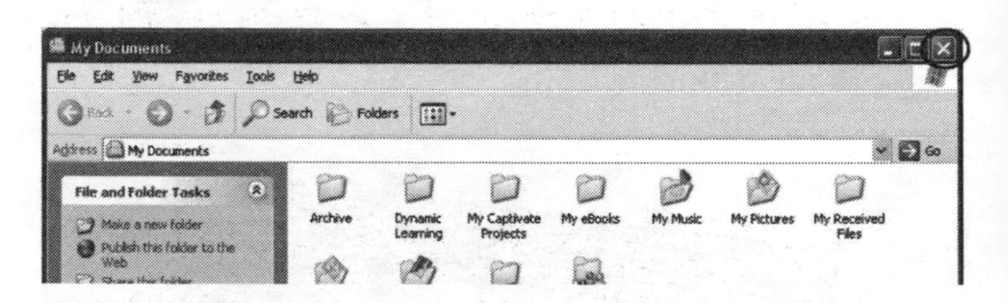

You have now used a double click and a click to open and close a window. You are now back at the desktop.

8 Move the mouse somewhere on the desktop where there are no icons.

9 Right click.

A hidden **menu** is displayed. This menu will be different depending on where you press the right click.

10 Click somewhere else on the desktop and the hidden menu will disappear again.

Hints and tips

The scroll wheel comes in handy when you are looking at things on the screen that take up more than a screen-full. If this is the case you have to scroll, or move up and down. This is where the scroll wheel comes in. We will use this for the first time in Chapter 5.

4.4 Using the keyboard

This is a bit more straightforward as it works in the same way as a typewriter. That is, you press the keys on the keyboard and whatever you type will appear on the screen.

When you are on the desktop you don't really need to type anything, but you will use it a lot in other programs. There are a few keys on the keyboard that carry out specific functions. You will be introduced to these as you need them, but it is worth pointing a few out now.

> Throughout this book, when you need to press one of the keys on the keyboard, the name of that key be shown in capitals. For example, if you need to press the ENTER key, the instructions will read: Press ENTER.

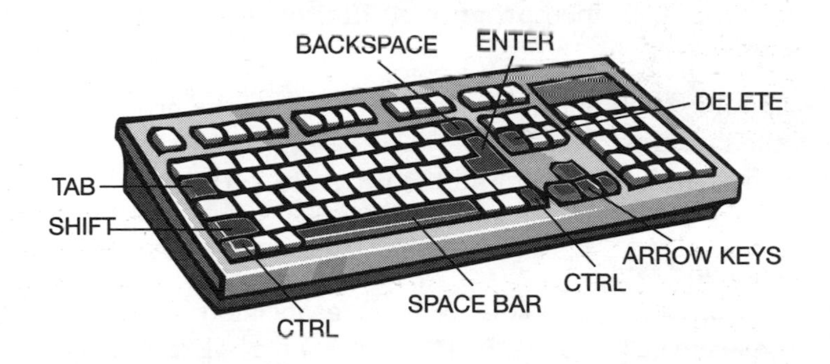

ENTER: You will use this key a lot. It is used to tell the computer you want to do something and is used when typing to start new lines.

SPACE: The space bar is used to add spaces between words when typing.

TAB: This is really useful when you are filling in forms when you are on the Internet. It will move you from one part of the form to the next and saves you having to click.

SHIFT: Allows you to type capitals and gives you access to all of the characters displayed at the top of the keys, for example above the numbers.

CTRL: Can be used for shortcuts. These are ways of doing things quicker. You will be told about these as you work through the book. CTRL is short for 'Control'.

BACKSPACE and DELETE: Used a lot when typing. They delete (erase) any characters that you have typed incorrectly.

ARROW KEYS: Can be used like the mouse to move the pointer on the screen around (in some programs).

4.5 Opening and closing programs

Programs are all of those things that you use your computer for, for example emailing, or surfing the Internet. To do these things, you have to open the appropriate program. You open programs from the desktop in one of two ways:

- Double click on the icon that represents the program on the desktop.
- Click on 'Start' and find the program in the list.

Hints and tips

All programs have little pictures associated with them. These are called icons. For example, Outlook Express® has an envelope with blue arrows; Internet Explorer® has a blue E. There is also a piece of text with the icon that tells you what program it is.

It is easiest to open programs from an icon, but sometimes the icon does not exist, so you have to go through the Start menu. To practise, we are going to open **Internet Explorer®**.

To open from an icon:

1 Double click on the 'Internet Explorer' icon.
Internet Explorer® will now open and will look like the image shown. Note that Internet Explorer opens what is called your **home page**. Your home page is the first

page the program will go to when you load it. On this computer, the home page goes to the Google™ website. It might be a different page on your computer.

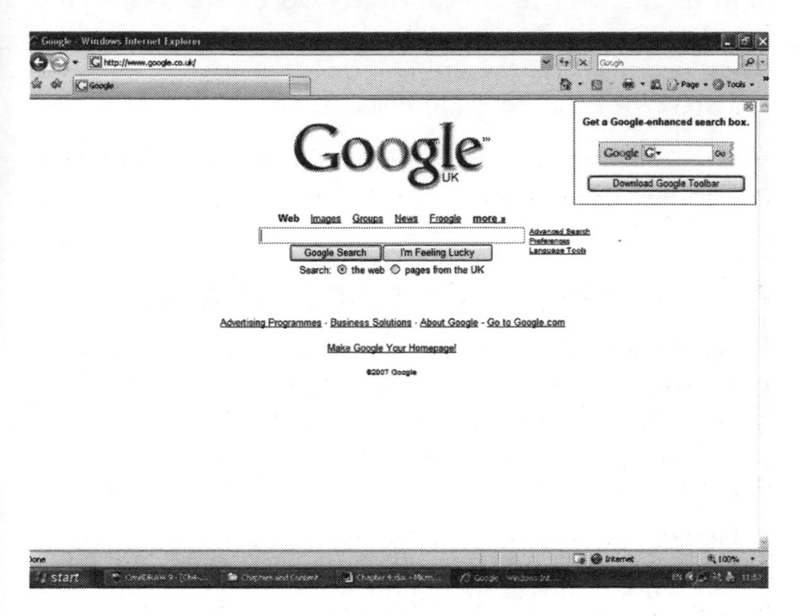

2 To close the program, click on the small cross in the very top right-hand corner of the window.

To open from the Start menu:

1 Click on 'Start'.
2 Find 'Internet Explorer' and click on it. If it is not there, move the mouse to 'All Programs'. A list will now be displayed which will have 'Internet Explorer' in it where you can click on it.
   The program will load.
3 Click on the cross to close the program.

The process of opening and closing any program is exactly the same. This means there will always be either an icon, or if there is no icon, the name of the program will appear on the list in the Start menu. All programs can be closed by clicking on the cross in the top right-hand corner.

4.6 Opening and closing folders

Folders are where you save your work. When you first start off there is a folder called My Documents, which has nothing in it. Think of folders like normal paper folders. They are just somewhere to put your work. All work (whatever it is) is stored in **files**.

> **Hints and tips**
> It might help to think of your computer as an electronic filing cabinet. The folders are where you will store all of your work.

Folders have their own icon, which is a little yellow folder! Whenever you see a little yellow folder, it means that there is some work stored in it.

As a practice:

1 From the desktop, double click on the 'My Documents' folder.

2 This will open a new window that will show you all of the work that is stored in this folder. If it's a brand new computer, there will be nothing in the folder. You will probably see two other folders within this folder: one called My Music and one called My Pictures. This is where you can store music and pictures if you want.

3 Now go to 'Start' in the bottom left-hand corner and open Internet Explorer® again.
You have now got two things open: My Documents and Internet Explorer®. You are now multi-tasking! This means that you are doing more than one thing at the same time. To switch between the two things that are open, you just click on them in the taskbar at the bottom of the screen as described previously. Try this now.

4 Click on 'My Documents' in the taskbar and then click on the cross in the top right-hand corner of the window to close it.
Internet Explorer® will still be open. Leave it open for now, as we will use it to look at some of the standard features of the software.

4.7 Internet Explorer® basics

In this book we will be visiting lots of different websites. You will be using Internet Explorer® to find and view all of these sites. Internet Explorer 7 is shown below. From here you can access the millions of pages of information that exist across the world.

Most of the screen is used to display the contents of the website (Google™ in this case). Notice at the top of the screen, what is called the **address bar**. All websites have a unique address, and this is where you can type in that address (if you know it) and Internet Explorer® will then display that website. The address shown here is for the Google™ website.

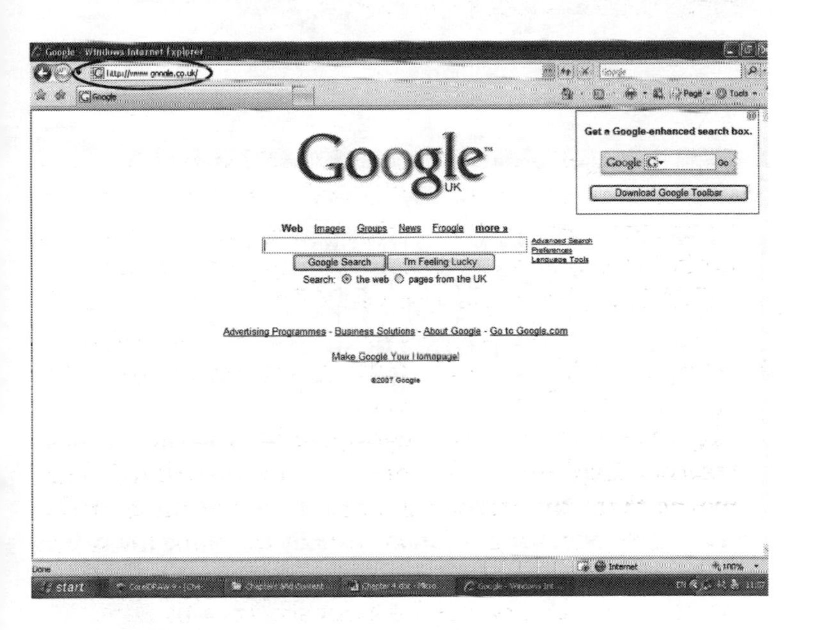

For example, to get to the BBC website:

1 Click in the address bar. Notice the little line flashing. This is the **cursor** and it shows you where you have clicked on the screen. When you start typing the text will appear wherever the cursor is.

2 Type: www.bbc.co.uk into the address bar and press ENTER. The BBC website is now displayed.

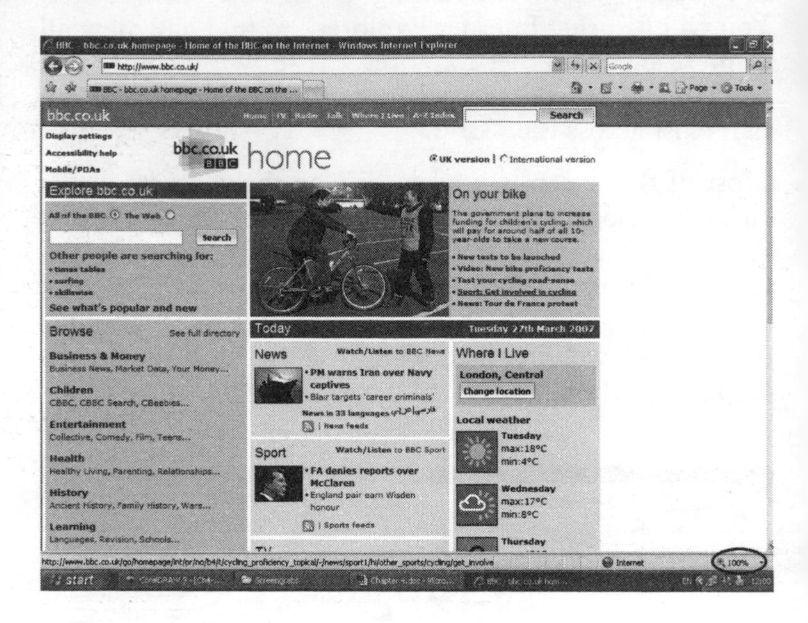

3 If you find that the text is too small, you can click on the little magnifying glass in the bottom left-hand corner until the text size is suitable for you.
4 Now close down Internet Explorer® by clicking on the cross in the top right-hand corner.

Hints and tips
Note that the term 'websites' and 'sites' are used interchangeably because they mean exactly the same thing.

4.8 Switching off the computer

You might not want to do this just yet, but it is worth having a practice now. Remember that you don't actually press the on/off button to switch it off – that would be far too easy. Instead you do the following:

1 Click on the 'Start' button in the bottom left-hand corner.
2 Select **'Shut Down'**.
3 Select 'Shut Down' again from the options listed.
4 Click 'OK'. Your computer may take a while to switch itself off, but after a few seconds it will shut itself down.

Hints and tips

It is important that you shut down the computer using this method. It carries out various checks as it shuts down to make sure that it is done properly. Switching off using the on/off key will cause problems when you come to switch on again.

When the computer shuts down it will also turn off the monitor, so you do not need to switch this off separately. You now need to switch your computer back on again so you can carry on with Chapter 5.

Summary

In this chapter we have discussed:

- How to switch on the computer and shut it down properly
- How to use the mouse
- How to click, double click and right click with the mouse
- How to use the keyboard
- How to open and close programs and folders
- The basics of Internet Explorer®

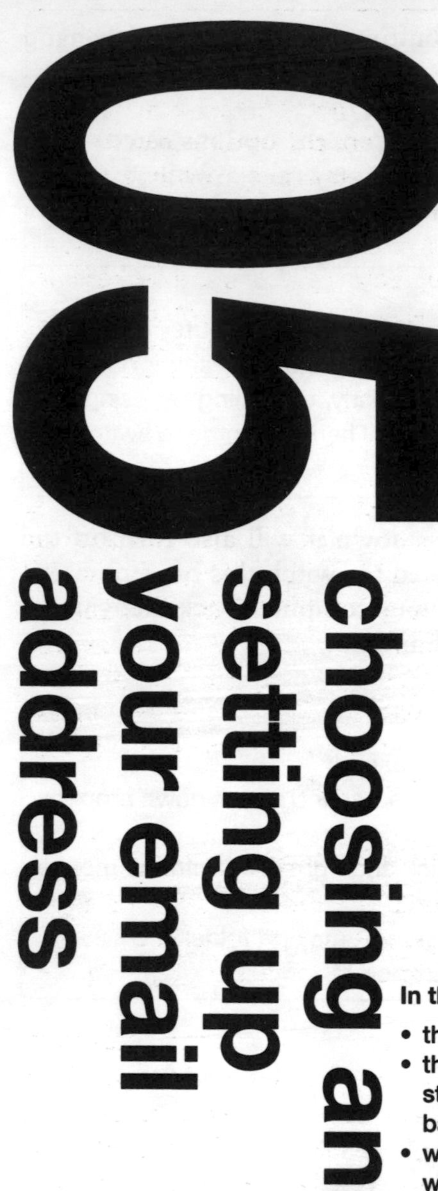

05 choosing and setting up your email address

In this chapter you will learn:

- **the basics of email**
- **the difference between standard email and web-based email**
- **whether to use standard or web-based email**
- **how to set up web-based email software**
- **how to set up Outlook Express®**

Aims of this chapter
This chapter introduces email and explains the different ways in which you can access it. There are two main ways of using email: one is to use standard email software like Outlook®, and the other is to use email based on the Internet (web-based email). This chapter will explain both, and help you make a decision about which one to choose. Finally, it will show you how to set up both types of email address. If you already know what email software you want to use and already have an email address, you can skip this chapter.

5.1 Email software

There are two main types of email **software**. The first is **standard email software** such as Microsoft Outlook® or Outlook Express®, which comes as part of the Microsoft® Office package. These are usually already **installed** and set up on your computer and you run them from your **desktop** in the same way as other programs. If you have had a new computer set up by your supplier, this might have all been set up for you. If not, then section 5.5 of this chapter will show you how to do it.

Hints and tips
If you are buying a new computer you should ask the supplier if they would set up an ISP and an email address for you. It can be quite tricky to do at this early stage of your computing career!

The second type is what is called **web-based email**. With these, you do not need to have email software installed on your computer, as you can get access to it using the Internet. Web-based email is generally free. For example, Microsoft **Hotmail**®, Google's Gmail™ and Yahoo!®Mail are all free-to-use web-based email. You may also be given free **email addresses** from your **Internet Service Provider** (the company from which you get your Internet connection). For example, BT, AOL and Tiscali all provide free web-based email too.

> **Hints and tips**
> There are so many different email providers that it is difficult to know which to choose. Some people have several different email addresses that they use for different things. When you are starting out, it's best to choose one email address and stick with it.

All email software has the same basic functions whether you use a standard or web-based one. Whichever one you choose, you will need to know your email address (i.e. if the supplier has set up one for you) or create an email address if you are setting up for yourself.

5.2 Email basics

Email stands for electronic mail and the easiest way to think of it is as an electronic letter. You do not have to print it out and send it – instead, it is sent electronically over the Internet. Therefore, you must have Internet access in order to use email.

Like normal mail, emails are sent and received using addresses. All email addresses follow the same format. For example: marjorie.franklin@googlemail.com The bit before the @ sign is usually used to identify the individual, and the bit after is the name of the **email provider**.

> **Hints and tips**
> Email has been around for many years now and has millions of users. Therefore you may not get the email address you want, as there is probably already someone out there with the same name as you who has already bagsied the address.

5.3 Choosing which email software to use

Choosing which email provider to use can be quite difficult. There is a lot of debate over which is the 'best'. Much of it depends on your personal preferences and the way in which you want to access your emails. It also depends on what software is already installed on your computer.

Reasons to choose web-based email

- You can access your email from any computer. Therefore, if you don't have your own computer, or are away from home and want to access your emails perhaps from a library or Internet café, then this is the choice for you.
- If you do not already have email software on your computer and you don't want to buy or **download** any, then it is simpler to set up and use a web-based email service.
- It's completely free and you can have several different addresses if you want to.
- You get access to other websites. For example, if you get a Gmail™ account with Google™, you can then use their **chat rooms** and **blogging** websites without having to register again.

Reasons to choose standard email

- You may already have the email software on your computer, and it may already have been set up for you when you bought it. If this is the case, this will save you the time of setting up a web-based email.
- Web-based emails can be cut off if you don't use them for a while. Most web-based emails will be cut off after a month if you have not sent or received an email in that time.
- If your connection to the Internet is not available for any reason, you cannot get at old messages with web-based mail, but you can with standard email.
- It is claimed that it is more secure as your emails are stored on your computer rather than on the Internet. See Chapter 16 for more advice on keeping your information secure.

5.4 Setting up a web-based email address

In this example, we will be using Gmail™, which is a free email service provided by Google™.

1 Open **Internet Explorer®**, by double clicking on the **icon**, or click on 'Start' and click on it from the list.

2 In the address bar, type: www.gmail.com as shown:

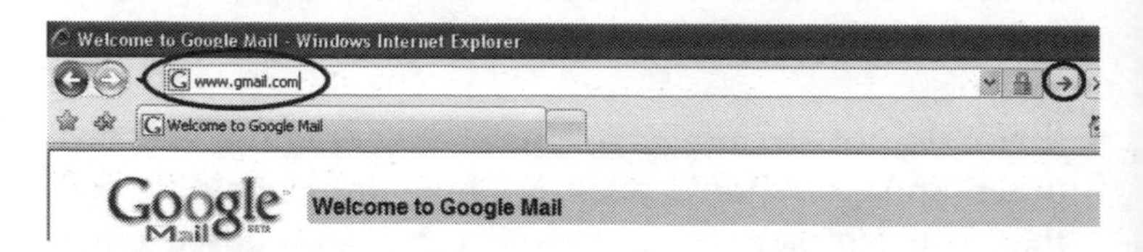

3 Press ENTER or you can click the green arrow.
The Gmail™ web page will now be displayed in the main window:

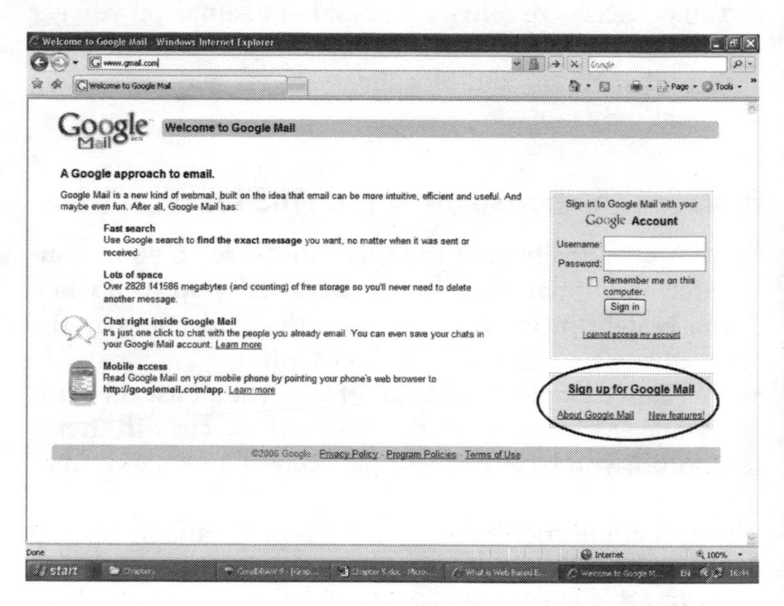

Many services are provided free on the Internet, but the websites offering these services do make you register with them first. This involves filling in an **online form.** You will get very familiar with this process as you start to use the Internet more and more, although it might take a while the first time you do it.

4 Move the mouse over the text that reads 'Sign up for Google Mail'.
You will notice that the pointer changes to a hand with one finger pointing. When the pointer changes to a hand like this, it means that you are on a **hyperlink** or **link**. This will take you to another page.

5 Click on the text 'Sign up for Google Mail'. You will now be asked to fill in the form.

6 Click in the box where an answer is needed e.g. First name

7 Type in your answer. Use the SHIFT key if you want letters in capitals.

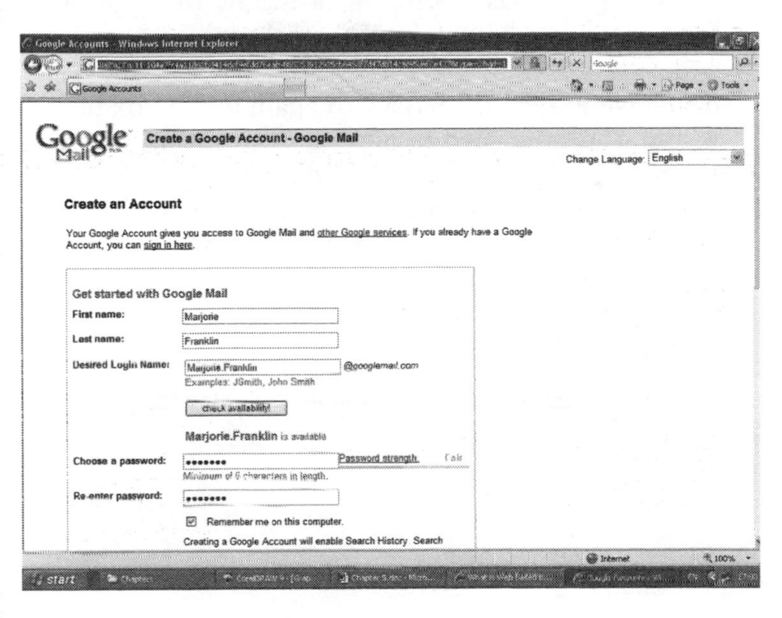

8 Carry on doing this for all of the boxes, filling in the information that is asked for. In this example, we have set it up for someone called Marjorie Franklin, but you will need to choose the name that you want to use.
You can tell which box you are in by looking for the cursor (the small vertical flashing line).

> Your email address does not have to be your real name. Remember that you will be giving this address to people so they can email you. Bunnykins@gmail.com might not be appropriate if you are going to be emailing the vicar!

9 After you have typed in what you want your email address to be, click the 'Check availability!' button. This will tell you whether someone else has already got that address. If your name is John Smith, then you're in trouble! You are now asked for a **password**. Passwords mean that only you can log on to this email address, so they are very important.

10 Choose a password that you will remember. It also has to be a good password, which means that you have letters and numbers in it. (This makes them harder for people to guess).

11 You have to type the password again in the box underneath. You now need to move down the page to fill in the rest of the form. You can either:

12 Use the scroll wheel on your mouse (if you have one) or click several times on the arrow on the right-hand side of the screen as shown below. Either way the page will move down.
This is called **scrolling**.

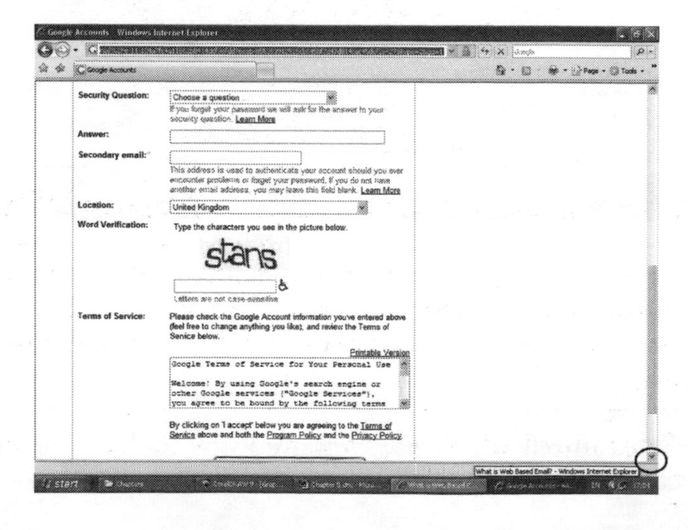

13 You need to complete the Security Question and Answer box. But you can leave the Secondary email box empty. The idea of the security question is that if you forget your password, you can get a reminder by entering this information.

14 You now need to fill in the Word Verification box. This is a security measure.
Type the words shown into the Word verification box. In this case it is 'stans' but it will be something different on your screen.

15 Now **scroll down** to the bottom of the page and click 'I accept. Create my account' button. You should now see this screen, which tells you that you have successfully set up your Gmail™ account.

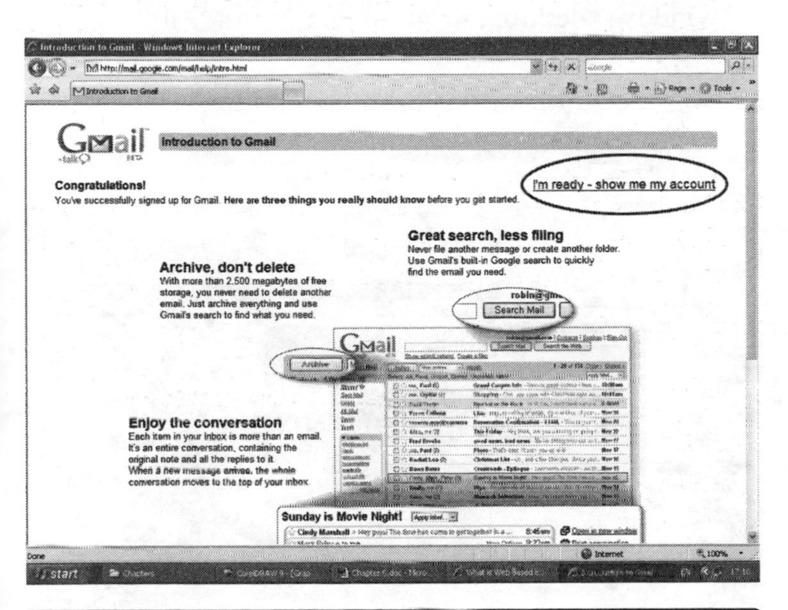

You have to type your email address and password in every time you want to check your email so it is important that you remember them, or you will have to set them up all over again.

Congratulations – you have now set up your email account.

16 Click on 'I'm ready – show me my account' and you are ready to send and receive emails.

5.5 Setting up Outlook Express®

This process is a little bit complicated so it is preferable to get this set up by the computer supplier when you buy your computer. It is complicated because you need to know some technical details from your email provider. In this example we will use Gmail™ as our email provider, and will set it up so that we can use the Gmail™ address through Outlook Express®.

1 Double click on the Outlook Express icon on the **Windows®desktop,** or go to 'Start' and 'All Programs' and click on it from the list.
2 Click on 'Tools' and select 'Accounts'.

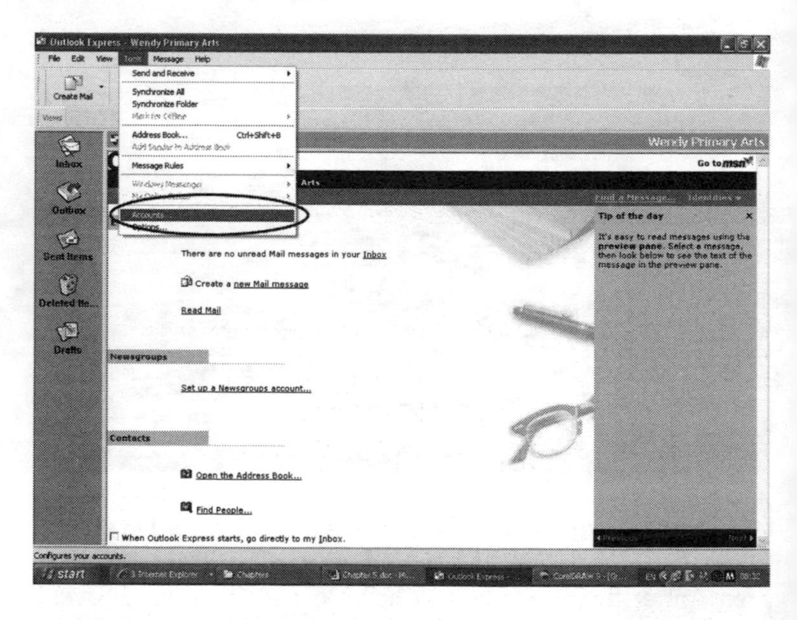

3 Click on 'Add' and then click on 'Mail'.
4 Now type in the name that you want to appear on your emails when you send them to people and click 'Next'.

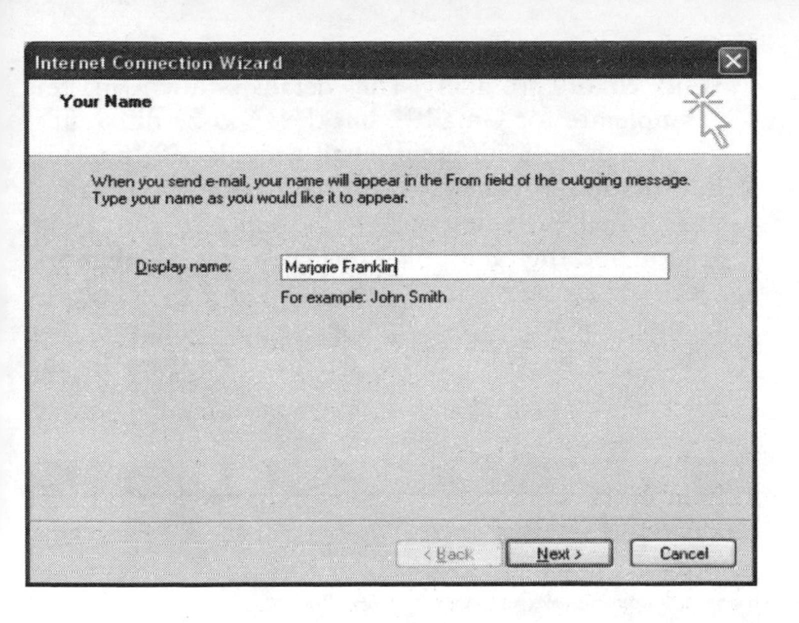

5 On the next screen, type in your email address and click 'Next'. You need to know your email address at this point. In this example we are using marjorie.franklin@googlemail.com

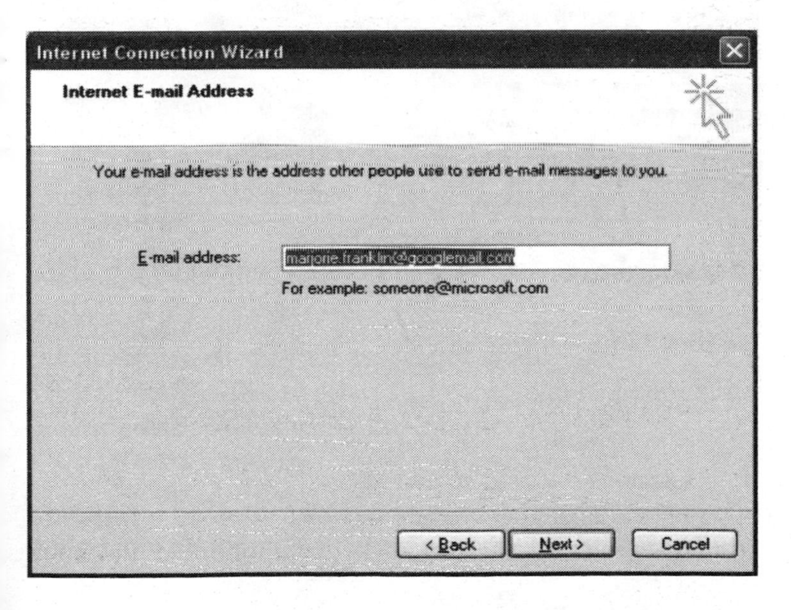

6 You are now asked for some technical details about your email provider. The details shown in this example are for Gmail™, but they will be different if you are using a different email provider. To find this information you need to go to the main website of your email provider, follow the links to the 'Help' section and then find the information on 'Configuring Outlook Express'. You can also get the details by phoning the technical help line of your email provider. When you have found the details, type them in and click 'Next'.

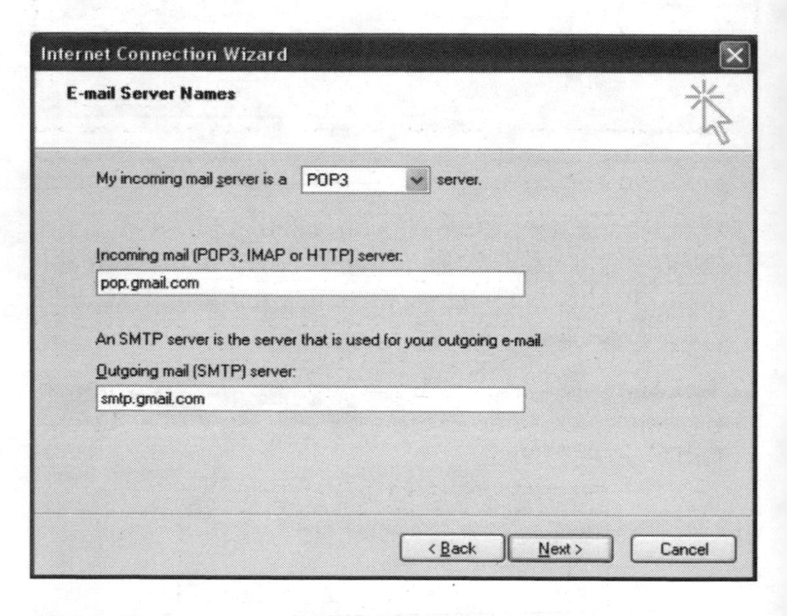

7 On the next screen, type in the full email address and the password.

8 Click 'Finish'. You will see this screen:

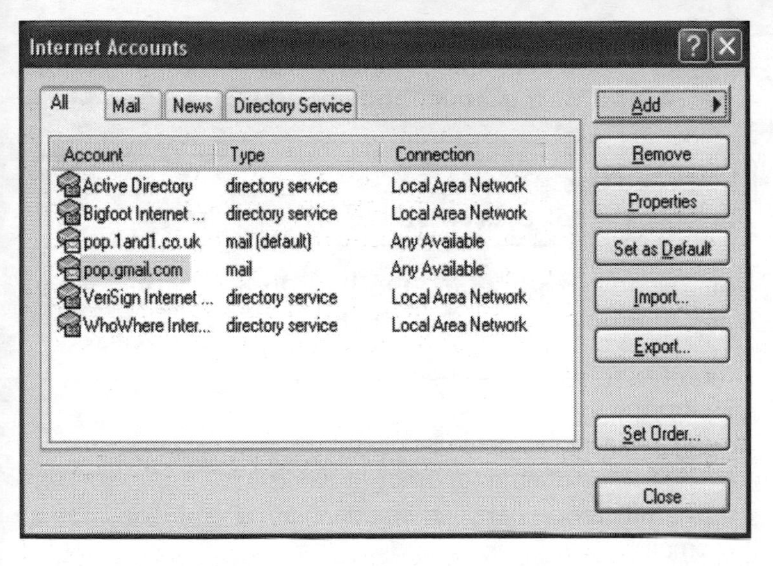

9 Click on pop.gmail.com and click on 'Properties' (or the pop address that you typed in step 6).
10 Click on the 'Advanced' **tab.**
11 Tick the box next to 'This server requires a secure connection (SSL)' under 'Outgoing Mail (SMTP)' and enter '465' in the 'Outgoing mail (SMTP)' field.
12 Tick the box next to 'This server requires a secure connection (SSL)' under 'Incoming mail (POP3)'. The port will change to 995.

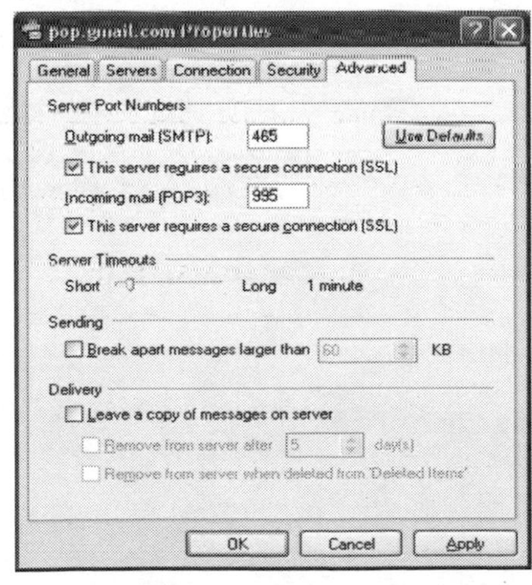

13 Click 'OK'.

14 Click on the 'Servers' tab and tick the box for 'My server requires authentication' and click 'OK'.

Hints and tips

To 'untick' a box click on it again.

You are now ready to use Outlook Express®. We will be using Outlook Express® in Chapters 6 to 8.

Summary

In this chapter we have discussed:

- The basics of email and how it works
- The difference between standard email and web-based email
- How to set up web-based email software
- How to set up Outlook Express®

09 sending and receiving emails

In this chapter you will learn:

- **how to open your email software**
- **how to look at messages that you have received**
- **how to send a message**
- **how to read and reply to messages**

Aims of this chapter
This chapter is the first of three that will show you how to send and receive emails (including attachments) and manage all of your messages and contacts. This chapter focuses specifically on opening up your email inbox and reading and replying to messages. It also shows you how to send an email to someone.

6.1 Introduction

If you do not already have an **email address**, you will need to go back to Chapter 5, which shows you how to set one up. As you may have seen in Chapter 5 there are lots of different **email providers** to choose from and each one is slightly different. However, they all share some common characteristics.

This chapter will use Outlook Express® 6 as an example. At the time this book was written, this was one of the most widely used email programs. What this means is that if you are using another type of email such as Gmail™, Yahoo!®, or Tiscali for example, then your screens will look different from those shown here. However, the basic principles remain the same whichever email you are using.

6.2 The basic functions of email

To start with, we will have a look at the standard features of email and what they do.

1 Double click on the Outlook Express **icon** (little picture) or click on 'Start' and select it from the list.
2 The main window will now open. Most of what you do can be done from here. We have labelled the three main areas that you will use:

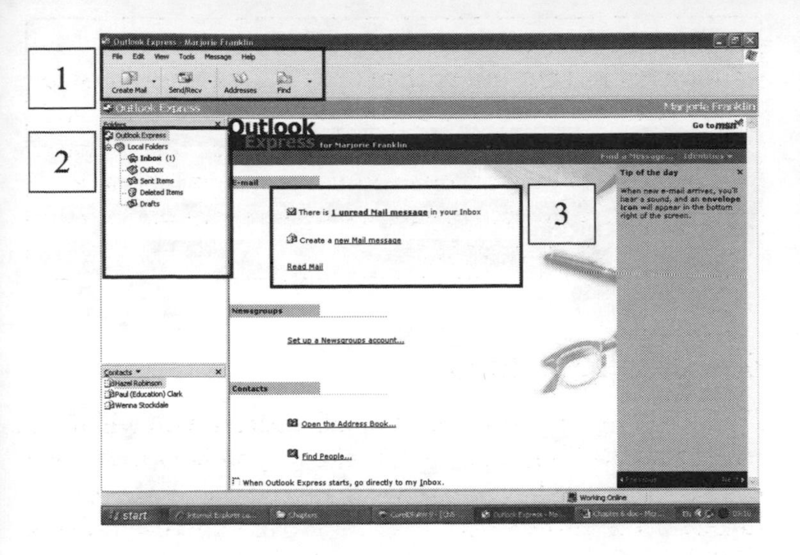

Area 1: This is where you can send an email, check for new messages, organize your contacts list (of other people's email addresses) and find email addresses. Notice that there are **icons** that you can use and the words across the top, for example File, View, Edit, which are called **menus**.

Area 2: These are called the **folders**. The main folder is the **Inbox** where all messages that you receive are saved. There is also a 'Sent Items' which saves messages that you have sent to people.

Area 3: There are two very useful **shortcuts** here to the two main email operations: looking in your Inbox for messages, or creating messages to send to other people.

Hints and tips

You will need to know the email address of someone else so that you can practise sending and receiving emails with them.

There will already be one message in your Inbox and this will be from Outlook Express® welcoming you to the **software**.

1 To view this email, click on 'There is 1 unread Mail message in your Inbox'.

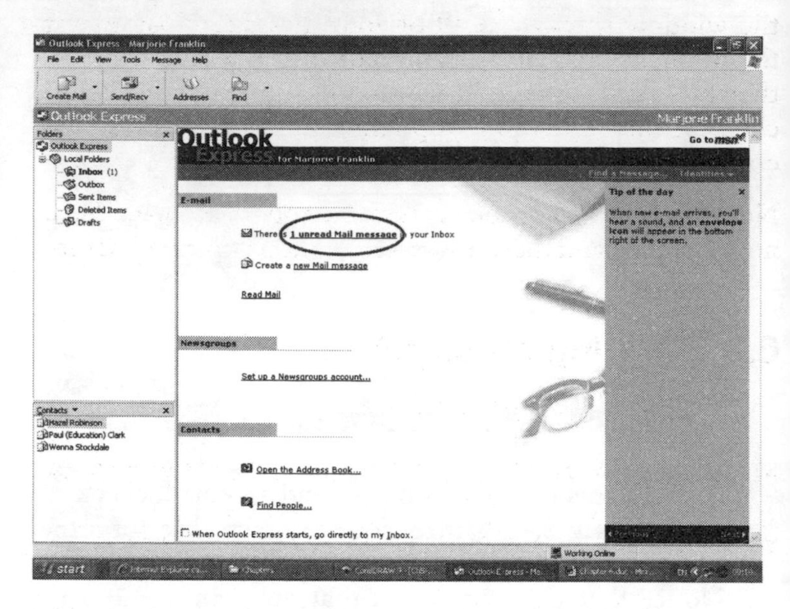

2 The Inbox will now open. All the messages that you receive will automatically be put in here.

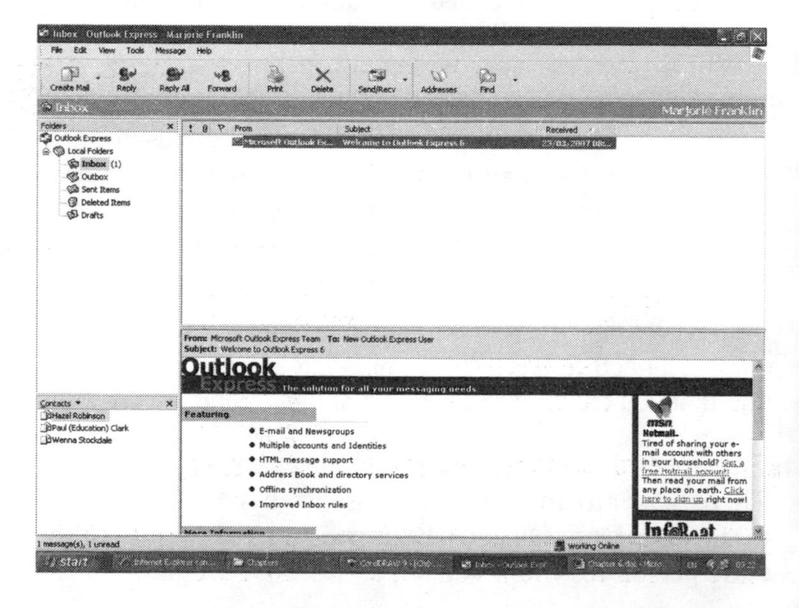

Notice that the folders on the left-hand side are still visible but that the main window has changed. The top half of the window shows you all of your messages (just one at the moment) and the bottom half of the window shows the message itself. If you had more messages you would click on each one in the top half and it would show the contents of the message in the bottom half.

Notice too that the icons across the top of the page have now changed and there are several options to choose from.

6.3 Sending an email

1 Click on the 'Create Mail' icon.

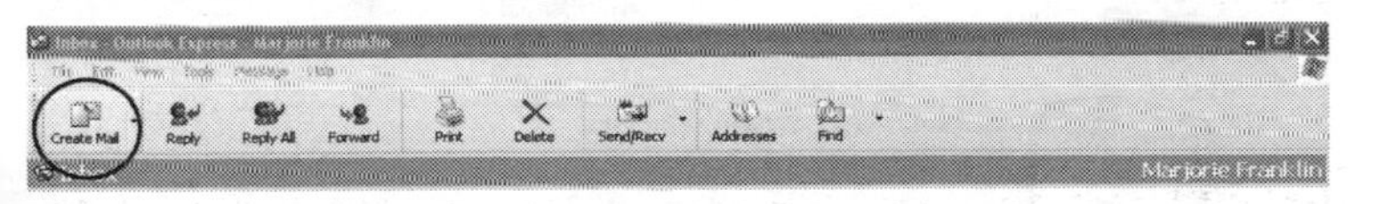

2 A new window will open in the middle of the screen. You can make this bigger if you like by clicking on the '**Restore**' button.

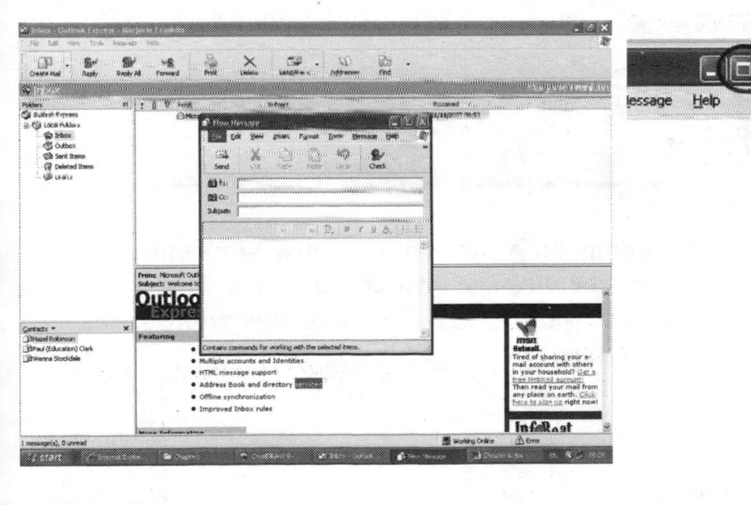

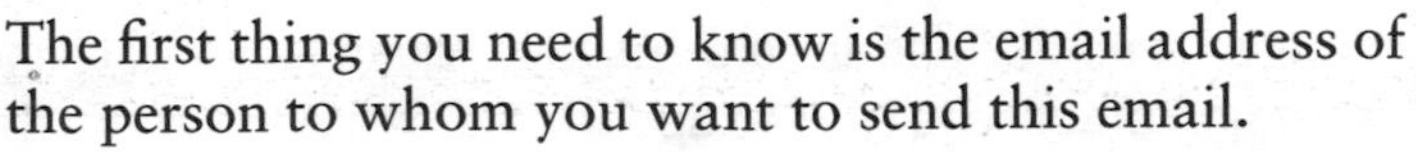

The first thing you need to know is the email address of the person to whom you want to send this email.

3 Type the email address into the box next to where it says 'To:'. It is important that you get the email address exactly correct or your message will not be sent.
The 'Cc' option here can be used to send the same email to someone else. If you want to do this, you should type the email address of the second person in here. If not, you can leave it blank.
4 In the 'Subject:' box, type a heading for what your email is about.
5 Then click in the big white box. This is where you will type in your message.

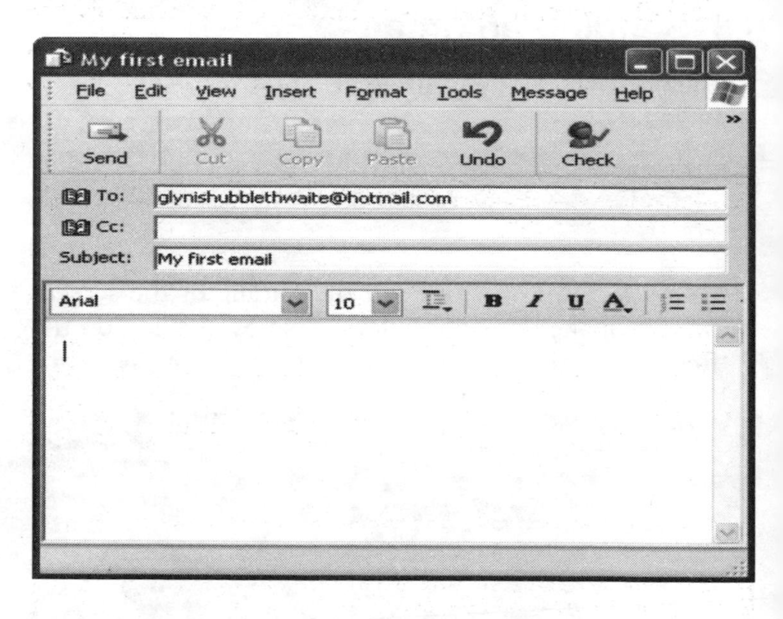

Depending on your typing skills, you will either fly through the message or it could take a while to type in what you want to say. Think of this white space as a piece of paper on to which you are writing (typing) the message that you want to send. It can be as short or long as you like.

Hints and tips

Emails among friends are usually quite informal and common practice is NOT to spend ages worrying about the layout and format, as you might do, for example, with a business letter.

6 Start your message with a salutation. Common practice seems to be 'Hi', but you don't have to do that. So type Hi Glynis and press ENTER twice. Notice that pressing ENTER starts a new line, so pressing it twice leaves a blank line.

7 You now type your message. You can just type away and it will automatically start on a new line when it needs to. If you want to start a new paragraph just press ENTER twice. If you have **maximized** the window the box will appear to be bigger as it is using the full screen. Alternatively, you can use this smaller window. It's up to you.

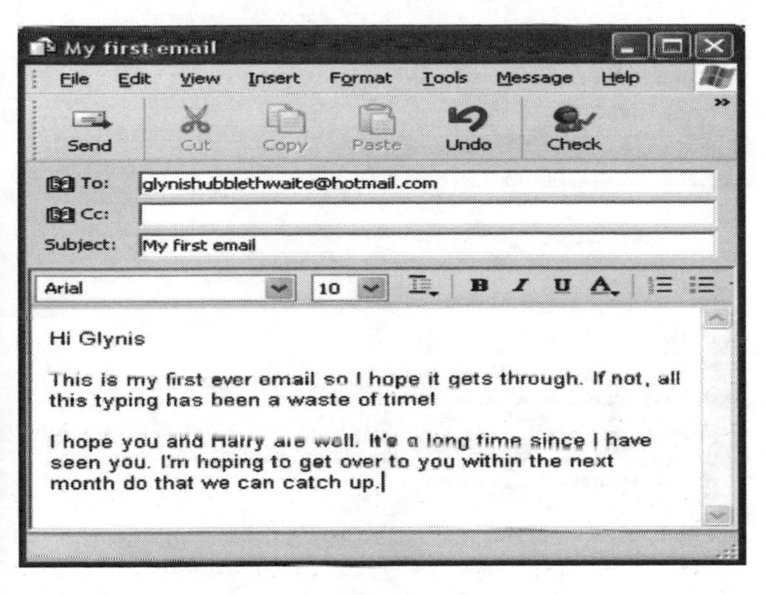

Notice that lines have been left between the paragraphs in this case. Also notice the standard use of capital letters, which is achieved by holding down the SHIFT key as you type the letter that you want to be a capital.

If you make a mistake when typing use the DELETE key

or the BACKSPACE key to delete the error and then re-type. For example, if you spelt Glynis incorrectly:

8 Move the mouse pointer to just before or just after the error and click. There is a small line called the **cursor**, which shows you where you are. If you start typing now it will put the text where the cursor is.

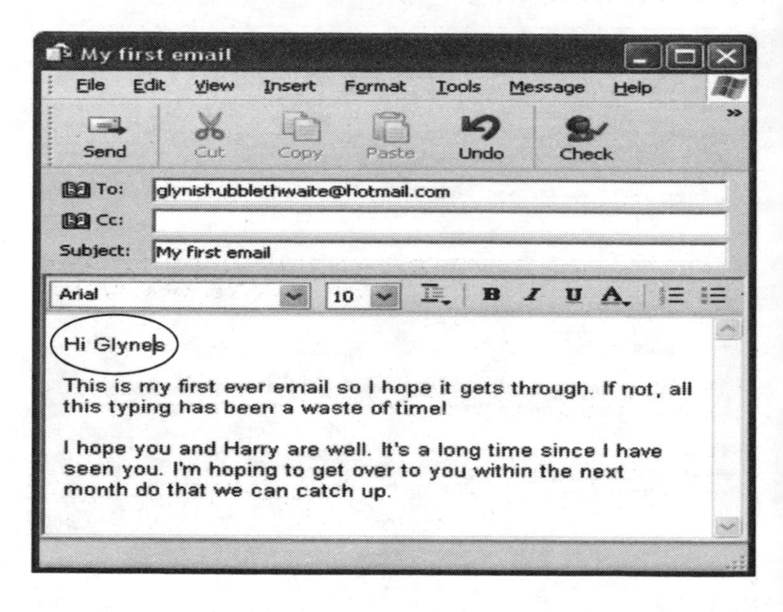

9 Delete the letter e by pressing the BACKSPACE key and then type the letter i. Note that BACKSPACE deletes the character to the left of the cursor and the DELETE key deletes the character to the right.
If you want to delete lots of text, you keep pressing BACKSPACE or DELETE. An alternative method is to

highlight the text you want to delete and delete it all in one go. For example, to delete the whole of the first sentence:

10 Point the mouse just before the T of 'This' on the first line, then hold down the left button of the mouse. Move the mouse to just after the exclamation mark. You will see that all of the text in-between is now **highlighted.**

11 Let go of the left mouse button and press the DELETE key. The whole block of text is gone.

Hints and tips

You can use this highlighting technique in any program. It may take a while to get used to holding the mouse button down and moving the mouse at the same time.

12 Common practice is to put your name at the bottom of the email, perhaps with an informal sign off such as 'Regards' or 'Cheers' but there are no hard-and-fast rules.

13 Click 'Send'.

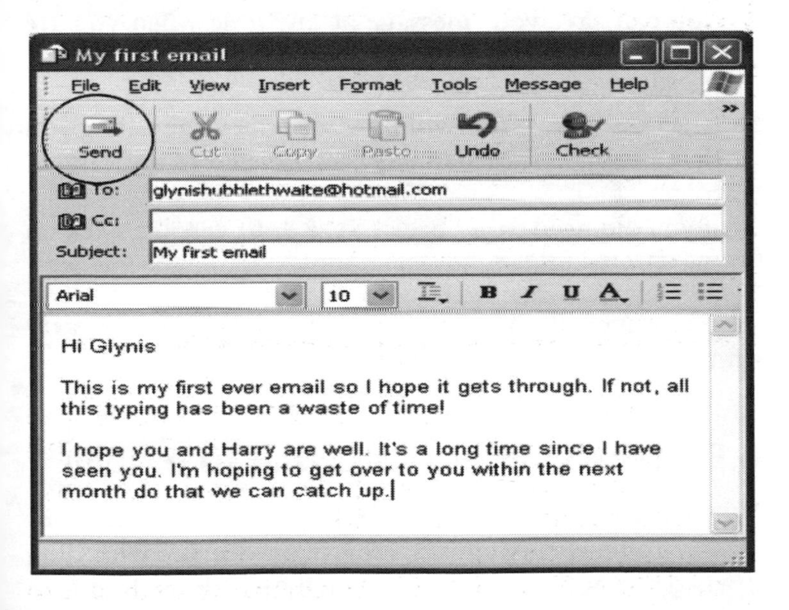

That's it. Your message now flies across cyberspace and will appear in the inbox of the person to whom you sent it. In most cases, this will be almost instant, but sometimes it may take a few minutes or even hours for the message to be received.

6.4 Saving your email

When you send an email a copy of it will be stored automatically in the 'Sent Items' folder. If you want to go back to an email you have sent previously, you can click on 'Sent Items', find the email in the list and double click on it to read it.

You might also find it useful to save your email as you go along. For example, if you were typing quite a long email and then something went wrong or you deleted it by accident, you would have to start typing all over again. What you can do is save a 'draft' version of the email so that if this did happen you can go back to the saved draft. To do this:

1. You can save your message at any time when you are typing it by clicking on 'File' from the menu options at the top of the screen.
2. Click on 'Save'. You will now see a message telling you that a copy of the email has been saved into the 'Drafts' folder.
3. If you did need to get back to the draft version, click on the 'Drafts' folder and then double click on the message.

The message will then be on the screen and you can carry on typing, or send the message.

6.5 Receiving and replying to emails

When people send you an email it will appear in your inbox. You have already seen this in Section 6.2 when you opened the welcome email from the Outlook Express®

team. All the messages received go into your Inbox and are stored there whether you have read them or not. When you load your email it will show you how many new emails you have got. You can then open up your inbox and read them. If you are using email for the first time, you might have to wait for your friends to reply to the message you have just sent, or you could give someone who you know uses email your new email address and ask him or her to email you so you can check everything works correctly.

In this example, Marjorie has received an email from her friend Glynis. This screen shows lots of other messages too and gives you a good example of how quickly an inbox can fill up. Later, we will look at deleting some of these messages, but first, let's read and reply to Glynis.

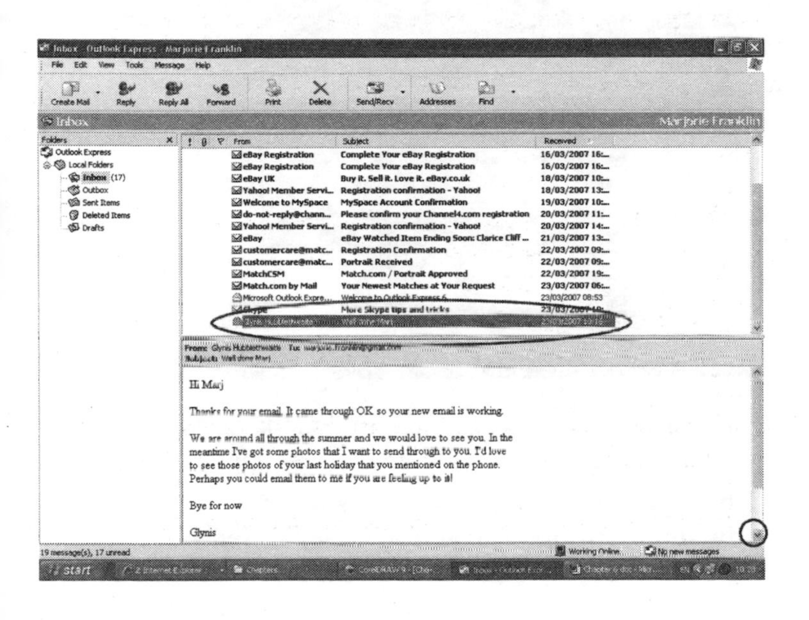

1 The Inbox was open when the email was received so it just appeared at the bottom of the list. It is in bold (darker text) which indicates that it has not been read yet.
2 Click on the message so that it is highlighted as shown. The message itself can now be seen in the bottom half

of the screen. If the message is too long you can click on the little arrow on the right-hand side as shown so that the rest of the message can be read.

This image shows 17 unread messages, with the message from Glynis highlighted. Also circled is the little arrow that lets you **scroll down** to read all of the message.

3 To reply to this message, double click on the message on the top half of the screen.
4 The message opens in a new window in the middle of the screen. Click on 'Reply'.

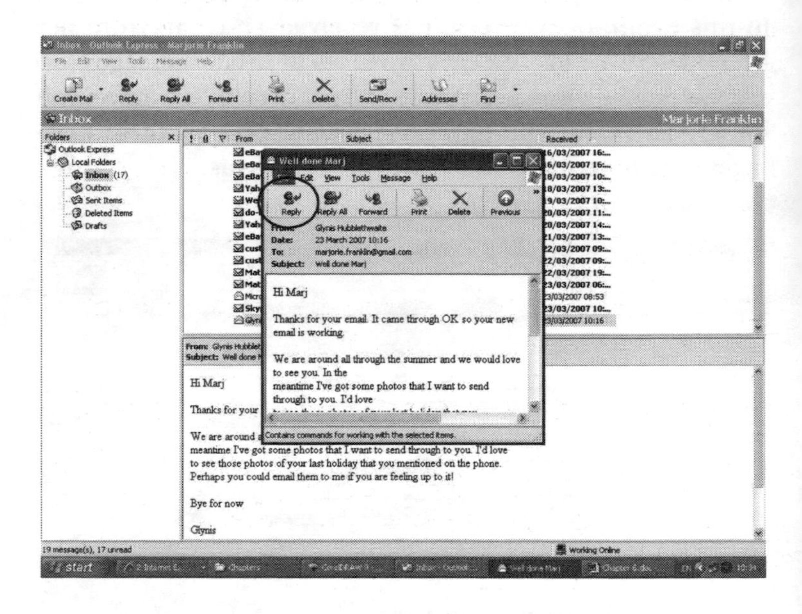

5 Replying to a message is exactly the same as sending one as described in section 6.3. It is actually slightly easier because you will see that it has put their email address in automatically so you don't need to remember it.
6 Type your reply and click on 'Send'.

6.6 Printing and deleting emails

Every time you go into Outlook Express® from now on you will need to check your Inbox to see if you have got any new messages. You can then read them and reply to them if you want to. All emails will just sit in your Inbox for ever until you delete them. You can delete messages after you have read them, or you can keep them if you think you need to. You may want to print an email out, either to keep as a record, or if you need a paper copy for some other reason.

Some emails you get will be junk email (called **spam**) and you should just delete it without even reading it. Some email software has a separate folder called 'Spam' where it automatically puts emails if it thinks they are junk email. As a general rule, you should never open an email unless you recognize who it is from – you should just delete it. Sometimes real emails can get put into the Spam folder by mistake so it is always worth checking to see if you recognize the email address before you delete them.

To delete an email:

1 Click on the email you want to delete in the top half of the screen so that it is highlighted.

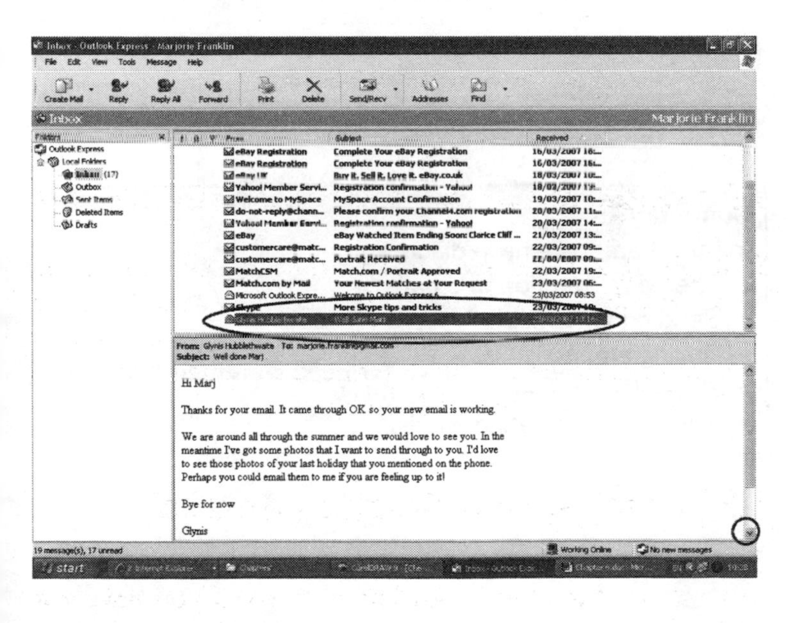

2 Press the DELETE key. It's as easy as that.

To print an email:

1 Double click on the email you want to print in the top half of the screen. It will then open in a new window.
2 Click on the 'Print' icon.

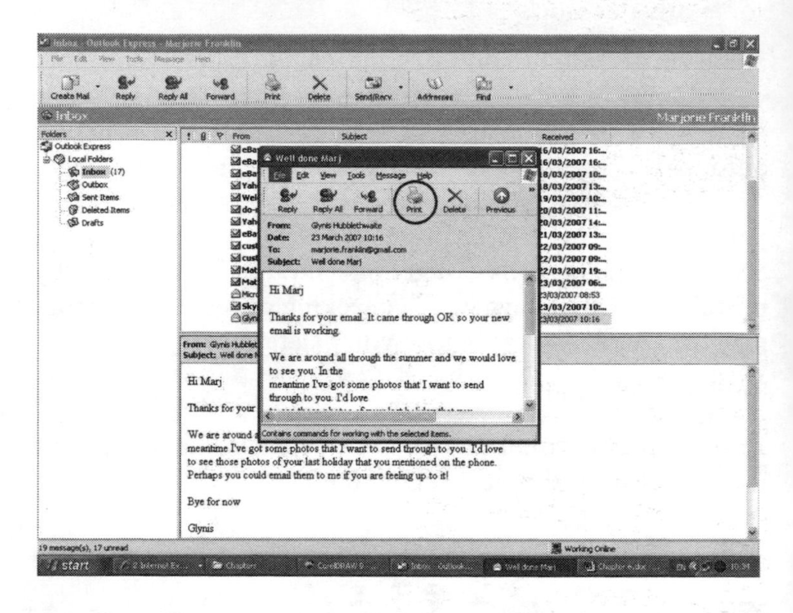

Notice that you can also delete the message from here too.

Summary

In this chapter we have discussed:

- The basic function of emails
- Sending an email
- Saving emails
- Receiving and replying to emails
- Printing and deleting emails

sending and receiving email attachments

In this chapter you will learn:

- **what an attachment is**
- **what can be attached and sent using email**
- **how to find what you want to attach**
- **how to send an attachment**
- **how to receive an attachment**

Aims of this chapter

This chapter will show you how to attach things to your emails so that you can send them to other people. These attachments could be any kind of computer file including photographs and documents. The chapter will also touch upon how to make sense of the folders that your computer uses to store information.

7.1 Introduction

When you send an email, you are sending some text from one computer to another. If you want to send other things too, you can do this using an **attachment**. Everything that is on your computer whether it is a document, a photograph, a piece of music, or a video clip, is stored in a **file**. In turn these files are stored in **folders**. To send an attachment, you are basically attaching one of these files to your email and it will be sent at the same time as the text message.

This does present a small problem in that you need to know which file contains the information you want to send, and which folder it is stored in. For example, if you had a photograph that you wanted to send to someone, you would have to know the name of the file that contains the photograph, and the name of the folder in which the file is stored.

Hints and tips

Think of your computer as a giant filing cabinet full of folders and files. Like a real filing cabinet you need to know where everything is filed if you ever want to find it again.

7.2 Understanding folders and files

We had a quick look at folders in Chapter 4. It is worth explaining them in a little more detail here as when you send or receive an attachment you have to send it from, or receive it into a folder. There are lots of folders on your computer already, and you can create your own if you want to. When you first start using a new computer, it will have one main folder for you to use called 'My Documents'.

1 To open the 'My Documents' folder, click on 'Start' and select 'My Documents'.
The 'My Documents' folder will be slightly different on every computer you use, so yours may not look exactly the same as this. You should, however, have several little yellow folders with names like 'My Music' and 'My Pictures'.

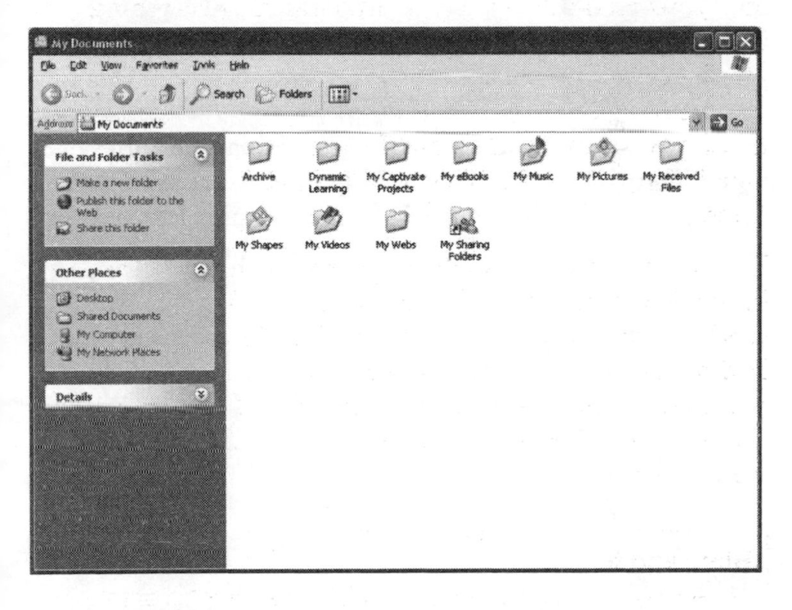

A folder can contain files, for example documents, photographs, music, etc., and it can contain further folders.

2 To find out what is in a folder, double click on it.
In this example, the 'My Music' folder has been clicked on. Inside it there are three further folders.

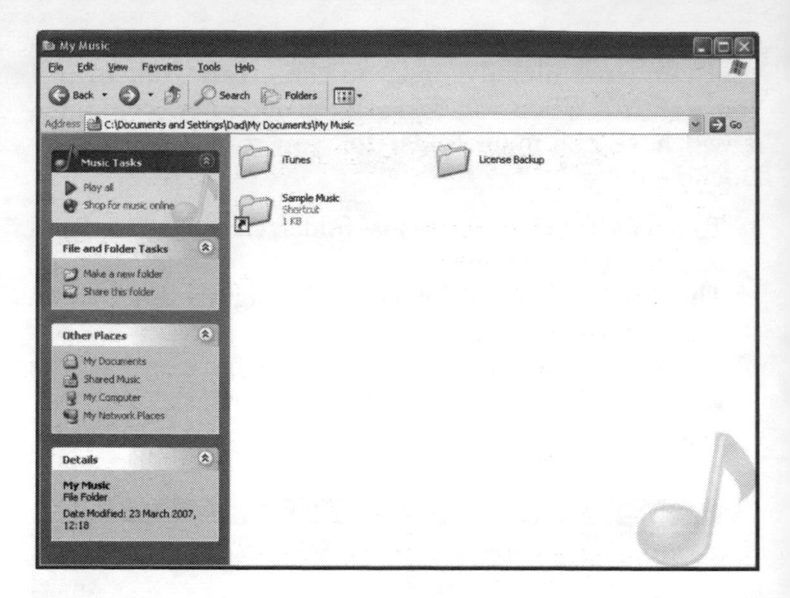

3 To see what inside any of these folders, double click on them.
For example, the **iTunes**™ folder contains lots of music files. You will probably be using your computer for other things as well, such as writing letters, or storing digital photographs. If this is the case, you will have come across folders, because every time you save anything, you are asked which folder you want to save into.

4 Click on the cross to close this down. We will now look at how you use email to send and receive any of these files.

> **Hints and tips**
> It would be useful if you could find a file, perhaps a photograph, that you can send to someone as a test.

7.3 Sending an attachment

1 Open Outlook Express® by double clicking on the **icon,** or clicking on it in the 'Start' menu.
2 Click on 'Create Mail' in the top left-hand corner.

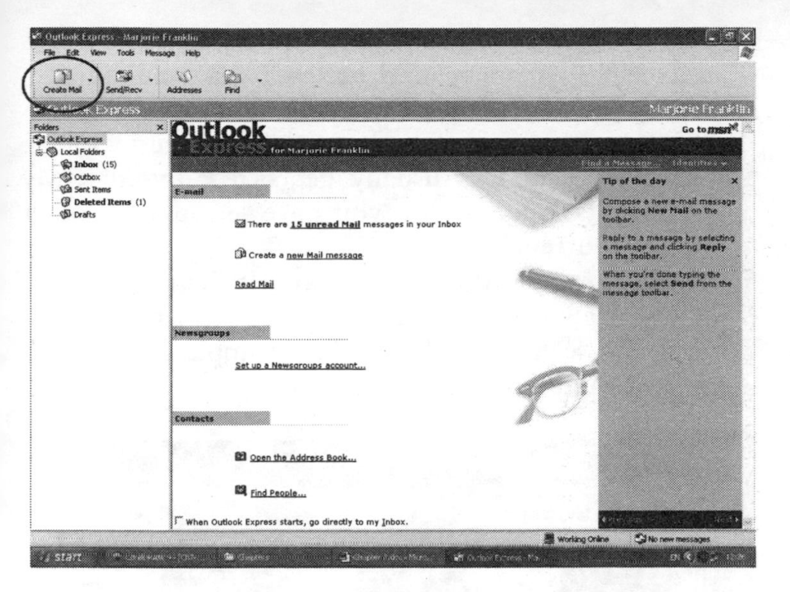

3 You can now write your email as described in Chapter 6, adding the **email address** of the person to whom you are writing, and filling in the subject line, and then typing your message.
4 To add an attachment, click on 'Insert' and then 'File attachment'. The My Documents folder will now open. Yours may not look exactly the same as this.

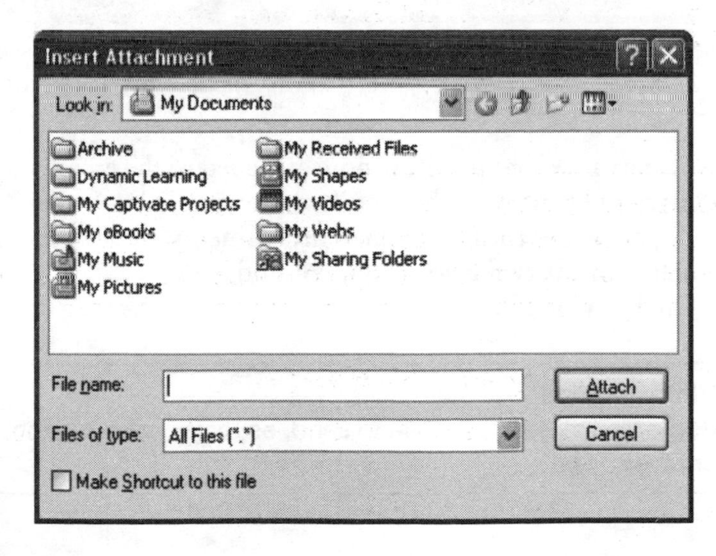

This is where you need to know the name of the folder and the file that you want to attach. If it is a photograph, it is most likely that it will be in the 'My Pictures' folder. If it is music, it is likely to be in the 'My Music' folder. Other types of files usually get saved into the 'My Documents' folder unless you have set up some other folders yourself.

5 For this example, double click on 'My Pictures'.
6 Double click on the file that you want to send, or click on it and select 'Attach'. In this example it is the one called Grandkids.JPG

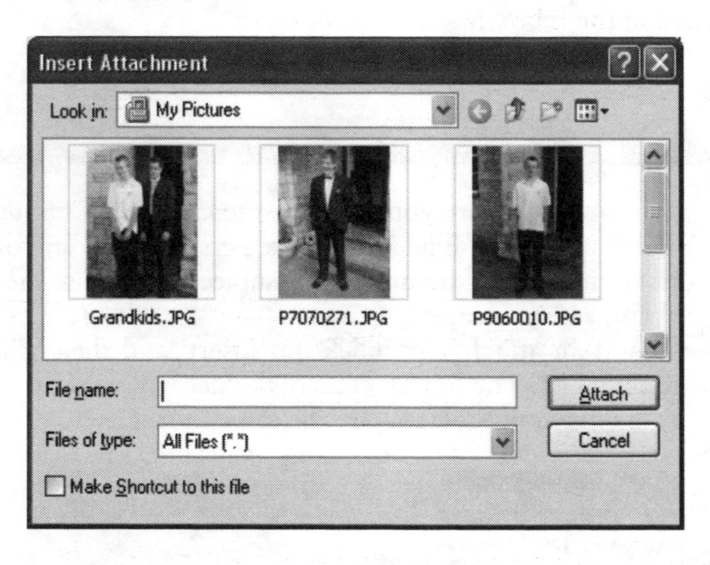

7 You can see that the file is now attached to the email and it will be sent with the email when you click on 'Send'. If you want to add further attachments, repeat these steps for every file you want to send.
8 Click on 'Send'.

Hints and tips
Some files may take a while to send, especially photograph or music files.

7.4 Receiving an attachment

When you receive an attachment you can view the file and save it onto your computer. For example, if someone sent you a photograph as an attachment, you could view the photograph and then save it onto your computer so you have got your own copy of it.

You will know that an email has an attachment because you will see a paper-clip symbol next to the email when you look in your Inbox. In this example, the paper clip is very small but you can see where it will be displayed. The last email in the Inbox has an attachment.

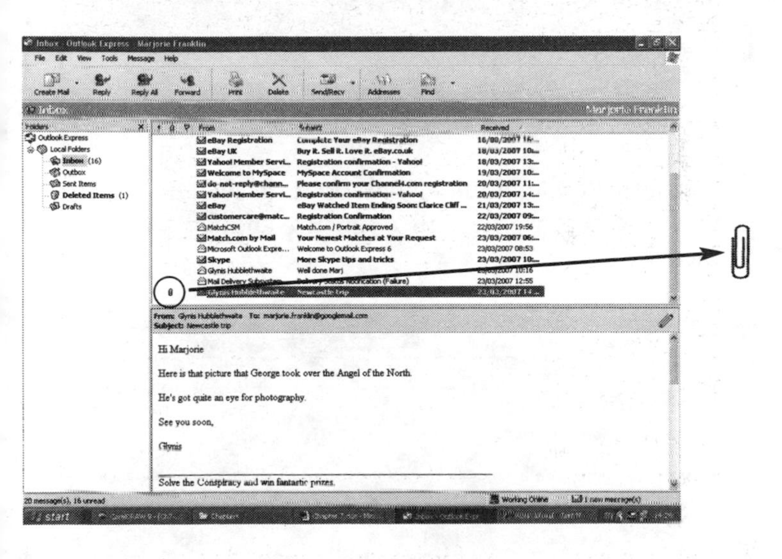

1 Move the **mouse pointer** to the message and double click.
2 The message will now open in its own window and you can see the name of the file that has been attached. In this case the file is called Angel of the North.jpg.

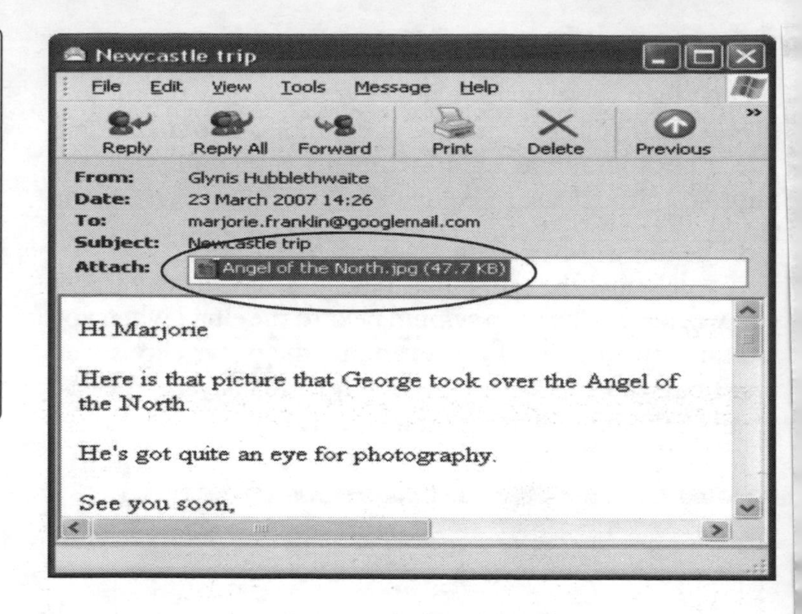

3 To view the file, double click on it. It will then open. As this is a picture, it will open up and let you see the picture.

4 To close the file click on the cross in the top right-hand corner.
5 To save the picture onto your computer, right click on the file name, in this case Angel of the North.jpg.
6 Click on 'Save As'. You will now see the folders again.
7 Double click on 'My Pictures'.
8 The file will be saved as 'Angel of the North.jpg'. You can change the name if you like, but don't change the **.jpg** bit.

9 Click 'Save'. You can now go back to your email and reply to it, or delete it. You can safely delete the message now because you have saved the attachment onto your own computer. If you deleted the message without saving the attachment first, you would delete the attachment too.
10 You can now view the photograph at any time without having to use email. Click on 'Start' and then on 'My Documents', and then on 'My Pictures'.
11 Find the 'Angel of the North.jpg' file and double click on it. It will then open for you to view.

Summary

In this chapter we have discussed:

- Email attachment
- What can be attached and sent using email
- Finding the file you want to attach
- Sending and receiving attachments
- Folders and files

In this chapter you will learn:

- how to manage folders in email
- how to add and remove contacts from your address book
- how to send emails to people in your address book

Aims of this chapter
This chapter will show you how to keep track of the folders that are used to store all of the email messages. There are five standard folders and you can make your own if you want to. It will also show you how to manage your contacts lists, known as an address book.

8.1 Introduction

Even if you use email only occasionally, it is worth being organized. Every time you send and receive an email, a copy of the email is stored in **folders** within the email **software**. After a while these folders can get full which can make it hard to find old messages if you need to, and it can make the email program run slower.

Also you will be using **email addresses**. All email software allows you to manage your contacts. This is normally called an **address book** and it works just like a normal paper-based address book in that you store people's names and (email) addresses in it.

This chapter will show you how to keep track of the folders and how to manager your address book.

8.2 Organizing the folders

In Chapter 7 we looked at the way that your computer has folders that it uses to store **files**. Email works in a similar way in that it has folders, which it uses to store emails. Let's look at the folders now.

1 Open Outlook Express®. The folders are listed on the left-hand side.

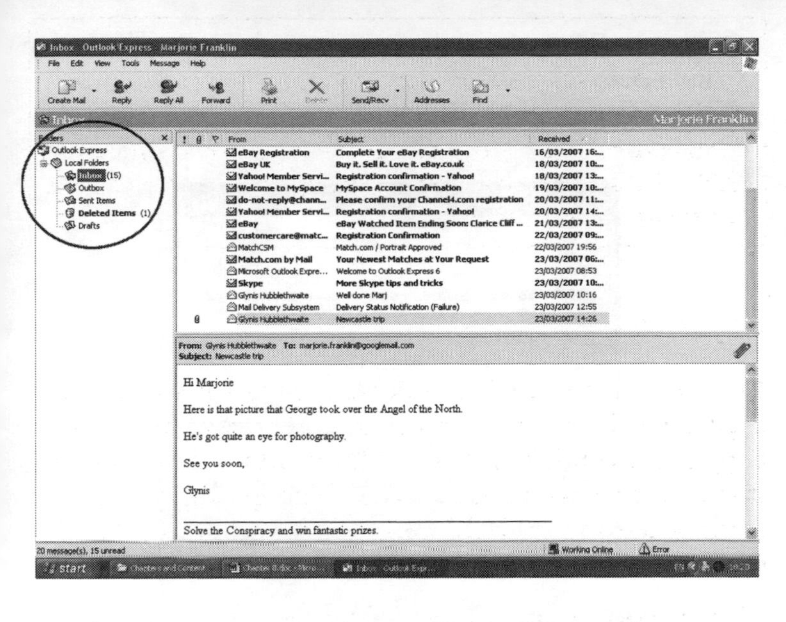

There is an alternative way of viewing folders, shown below. If you prefer this view (notice that the folders are replaced with **icons**), then follow steps 2 to 4. If you are happy with the current layout, go straight on to step 5.

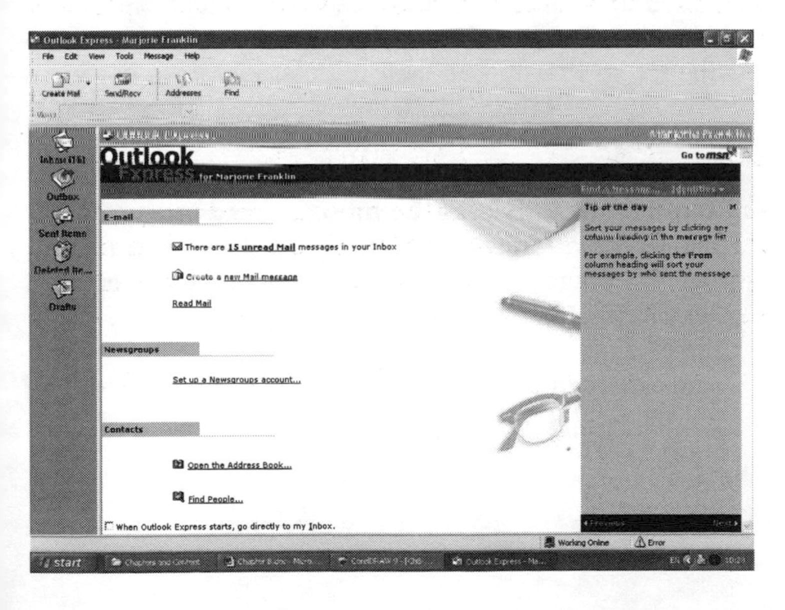

2 Click on 'View' from the options at the top of the screen and select 'Layout'.
3 This screen will be displayed:

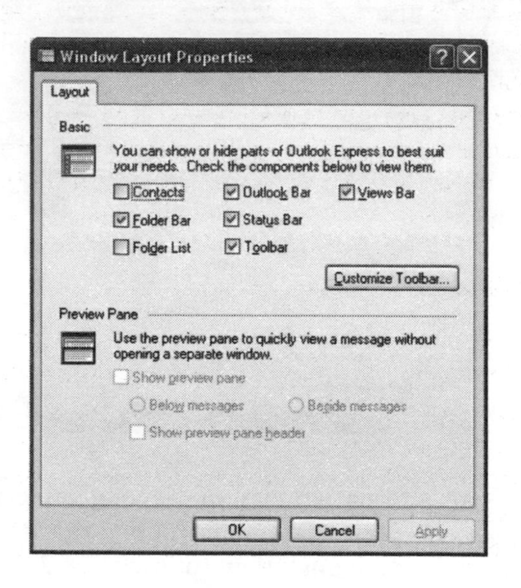

4 Tick the boxes as shown. The boxes that should be ticked are: Outlook Bar, Views Bar, Folder Bar, Status Bar and Toolbar. Then click 'OK'. The layout will change so that rather than folders, you have got icons that represent the folders.
The basic set-up for the folders is that every message you ever receive is stored in a folder called the **Inbox**. You have already used the Inbox to read messages. The messages will stay there until you delete them. Also, every message you ever send is stored in the folder called Sent Items. Again, these will stay here until you delete them.
The three other folders are: Outbox, Deleted Items and Drafts.

Outbox

There may be occasions when you want to use Outlook Express®, but you are not connected to the

Internet. Perhaps you are having problems with the connection. You can still use Outlook Express® to write your emails in the normal way. The email will be saved in the Outbox folder. Next time you **log on** to the Internet, any messages in your Outbox will be sent automatically.

5 To use this feature you simply compose your email in the usual way and if you are not **online**, it will automatically store it in the Outbox and automatically send it the next time you connect to the Internet.

Deleted Items

When you delete an email message it is removed from your Inbox but a copy of it is stored in the Deleted Items folder. The logic behind this is that you might delete something by accident. If you do want to retrieve a deleted message you can click into the Deleted Items folder and you will find it there.

6 To access the Deleted Items folder, just double click on it.

Drafts

There may be an occasion when you are typing an email message but don't want to send it straight away. Sometimes you might be typing a long email but are interrupted and want to save your message. In this case you can save the email into the Drafts folder. You can then retrieve it from the Drafts folder, and send it in the normal way.

7 To save something into the Drafts folder, start composing your email in the normal way.

8 When you are ready to save it, click on 'File' and then 'Save'. The message is then saved in the Drafts folder.

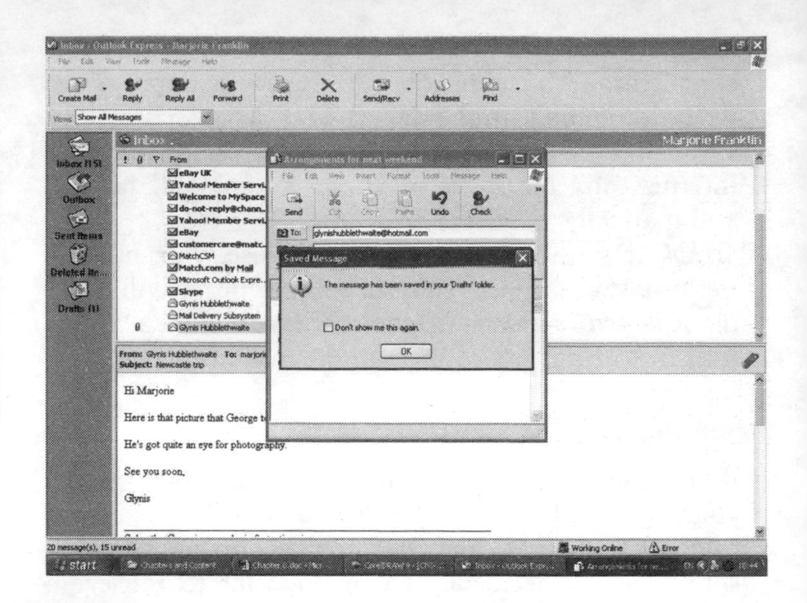

9 To retrieve to this message, click on the Drafts folder and then double click on the message. You can now finish it off in the normal way and send it.

In addition to these five standard folders you can also create your own.

Hints and tips

It is suggested that you create your own email folders only if you use email a lot for different reasons and need to keep messages separately, or if you are one of those really organized people!

10 To create a new folder, click on 'File' and then on 'Folder' and then on 'New'.

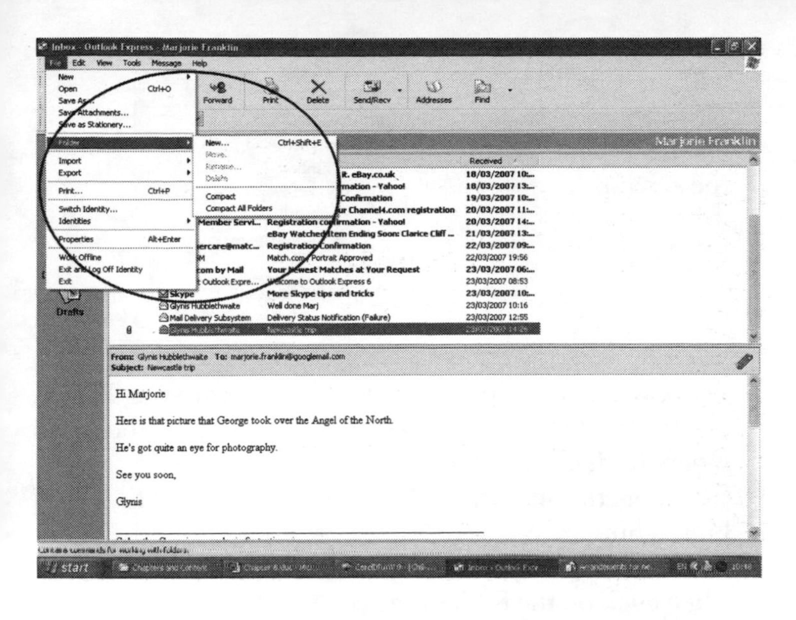

11 In the next window, click on 'Local Folders' and then in the box under 'Folder name:', type a suitable name. This example shows a new folder called 'Work related'.

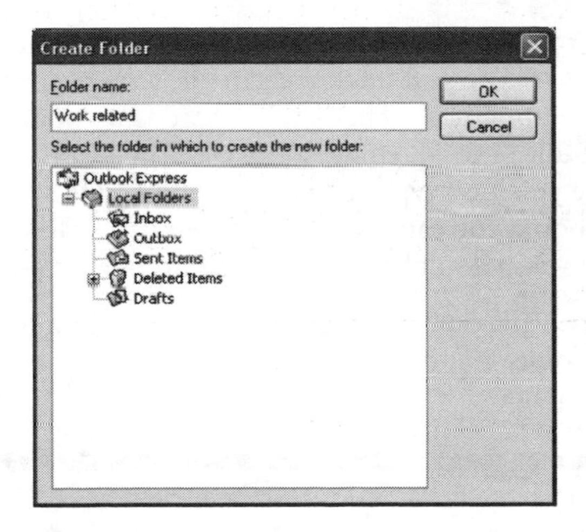

12 Click 'OK'.
13 To see any new folders you need to have the folders list displayed. To do this, go to 'View' and 'Layout' and then un-tick the box for 'Outlook Bar' and click 'OK'.

The new folder will now be displayed on the left-hand side of the screen.

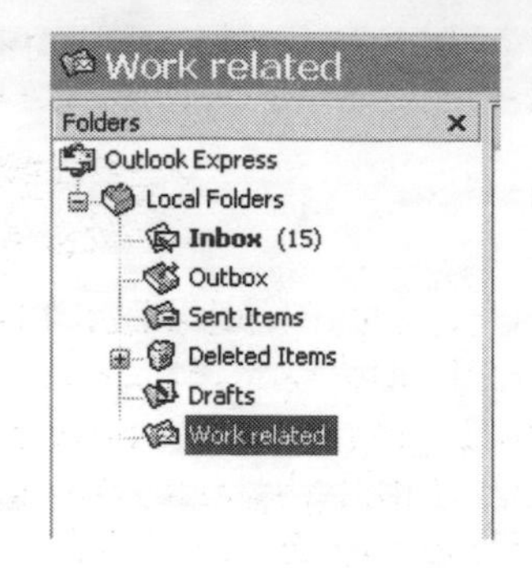

All new emails will automatically go into your Inbox. You may want to move messages out of your Inbox into a new folder. To do this:

14 Click on the message you want to move so that it is highlighted.

15 Click on 'Edit' and select 'Move to folder'.

16 Then click on the folder that you want to move it to, and click 'OK'. The message has now been moved.

8.3 Using the address book

You can't possibly remember every single email address that you will ever use and having them all written down somewhere is impractical. That's why there is an address book facility built in to all email software. The beauty of this is that once you have typed someone's email address into your address book, you can just click on their details to send them an email – you don't have to type the address in ever again.

1 To open the address book, open your Inbox (or any of your folders) and click on the 'Addresses' icon at the top of the page.

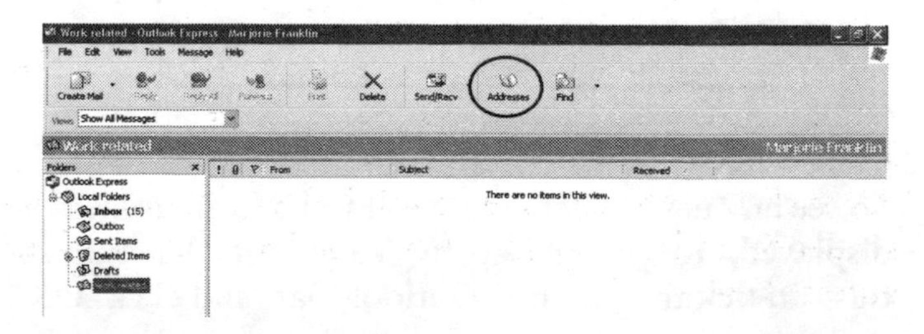

2 The address book will open in its own window, **maximize** this by clicking on the '**Restore**' button.

3 Click on 'New' and select 'New Contact'.

4 You will now see this screen where you can type in the contact details. This example shows the details for Glynis Hubblethwaite. You actually have to type in only the name and the email address – the rest is optional.

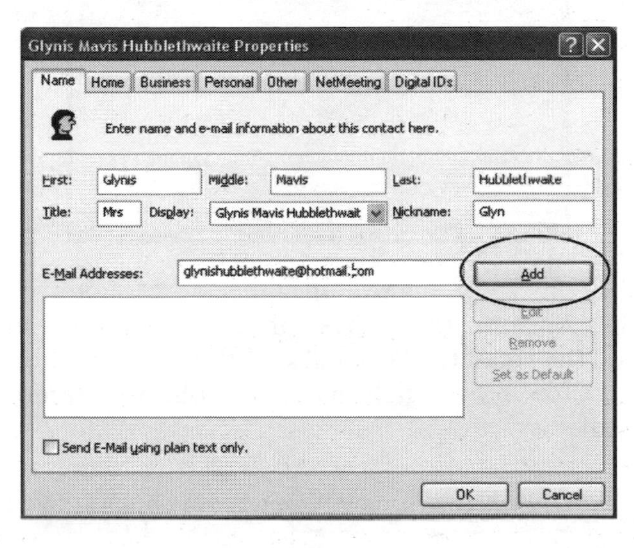

5 Click on 'Add' and then 'OK'.

6 Repeat this process every time you want to add a new contact.

7 To change any of the details, double click on the contact and then click on 'Name' and you get back to the same screen to make changes.

8 Click on the cross to close the address book.

Sometimes you will be sent an email from someone who is not in your address book. To add that person to your address book:

9 Right click on the email in your Inbox and click on 'Add sender to address book'. Their email address is added automatically.

10 To send an email to someone in your address book, click on 'Create Mail' in the usual way. This screen is displayed:

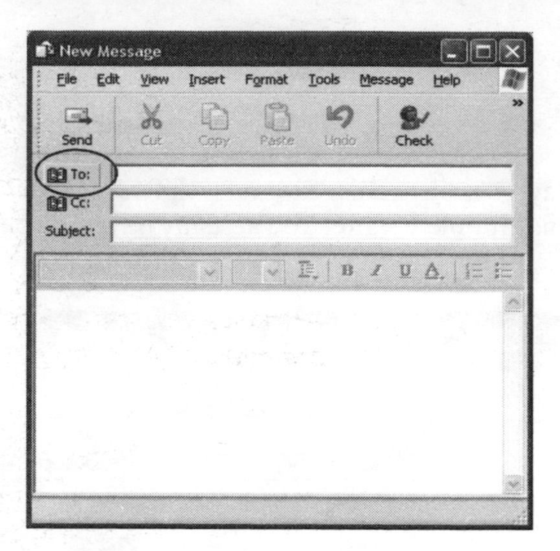

11 Click on 'To:'. This will open the address book.

12 Click once on the address of the person you want to send the email to. Then click on the arrow as shown. It will show on the right-hand side who will receive the email.

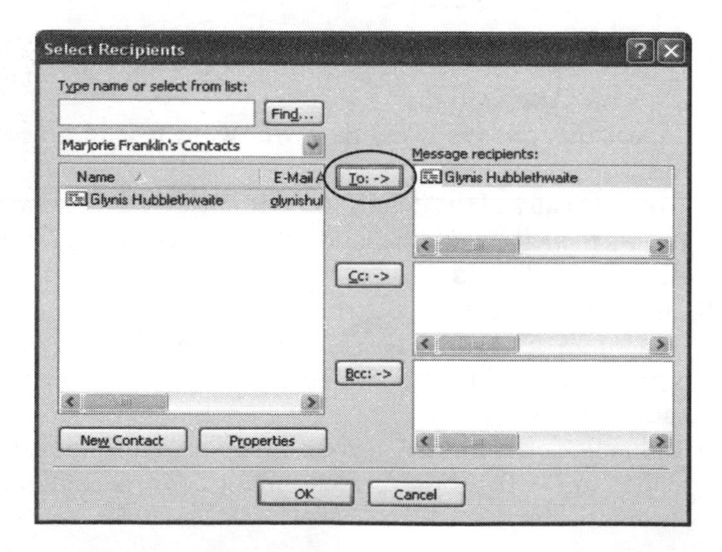

In this example there is only one person in the address book but you are likely to have lots of people in yours. If you want to send the same message to lots of people, then repeat step 12 for all the people you want to receive the email.

Hints and tips

The Cc box indicates 'copy to' which means that you are sending them a copy for information although they are not the main recipient. The main recipient will know that this other person has also got the email. The Bcc is a blind copy, which means you can send someone else a copy of the email and the main recipient won't know that this person is also getting a copy.

13 Click on 'OK'. The normal screen will now open but you will see that the email address or addresses are already in place, so you don't have to type them in manually.

Summary

In this chapter we have discussed:

- Organizing email folders
- Organizing an address book
- Using an address book to send emails

getting started on the Internet

In this chapter you will learn:

- **what the Internet is**
- **how to type in a 'web address'**
- **what a hyperlink is and how to follow one**
- **how to move forward and back through web pages**
- **how to use a 'search engine'**
- **how to assess whether a website is reliable**
- **what to do when websites don't work**

Aim of the chapter
The aim of this chapter is to help you to search the Internet to find what you want. It will also give advice on how to work out whether the information you find is reliable and trustworthy. The skills that you learn in this chapter are essential to being able to find what you need on the Internet. Once you have mastered these skills, you will be able to surf the net for anything you want.

9.1 Introduction

The Internet is a worldwide connection of computers. It is also referred to as the **World Wide Web (www)** and is made up of millions and millions of pages of information. These pages are called **web pages**. A collection of web pages is called a **website**. All sorts of organizations and individuals might create a website. In many cases these are businesses trying to sell things, but it also includes government organizations, charities, clubs and private individuals.

This presents a few problems. The first is that there is so much information available that it can be difficult to find what you need. The second is that there is an awful lot of rubbish in among the good stuff. The third is that the information on the Internet is constantly changing. New websites are being put on the Internet all the time, websites are being removed and also the content of individual websites is constantly changing.

Hints and tips
The Internet or net refers to the global connection of computers. The World Wide Web (www) or web refers to all of the information that is available on the Internet. The two terms basically mean the same thing.

9.2 Finding a website when you know the web address

The easiest way to find a website is if you know the address. Website addresses are unique, so no two websites can have exactly the same name. Most organizations advertise their web addresses and include them in their advertising. For example: www.oxfam.org.uk

Hints and tips
Internet Explorer® is what is known as a web **browser** that allows you to look at websites. Internet Explorer® is the most common but there are other web browsers available such as Mozilla, Opera and Netscape. These work in exactly the same way, but look slightly different.

To go to a website if you know the address:

1 Double click on the 'Internet Explorer' **icon** on your **desktop**.

If you have not got one, click on 'Start' and select it from there.

Internet Explorer® will now load and a web page will be displayed. This is known as your **home page** and is always the first page to be shown. In this case, the home page is Tiscali, which is an **Internet Service Provider (ISP)**. Yours might be something completely different.

Circled at the top of the page is the **address bar**. This is where it will show you the web address of the page you are on, and where you type in the web address of the page that you want to go to next.

2 Click in the address bar and type in the address of the website you want to go to (in this case www.oxfam.org.uk). It is very important that you type the address exactly as shown with the correct slashes and full stops where relevant.

3 Press ENTER or click on the green arrow to the right of the address bar.

After a few seconds, you will be taken to the page with the address that you have just typed in.

When you get to the page, it is probably the home page of the website. A home page is the main page of a website. This should contain general information that welcomes you to the site and tells you about the organization or person who is responsible for the site.

Once you are in the website, you may need to move to other parts of the website to find what you want. Nearly all web pages include **links** to other pages. These links are called **hyperlinks**. They might take you to another page on the same website, or to a page on another website.

Hyperlinks can be attached to anything. There might be a link from a piece of text, or from a picture. They try to make it easy for you to spot the links and explain where the link will take you. Also, the **mouse pointer**, which normally looks like this ↖ will change when you hover the mouse over an object on a web page. If it changes to a little hand like this 👆 that means that there is a link to another page.

4 Find a hyperlink (any hyperlink) and click on it. You are now taken to a different web page. This page will have lots of information on it, and it will also have lots more hyperlinks too.
   One of the problems is that you can quite quickly lose track of where you are up to. After you have clicked on a few hyperlinks, you have lost the page where you started. If this happens:
5 Click the 'Back' button, which is the arrow (pointing left) in the top left-hand corner of the page.

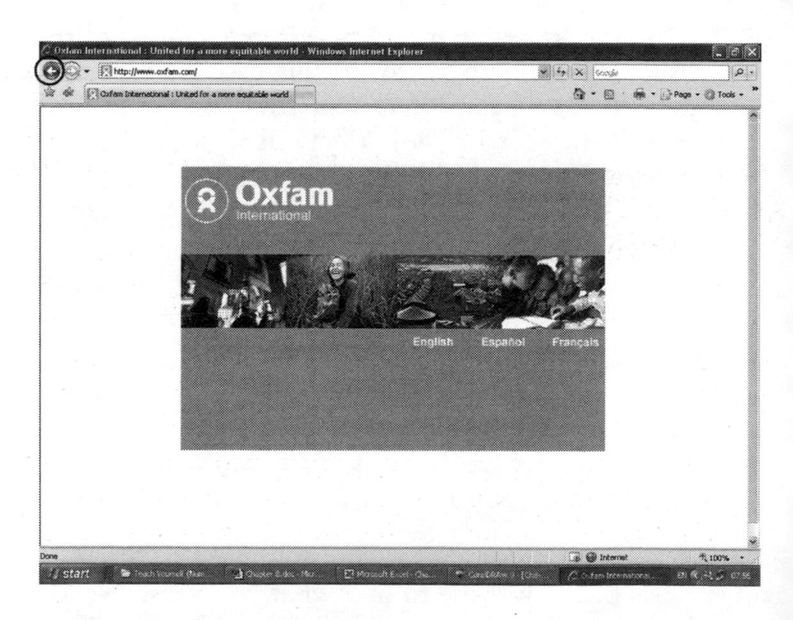

This will take you to the previous page.

6 Click the 'Back' button again.
This will take you back to the page before that, and so on until eventually you are back where you started.

Hints and tips
The 'Back' button will work only if you have already been to some web pages. Otherwise there will be nothing for it to go back to. If the arrow is in a blue circle it means that there are pages to go back to. If it is in a grey circle, then there are no pages to go back to.

Another problem is that sometimes when you click on a hyperlink, a new window opens up. This means that your original page is still open in the background. To get back to the original page in this case:

7 Click on the small cross in the top right-hand corner of the window. This window then closes, and your original page is displayed again.

9.3 Structure of web addresses

It is useful to be able to recognize the way that web addresses are put together. Sometimes it will give you a hint about the nature of the site. Most addresses look like this: www.hodder.co.uk

- The www means World Wide Web and most (but not all) addresses start with this. Sometimes you don't even need to type this in.
- The next part tells you the name of the individual or organization who owns the website. In this case it is Hodder Headline (the publisher of this book).
- The last part of the address tells you what type of organization or person owns the website and where it is in the world. The table below shows some common examples.

.com	Stands for 'commercial' and will be a business. Could be anywhere in the world.
.co.uk	This will be a business in the UK.
.org.uk	This will be an organization in the UK, but not a business, e.g. a charity.
.gov.uk	This is UK government website.
.ac.uk	This will be a UK college or university. The 'ac' is short for academic.
.au .it .de	These are country codes that appear at the end of an address and indicate which country it comes from. There are lots of these: in this example, Australia, Italy and Germany.

9.4 Finding the information you need using a search engine

If you do NOT know the web address, you will need to **search** the Internet to find the information you need. To do this, you need a **search engine**.

Search engines are free and you can access them using the Internet. There are lots to choose from but the most common ones are Google™, Yahoo!® and Ask™. They all do the same thing and it is up to you which one you use. The most popular one at the moment is Google™.

A search engine allows you to type in key words that describe what you are looking for. For example, let's say we want to make a donation to the British Red Cross and we need to find the website. You might start by searching for: charity. It will then search through the web to find web pages that contain information based on the key words you typed in. When it has found all the sites, it will display them all in a list. The list may take up hundreds of pages.

> **Hints and tips**
> Even the best search engine doesn't search every single page on the Internet. You may want to experiment with a couple of different search engines to find the one you like the best. The organizations that provide these search engines are commercial businesses so they will all tell you that theirs is the best.

1 Open **Internet Explorer®**, if it is not open already.
2 Type: www.google.co.uk into the address bar. The Google™ home page will now load.

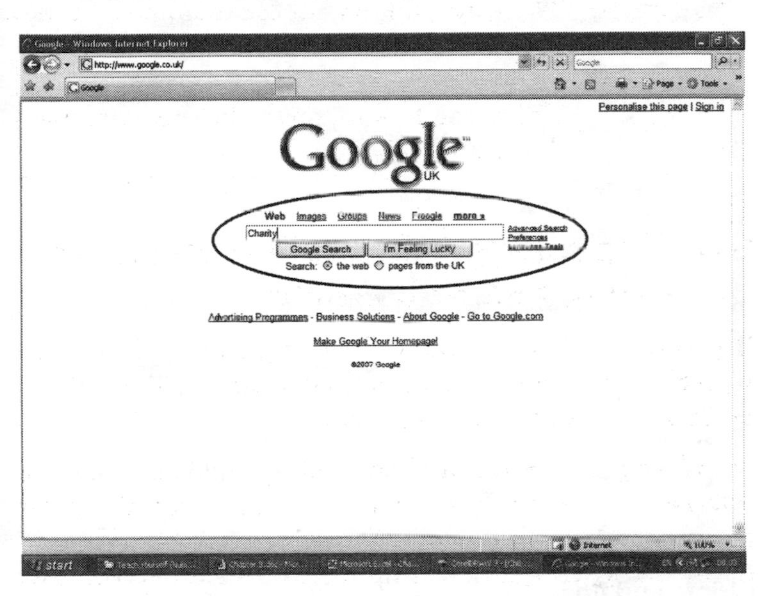

3 Type the word: Charity into the box as shown.
4 Click on the button for 'pages from the UK'.

> **Hints and tips**
> Clicking the UK button means that you should get only websites based in the UK, although some others do get through sometimes.

5 Click on the 'Google Search' button.

After a few seconds your screen will show the results pages listing all of the websites that contain information about charities.

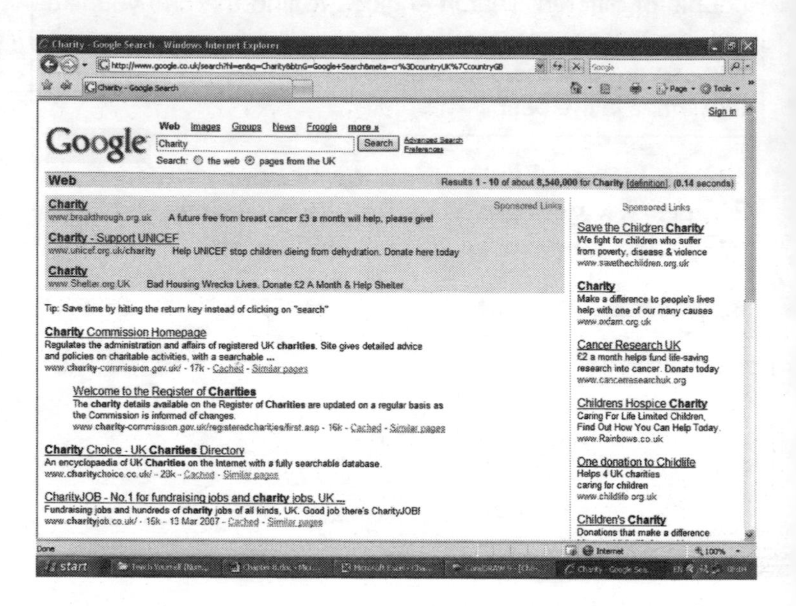

This page contains the first ten websites that contain information that meets your key words. It also contains some sponsored links, which mean that businesses have paid Google™ so that their websites will appear on this page.

> **Hints and tips**
> Each website shown on the results page can be opened by clicking on it. You can read what it says about the website and use this to decide whether it is worth clicking on or not.

In the top right-hand corner you will see how many pages the search engine has found. In this case it has found 8,540,000 pages. This is sometimes called the number of **hits**. It would take years to search through all of these, so we need to narrow down the search.

6 Scroll to the top of the page and type the words 'British Red Cross' into the box. You will find that this reduces the number of hits significantly, and that the website for the British Red Cross is first on the list on the first page of results.

We actually wanted to find out how to donate to the British Red Cross so we could this in two ways. We could:

7 Click on the link to the British Red Cross website.

8 Follow the hyperlinks to the donation section.

OR we could refine the search still further:

9 Type the words: "British Red Cross" + donation (exactly as shown).

Hints and tips

Putting words inside speech marks means that the search engine will show only websites that contain those words in that sequence. Using the + sign means that it will include sites that also only contain the word 'donation'.

10 Press ENTER. The results page will now show a direct link to the donations web page of the British Red Cross website.

9.5 How to tell whether websites are reliable and trustworthy

Just because a website is listed by a search engine, does not mean that it contains the information you need, or that the information is correct. Anyone can put information onto a website and there are plenty of strange people out there!

It is not always easy to tell how reliable a website is, but there are some general guidelines you can use:

- Rely on websites only if they are from organizations or businesses that you already know and trust.
- Check for an 'About Us' link to see if you can find out who is responsible for the site.

- Check the name of the site. If it is a .gov site for example, you know that it has come from the government (whether you trust it or not is up to you!). If it is .co.uk it could be from anyone.
- Most sites are trying to sell you something, so you need to be as cynical as you would be if confronted with a pushy salesman in a shop!
- Some websites are what is known as secure sites. There is more information on this in Chapter 15.

9.6 Dead links and redirection

Finally, it is quite common to click on a hyperlink and not to get the page you want. This might be for a number of reasons. The web page might no longer exist, or the link might have been set up incorrectly. These are sometimes called **dead links** as they don't take you anywhere. You will most likely get a message on the screen saying that the web page has not been found.

If this happens:

1 Click on 'Back'.
This will take you back to the page that you linked from. It is worth trying again, as sometimes you just get a bad connection. If you try again and you get the same message, then the link is probably dead and there is nothing you can do about it.
Sometimes you will be redirected to another website. Sometimes this is for genuine reasons, as the website may have been moved to a different address. Sometimes, it is an advertising ploy to take you to a site that then tries to sell you something. A bit like dead links, all you can do is:
2 Click on 'Back' OR click on the cross to close the window.

9.7 Common features of websites

As you will soon discover, every website you visit looks different. At first it can be difficult to find your way around some websites. However, many websites have similar features that you should look out for. For example, on many websites:

- The links to other pages are either across the top of the page or down the left- or right-hand side of the page.
- A registration process is necessary, usually requiring your email address and a **password**.
- You may have to fill in a form to register with the website.
- Where the website has masses of information there will be a **browse** or search facility to help you find what you are looking for.
- There may be the opportunity to **download** things, which means that you can take things like music or software from their sites and put them onto your computer.

Throughout the rest of this book you will need to use the skills learned in this chapter. We do use some websites as examples, although we should point out that we are not endorsing these sites and there will always be plenty of others to choose from. We would encourage you to find your own websites either on recommendation from others, or perhaps sites you have seen advertised. Alternatively, you can find suitable sites by typing appropriate search words into a search engine such as Google™.

Summary

In this chapter we have discussed:

- How to understand and use web addresses
- How to use a search engine
- How to follow hyperlinks and move between web pages
- How to tell whether a website is reliable
- What to do when you get a bad link
- Common features of websites

In this chapter you will learn:

- how to revisit websites you have been to before
- how to save websites in a 'favourites' list so that you can find them again easily
- how to change your 'home page'
- how to have several web pages open at the same time
- how to view a list of all websites that you have visited (called a history file)
- how to delete your history file

Aim of the chapter
The aim of this chapter is to keep organized when you are using the Internet. This will make it easier and quicker for you to revisit websites, and will stop your computer getting cluttered up with your past website viewing history.

10.1 Introduction

In Chapter 9 we looked at how you could find **websites** either by typing in the **web address**, or by using a **search engine**. What you will probably find is that there are some websites that you want to use over and over again. If this is the case, you want to be able to get back to them quickly. **Internet Explorer®** keeps a record of every **web page** that you have ever visited. This is called your **history file**. This chapter will look at how you can use the history file to revisit websites. It will also show you how you can create a list of favourite websites – the ones that you will visit the most often.

10.2 Revisiting websites using the address bar

This history file stores the web address of every address that you type into the **address bar**. This can be very useful if you want to revisit a website as it saves you having to remember the address. It can also be a pain, because it records every single web page that you ever go to, and after a while the list can get very long.

To see how it works:

1 Open Internet Explorer®, if it is not open already.
2 Type an address into the address bar, for example, www.bbc.co.uk
3 After a few seconds, the BBC **home page** will open.

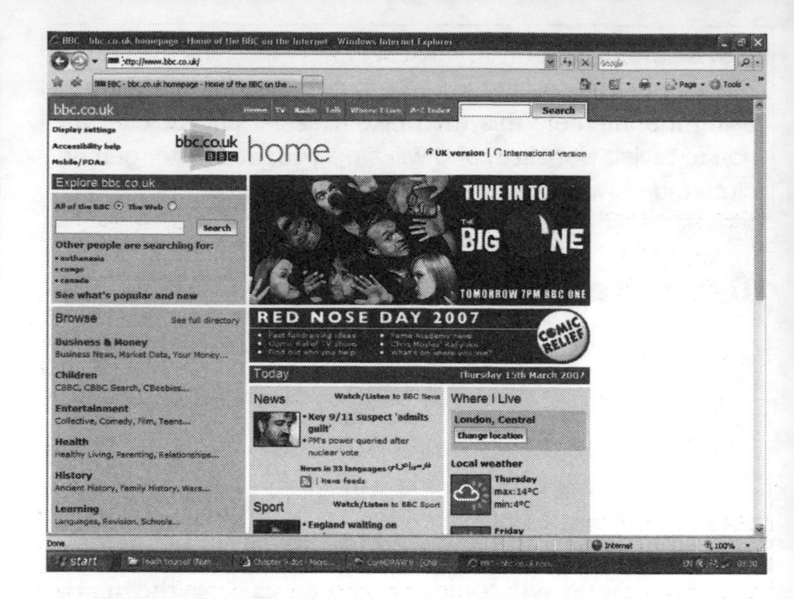

So far in this book, we have been to the Oxfam website and to the Google™ website. You might have been to a few other websites too while you have been experimenting. All these websites will be saved in your history file.

4 Click on the small arrow that is at the far right-hand side of the address bar as shown:

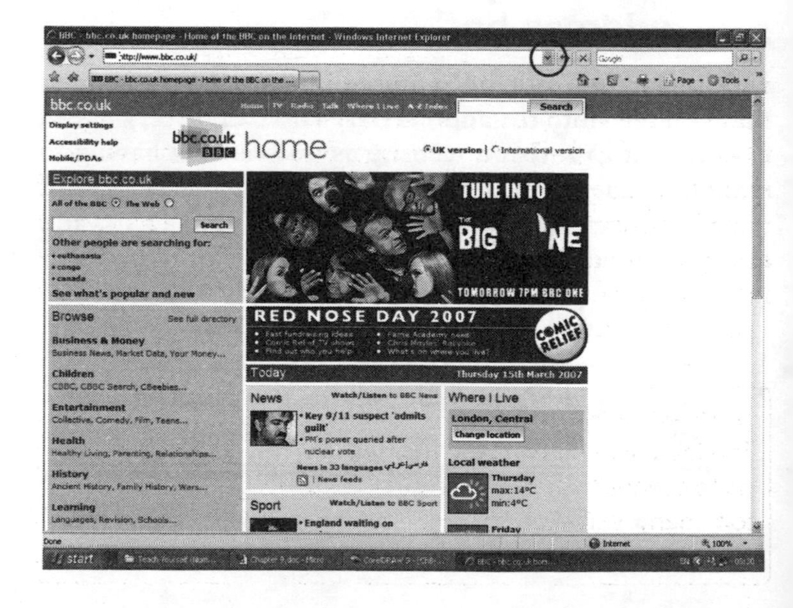

When you click on it, a list will appear. This list is every website address that you have ever typed in.
In this case there are three sites – but this list can get very long.

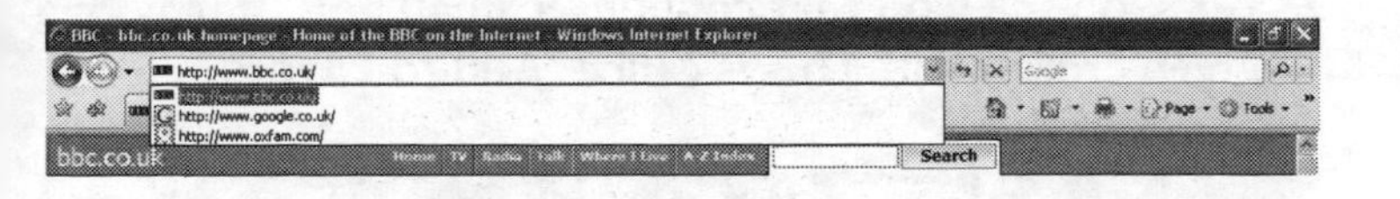

5 To go back to any of these sites, all you have to do is move the **mouse pointer** over it so that is **highlighted**, and then click on it.

> **Hints and tips**
> If something is highlighted it means it has been selected. If you move the mouse pointer up and down over this list you can see how the website that is highlighted changes as you move the mouse.

10.3 Saving websites into a favourites list

The problem with using the address bar to get back to websites you have been to before is that you still have to find the one you want in among what could be a long list of sites. If you find a website that you know that you will want to use again, you can save it into a special list, called your **Favorites** (notice the American spelling). The idea is that you should put only a small(ish) number of websites into your favourites list. These would be the ones that you visit most often.

> **Hints and tips**
> The idea of the favourites is to make it quicker and easier to go to a website that you are going to use regularly. If you put too many websites in your favourites list, it defeats the object because the list gets too long.

In this example, we will put the BBC website into your favourites list.

1 Open the BBC website, either by typing: www.bbc.co.uk or by clicking on the little arrow and finding it in the list.
2 Click on the **icon** that contains a small gold star with a green cross on it. This is called 'Add to Favorites'.

3 Click on 'Add to Favorites'.

A new window will now open in the middle of the screen:

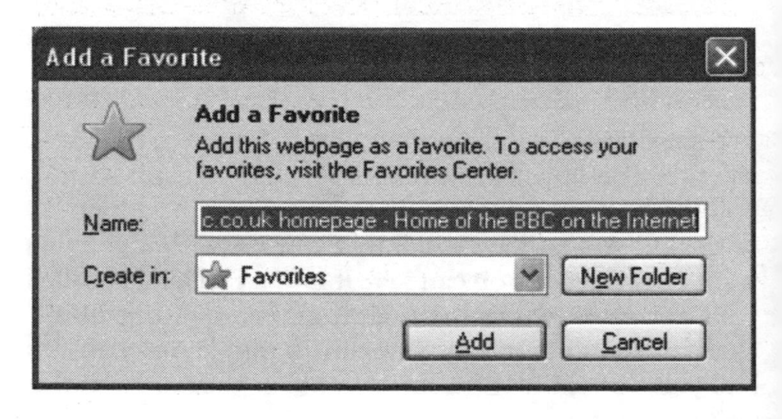

Notice that the Name has been put in automatically – you can type over this with a new name if you like.

4 Click on the 'Add' button. The BBC website is now saved in your favourites.
5 You can now go to this website at any time by clicking on the icon with the gold star:

This screen will now be displayed:

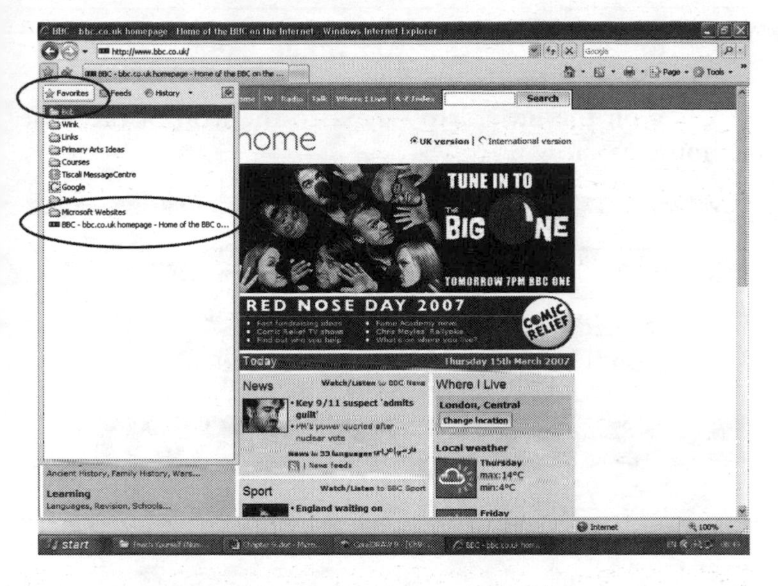

6 Click on 'Favorites'.
A list of every website that you have saved as a favourite is now displayed. In this example there are a few listed, and you can see the BBC website at the bottom of this list. On your computer, you may have only the BBC website in the list. To go back to the BBC website:
7 Highlight the BBC website in the list and click on it. You may want to test this out by changing to another website, and then following these steps to get back to the BBC website.

10.4 Changing your home page

As you have seen, when you first click on Internet Explorer®, a web page opens up. This is called your home page. The page it opens will depend on how you (or the supplier) set up the computer in the first place. You may want to change this to something else.

Hints and tips

You usually set your home page to the website that you use most often, like your email website, or perhaps the search engine you use most often.

1 Go to the website that you would like to set as your home page.
2 Click on the little arrow next to the icon of the little house as shown:

3 Select 'Add or Change Home Page'.
4 Click on 'Use this webpage as your only home page'.

5 Click on the 'Yes' button. The next time you open Internet Explorer®, it will now open this page.

10.5 Opening several web pages at the same time

In Internet Explorer®7, there are **tabs** that let you have more than one page open at the same time. This can be quite useful if you want to keep a page open and then go off and view a different page. You can actually have quite a few pages open at the same time if you want to.

To open a new tab:

1 Click on the New Tab icon as shown.

> **Hints and tips**
> A tab is the computer equivalent of tabs you might find in an address book in real life.

A new page will now open that will look like this:

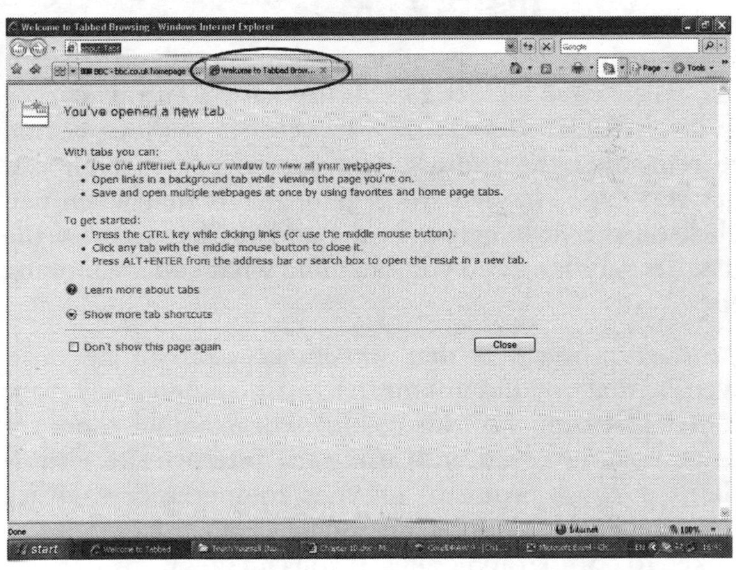

2 Type the web address of the page that you want to view into the address bar. For example, to open the Oxfam website type: www.oxfam.co.uk. You have now got two pages open: the BBC and Oxfam. You can flick between the two by clicking on the appropriate tab.

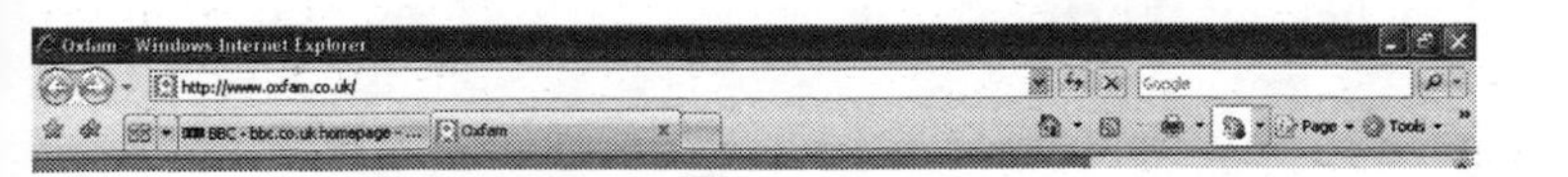

You can close an individual page by clicking on the cross in the tab.

If you close Internet Explorer® using the cross in the top right-hand corner, it will close all of your tabs.

Hints and tips

Having too may tabs open can get confusing. Note that the address that is displayed in the address bar relates to whatever tab is currently selected.

10.6 Viewing and deleting websites in your history file

Every website that you visit is automatically saved in a list called your history file. As we have seen this can be quite useful as you can revisit websites without having to remember the address. However, the history file can get very big. The disadvantage of this is that when you click on the little arrow in the address bar to view the list, it is very long and you can't find what you are looking for.

Another problem is that sometimes you end up on a website that you did not mean to visit, and you may want to delete it from your history file. For example, there are some risks involved with using the Internet like **viruses** that can cause problems on your computer, or **spyware** that records what you are doing. Sometimes you get linked to pornographic sites. If you end up on any of these websites, you may want to delete them from the history file.

To view your history file:

1 Click on the gold star again (where you got into your favourites).
2 Click on 'History'.

The history file is organized into days and weeks. In this example, you can see where it says 'Today'. This lists all the sites visited on this computer today.

3 To view it, click on 'Today'. The sites are now listed.
4 To go back to any of these sites, **highlight** the website and click on it in the list.
5 To delete any of these sites from the history file, highlight the website you want to delete and right click on it. Remember that a right click opens up hidden **menus**. In this case, a menu will appear with the options to Expand or Delete.

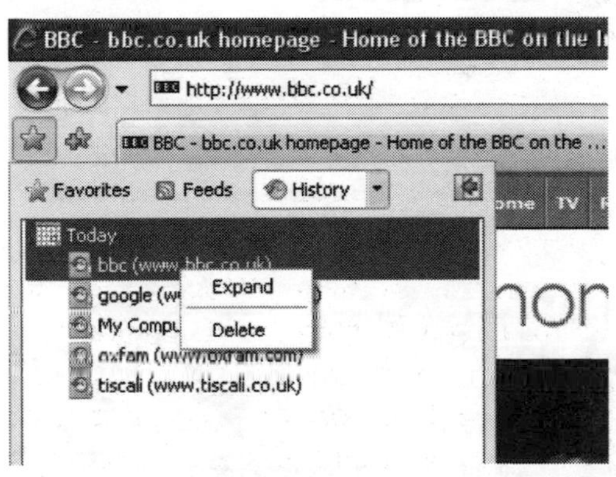

6 Click on 'Delete'. This now removes that website from your history file, and it will not appear in the address bar when you click on the little arrow.

10.7 Deleting your entire history file

Every so often your address bar gets so full of addresses that you just want to get rid of all of them from the list and start again.

Hints and tips
You should use your 'Favorites' to save websites that you definitely want to go back to again. This means that you can safely delete your history file from time to time without losing the addresses of your favourite websites.

1 Click on 'Start'.
2 Right click on 'Internet Explorer'. A hidden menu will appear.
3 Select 'Internet Properties'. This screen will now be displayed:

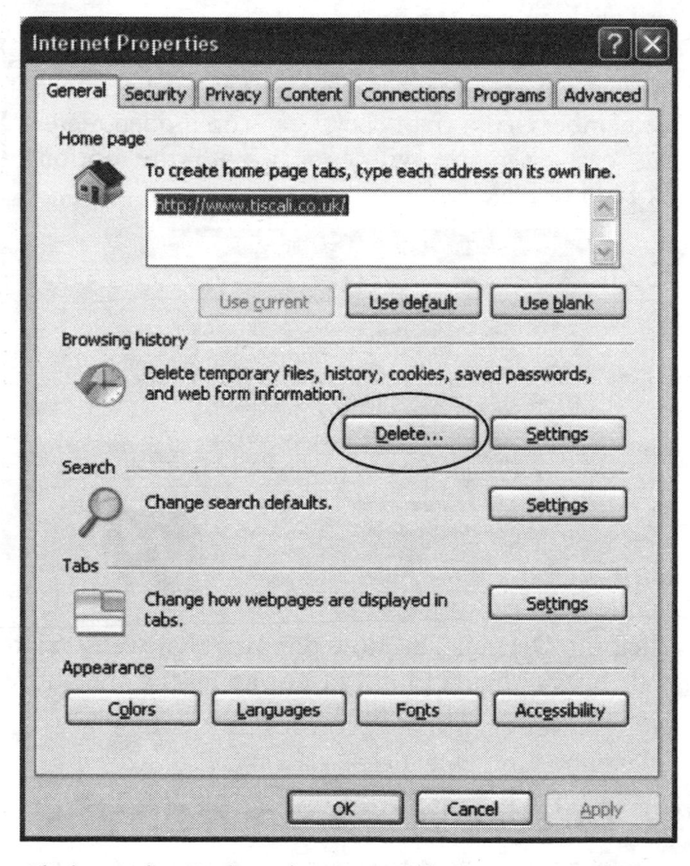

4 Click on the 'Delete' button as shown.
5 Click on the 'Delete all' button on the next screen as shown:

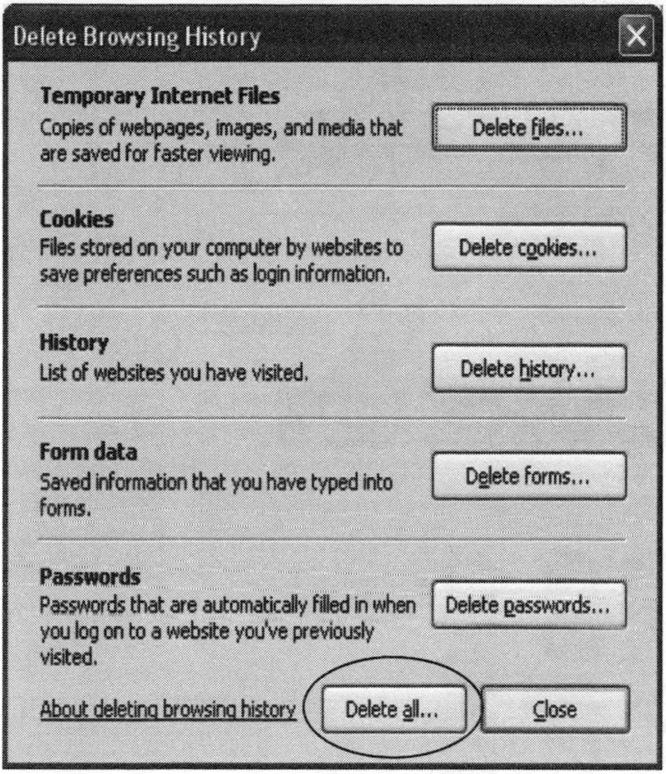

Delete Browsing History

Temporary Internet Files
Copies of webpages, images, and media that are saved for faster viewing. | Delete files...

Cookies
Files stored on your computer by websites to save preferences such as login information. | Delete cookies...

History
List of websites you have visited. | Delete history...

Form data
Saved information that you have typed into forms. | Delete forms...

Passwords
Passwords that are automatically filled in when you log on to a website you've previously visited. | Delete passwords...

About deleting browsing history | Delete all... | Close

It may take a few seconds or even minutes to delete the history file. When it has finished, this screen will disappear.

6 Click on 'OK'.

Summary

In this chapter we have discussed:

- Revisiting websites you have been to before
- Saving websites in a 'favourites' list
- Setting your 'home page'
- Using tabs to view several open pages at a time
- Viewing and deleting websites in your history file
- Deleting your entire history file

11 making phone calls over the Internet

In this chapter you will learn:

- **how to download software from the Internet so that you can make phone calls**
- **how to make phone calls over the Internet**
- **how to make video calls over the Internet**

Aims of this chapter

In Chapters 5 to 8, we looked at email, which is just one of several ways in which you can communicate with people over the Internet. This chapter will show you how to use something called VOIP, which allows you to use the Internet to make phone calls. It will also show you how you can use this service to make free phone calls.

11.1 Introduction

When your computer is connected to the Internet, you are part of a massive collection of computers all communicating with each other. It is possible to communicate using text, voice and video with anybody who is connected. Remember that the Internet works on the same basis as the telephone system – that is, that information is passed around through wires, cables and satellites.

In the same way that text and images are transferred around the Internet, you can also use it to transmit your voice.

You will need to **download** some extra **software** to enable you to do this and, to access most of these efficiently, you will need a **broadband** connection otherwise it may be too slow.

11.2 What is VOIP?

VOIP stands for Voice Over Internet Protocol, which is computer-speak for the ability to make telephone calls using the Internet. This means that you use your computer like a phone. You talk into your computer at your end and someone else on his or her computer at the other end can hear you and talk to you. If you have a **web cam**, it is also possible to see the person you are talking to and for them to see you. If you are both using the same VOIP **website**, the phone calls are completely free, even if the person you are talking to is in another country.

For this to work, you do need a broadband Internet connection, a web cam (which should have a microphone built into it) and some speakers. If you plan to do this a lot, you can also buy an Internet phone, which means that rather than talking into a microphone, you can have a normal hand-held phone. You may need to go back to Chapter 2 to find out how to add these to your **computer system** if you do not have them already.

11.3 Downloading the VOIP software (Skype™)

There are different websites from which you can get VOIP. This section will be using a popular one called **Skype™**. The first thing you need to do is download the Skype™ software onto your computer. You will also need to have someone with a computer and a web cam and Skype™ at the other end so you have got someone to talk to once the download is complete.

> **Hints and tips**
> This is the first example in this book of having to download software from the Internet. The first time you do it, it might take you a while. However, the process of downloading software is pretty much the same for any software, so once you have done it once, any other software you need to download will be much easier.

1 Open **Internet Explorer®**.
2 Type: www.skype.com into the address bar. The Skype™ **home page** will now open.

3 Click on the **link** to 'Download' as shown. It might take you to another screen, where you need to click 'Download now'.
After you have done this, you will see a screen that looks like this:

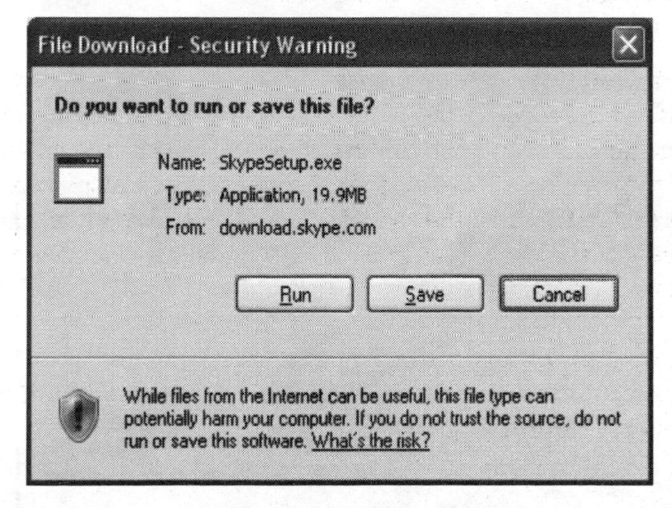

4 Click on 'Run'. You might get another screen asking if you are sure you want to run it.

5 Click 'Run' again if this happens. It may take a few minutes to download the software. You will see a **progress bar** that shows roughly how long this will take.

6 When the download is complete, Click 'Run'.

7 Another screen will now be displayed. You will need to click to accept the terms of the licence by ticking the box and then click '**Install**'.

8 The next screen you see will ask you whether you want to install a Google™ toolbar. Un-tick the box and click 'Next'.

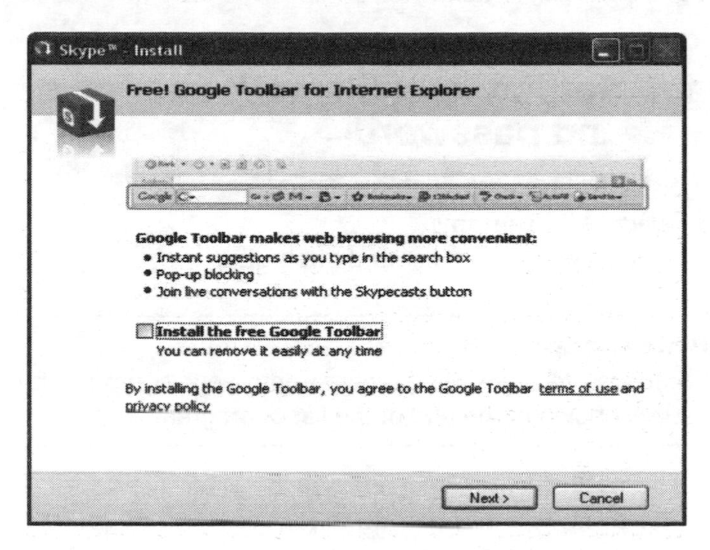

You will be shown one more screen:

9 Click on 'Start Skype'. You will now be connected to the Skype™ website so that you can make phone calls. You will not need to go through this process again as Skype™ is now installed on your computer.

10 Close down the Skype™ website by clicking on the cross. We have closed it down, just so we can see how to open it up again!

11.4 Setting up a Skype™ user name and password

1 To open Skype™, click on 'Start'.
2 Select 'All Programs'.
3 Find 'Skype' in the list and click on it.

> **Hints and tips**
> Whenever you put new software onto your computer it is usually shown at the end of the list of programs.

The main Skype™ screen will now be displayed. The first thing you need to do is register with Skype™ and set up your **user name** and **password**.

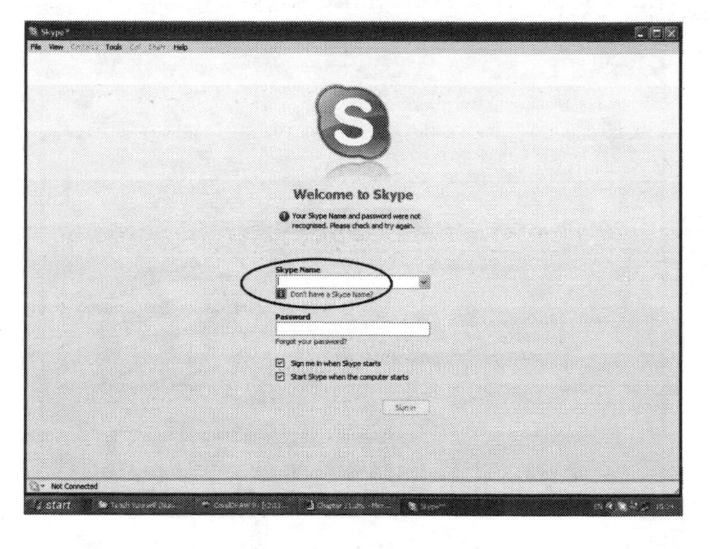

4 Click on 'Don't have a Skype Name?'
5 Complete the form with your details, like the example shown, and click on 'Next'.

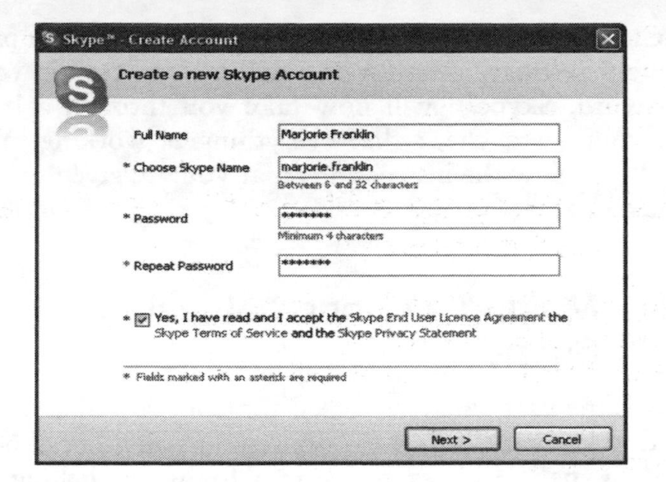

Make a note of the 'Skype Name' that you have chosen.

Hints and tips
Like email, because lots of people use Skype™, you might not get the Skype Name that you want. If this happens, you will be asked to fill in the form again with another name.

6 There is another form to fill in with your email details. Complete the form as shown in the example here and click on 'Sign In'.

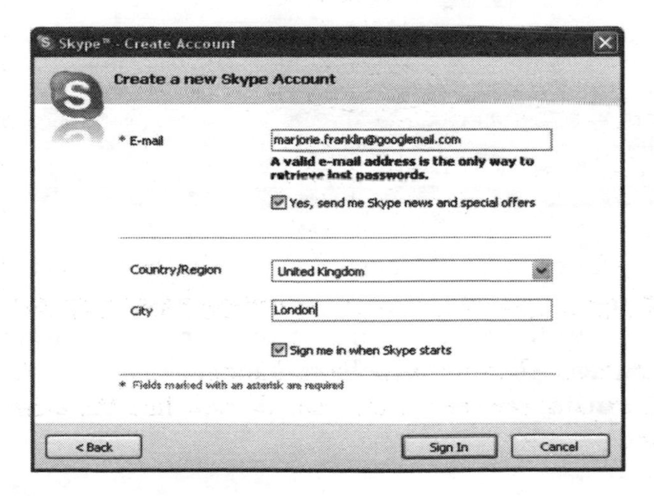

The next time you use Skype™ it will automatically pick up your settings, although you will have to type in your password. Skype™ will now take you through a little test routine to check that everything is working. You need to follow the instructions that you are given on the screen.

11.5 Making a phone call using Skype™

This is the part where you need someone to call and you need to know their Skype™ address. If you do not know their Skype™ address you search for it by clicking on 'Search for Skype Users'. It is probably easier to phone them and ask them what it is!

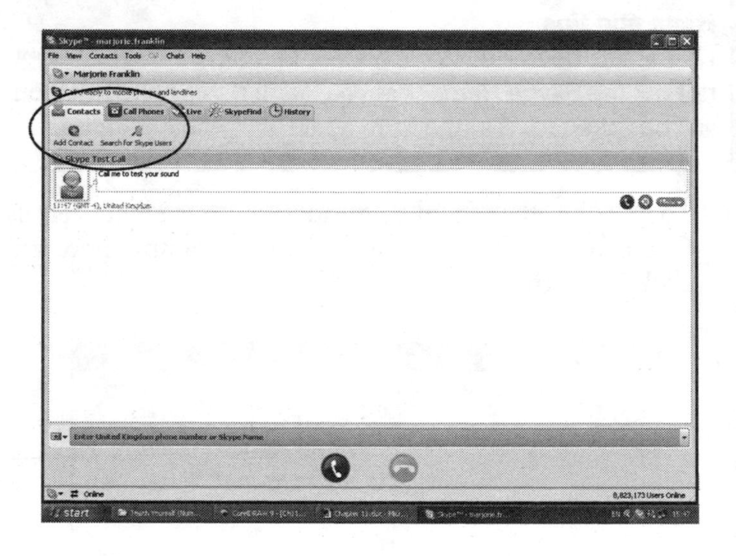

1 Click on the 'Add Contact' button in the top left-hand corner.
2 Type in the Skype Name of the person you want to contact. All your Skype™ contacts will be displayed in the main window. In this case there is just one contact:

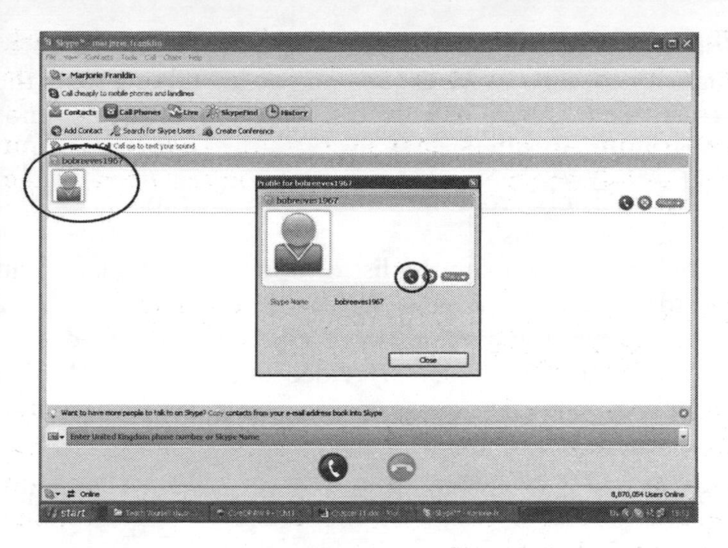

3 Now click on the 'Contacts' tab and click on this person's Skype Name.
4 A smaller window will open in the centre of the screen. Click on the green phone and it will dial this person's number.
5 If they are **online**, they will answer and you will hear their voice coming out of your speakers. You can now talk to them as if it were a normal phone call. If they are not there you will get a message telling you that they have not answered.
6 To end the call, click on the red phone symbol at the bottom.

If someone calls you using Skype™, you will hear your computer ringing and you will need to click on the green phone symbol to accept the call. Calls from one Skype™ user to another, like this, are free.

11.6 Video calls

Once you have established a voice connection, you will be given the option to video call with that person if you both have web cams set up on your computer.

If both web cams are working properly, you should automatically be able to see the person you are talking to on the screen. They should be able to see you too. If this does not work automatically:

1 Select 'Tools' from the menu across the top.
2 Select 'Options'.
3 Select 'Video' from the list of options on the left-hand side.
4 Make sure the 'Enable Skype Video' box is ticked.
5 Make sure the 'Start my video automatically' box is ticked.
6 Click 'Save'.

You should now be able to see the person you are talking to.

Hints and tips

Sending and receiving video images and sound requires broadband Internet speeds. Even with broadband, the sound may break up a bit, or the images may be jerky.

Summary

In this chapter we have discussed:

- How to download Skype™ software
- How to make and receive phone calls
- How to make and receive video calls over the Internet

12 chatting over the Internet

In this chapter you will learn:

- **how to download 'instant messaging' software that lets you chat with chosen people**
- **how to chat using text, sound and video**
- **how to find and enter public chat rooms**

Aims of this chapter

There are many ways of communicating with other people on the Internet. This chapter looks at 'instant messaging' and 'chat', both of which allow you to communicate with people in real-time using text, sound and video. You can do this just with people you know, or you can enter into public chat rooms. Some of these are for general chat, and some of them are on a particular theme. For example, there are some chat rooms just for the over 50s.

12.1 Introduction

Emails are a very popular way of communicating, but one of the problems with email is that it is not instant. You send an email, and then you wait for a reply. That might take a few minutes, hours or days. Sometimes you want to be able to have a live conversation with someone where you get an instant response. There are two main ways of doing this:

- Use **instant messaging software** such as MSN® Messenger. You have to **download** this onto your computer, but then you can use it to chat with people who you know – they would need to have this software on their computer too.
- Use a **chat room**. Generally speaking you don't need any special software to use a chat room, you just **log on** to a chat room **website** and you can join in the live conversations that are taking place.

12.2 Downloading MSN® Messenger

If you want to use instant messaging, you need to download the software first. We will be using MSN® Messenger, although other instant messaging (IM) software is available.

1 Type: messenger.msn.com into the **address bar** of **Internet Explorer®**.

Hints and tips
With many **web addresses** it is not always necessary to type the www before the main address.

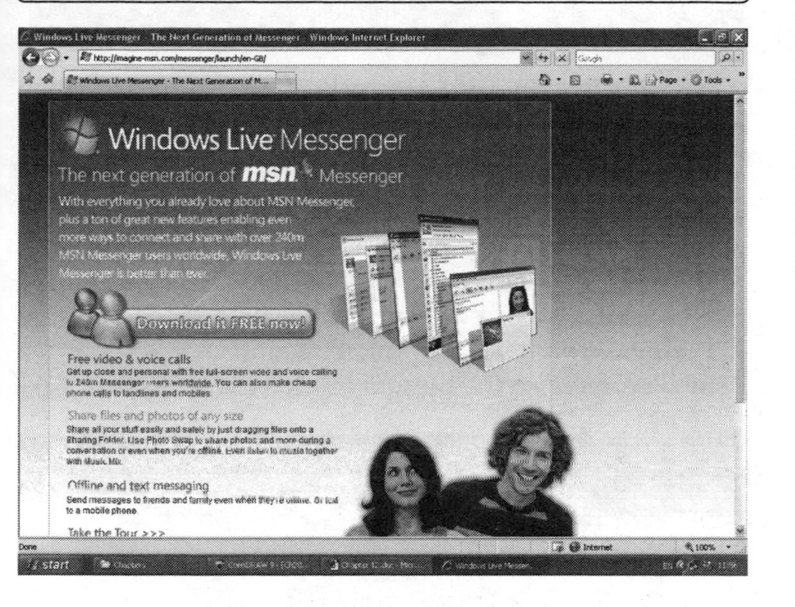

2 Click 'Download it FREE now!'.
3 Click 'Run' on the next screen. It may take a few minutes to download. A **progress bar** will be displayed with an estimate of how long it will take.

Hints and tips
Progress bars are quite useful as they let you know that something is happening and give you an idea of whether to sit and wait, or go for a cup of tea.

4 When it has finished downloading, you may be shown a further screen – click on 'Run'. You then need to work through the **install** process. You will be shown a series of screens.
5 Keep clicking 'Next' until it has finished. When the software is installed, you will never have to go through this process again, you can just go to 'Start', 'All

Programs' and click on 'Windows Live Messenger' on the list.

12.3 Sending and receiving messages

When you first log on, you will be asked for an **email address** and a **password**. You have to use a **Hotmail®** address for this to work.

1 Open 'Windows Live Messenger' (if it is not already open).
2 If you have a Hotmail® address, type it in now along with the password you use for your Hotmail® address.
3 If you do not have a Hotmail® address, click on 'Get a new account' at the bottom of the screen.

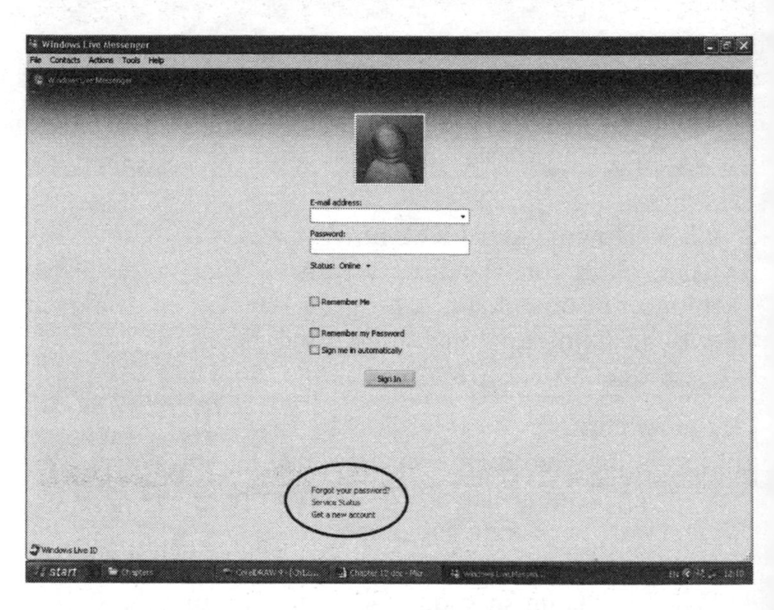

4 Click on the **link** to 'Sign up'. You will now have to complete a form. This will ask for the standard information such as your name, address, email address, etc.
5 Complete the form and tick the box that says you agree to their terms and conditions.

Hints and tips

You will soon become very familiar with filling in forms, as most websites you register with will ask you to fill in a form. You will notice that all forms are quite similar, and all ask for the same information. You do not have to disclose some of your personal information if you don't want to.

6 Close this website and go back to Windows Live Messenger.

7 Type in your details to log on. You can check the 'Remember Me' box, which saves you having to type in your details every time.

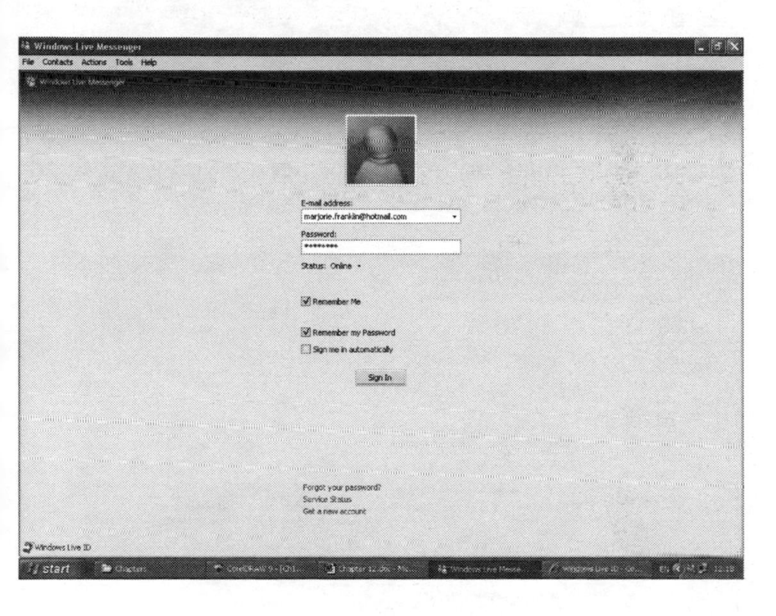

You will now be logged in to the Messenger software. Because it is the first time you have used it, you will be prompted to add some contacts. The advantage of using instant messaging software like this is that you can control who is in your list of contacts, and then you talk only to people who you know. In public chat rooms, anyone can enter.

8 Click on 'Add a Contact'.

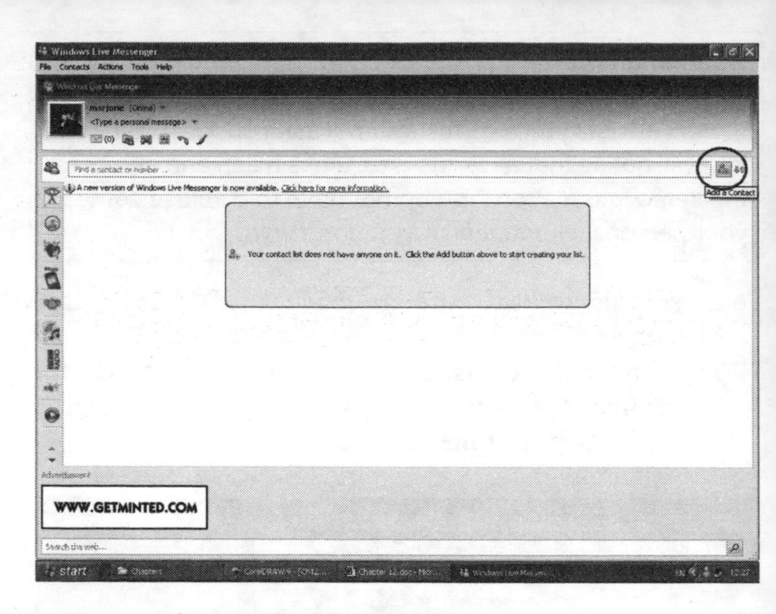

9 Type in the email address of the person you want to add into your contacts list and click 'Save'.

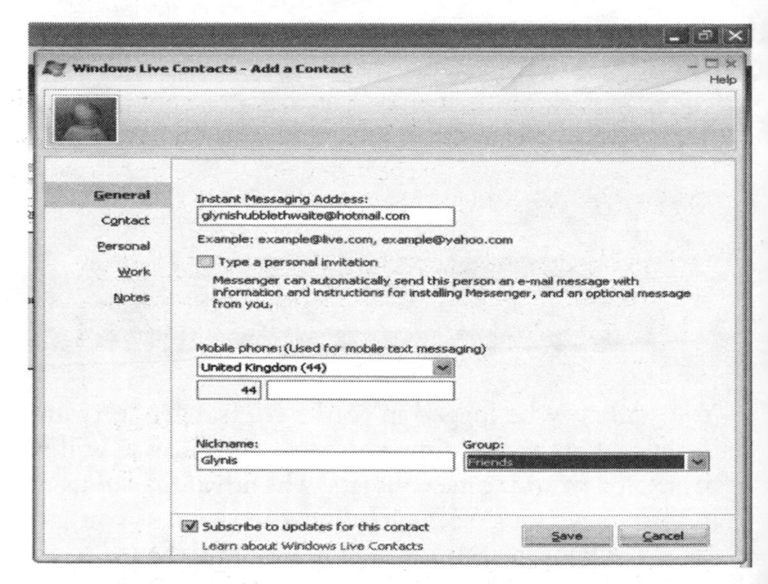

In this example, two new contacts have been added – Glynis and Harry. The way that Messenger works is that you have to accept an invitation to chat with

someone. This means that you can block people who you don't know. The person you want to chat with also has to be **online**. This means that they are using their computer and are logged in to Messenger.
In this case, Harry is online – the **icon** next to his name will appear in green on your screen.

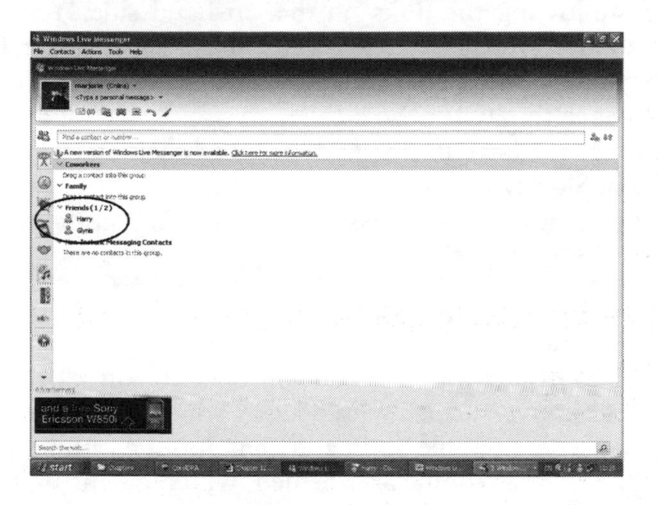

10 Double click on the person you want to chat with. This screen is now displayed. You can type in what you want to say and the person at the other end will see the message. They will type in what they want to say and on it goes.

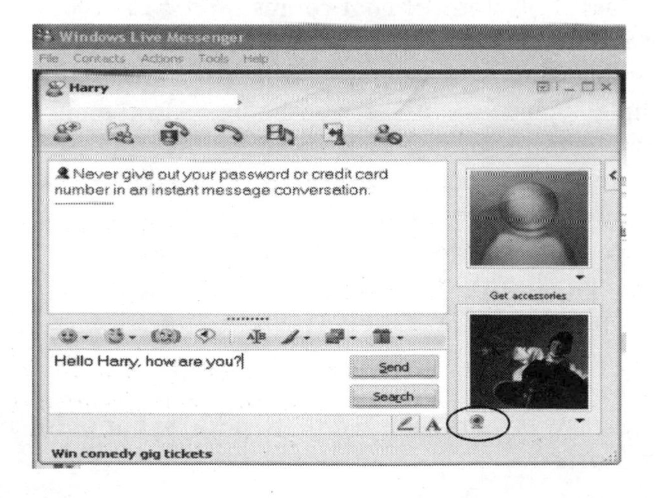

11 If you both have a **web cam**, you can set up a video chat, by clicking on the small web cam icon under the picture.

There are quite a few other options and links in Messenger that you may want to try out. For example, you can link to live radio stations, or to dating websites, by following the links on the left-hand side. You can also use Messenger to make phone calls, a bit like Skype™ that we looked at in Chapter 11, although you do have to pay for these calls.

12 When you have finished you need to click on 'File' and then 'Sign Out'.

13 You can then close Messenger by clicking on the cross.

12.4 Chat rooms

Chat rooms are public websites where you can have **real-time** conversations with people. Some chat rooms are general, where people go in and chat about anything they like. Other chat rooms are themed, which means that the chat is about a specific topic. Some chat rooms are regulated, which means that there is a moderator who keeps an eye on what is being said, in case it gets offensive. Others are not supervised, and anything goes.

There are thousands of chat rooms on the Internet covering every possible theme. You can find a chat room by using a **search engine** and typing in suitable **search** words, for example: "chat room" + gardening. Also, many well-known websites have a chat room facility; Google™ and Yahoo!® both operate chat rooms on a range of themes. Also, many charities now have chat rooms where you can find people with the same interests and concerns. Many medical and health charities, for example, have chat rooms for people affected by illness.

This example will use Yahoo!® chat rooms.

1 Type: www.yahoo.co.uk into the address bar of Internet Explorer®.

2 Click on the link to 'Chat'.

3 You will have to register with Yahoo!® before you can start chatting. This involves the usual information including a name, password and email address. They may also ask for gender and date of birth.

4 When you have logged on, click on the link to 'Chat'. You will see the main chat screen, which in Yahoo!® looks like this. Each line of text is a message from someone in the chat room.

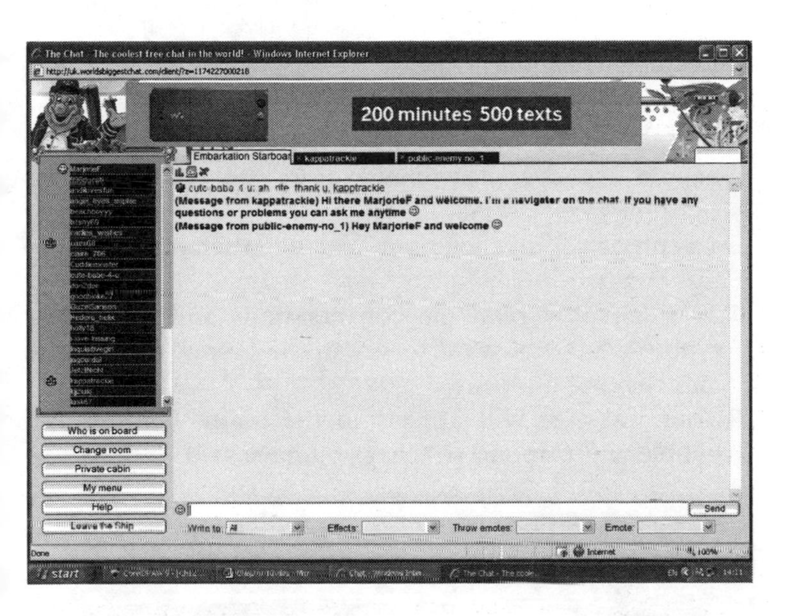

The main problem with chat rooms can be finding like-minded people who are online at the same time as you. You may enter a few rooms to find people who you want to chat to. The names of the rooms usually give you an idea as to what the chat is about. Yahoo!® has a number of rooms:

5 Click on 'Change room' in the left-hand corner. Yahoo!® will then list the rooms that are available and show you how many people are in them:

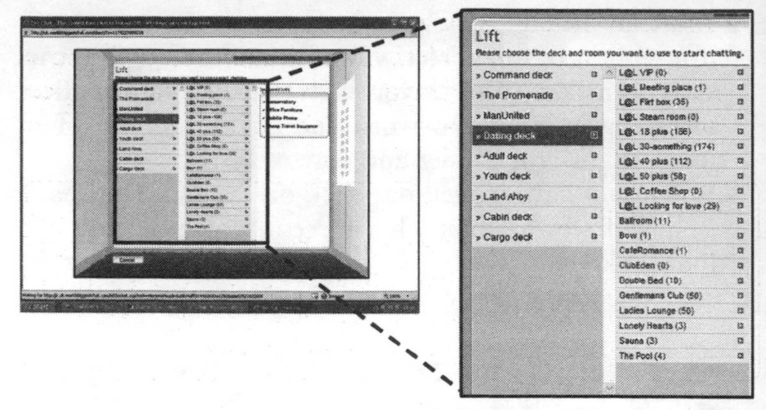

In this example, you can see the rooms have names like '50 plus'. The number in brackets shows how many people are currently chatting in the room. In this example there are 58.

6 To enter a room, click on it. You will then be taken into this room.

7 You can now read the conversations and join in by typing what you want to say in the box at the bottom and clicking on 'Send'.

8 Your message will appear in the main window and people will respond to what you have said.

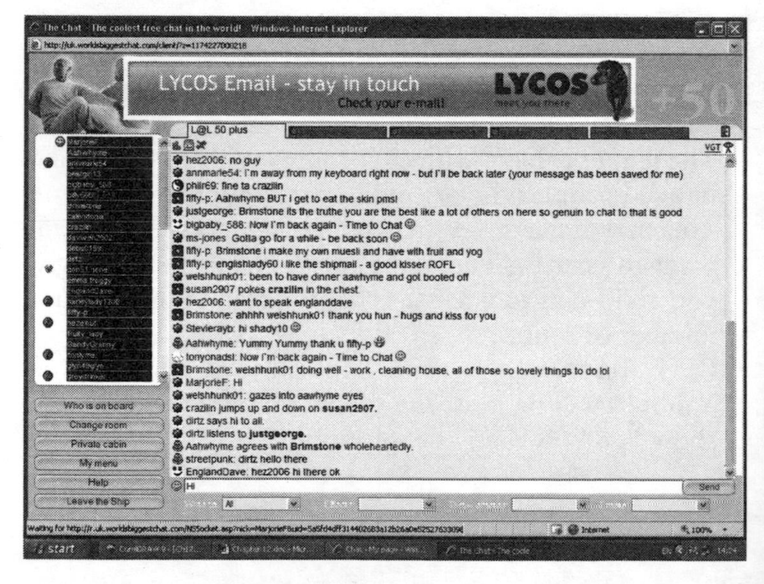

9 You may receive messages from people asking you if you want a **personal chat.** This means that you would enter into a one-to-one chat with that person. You can accept or decline this offer.

Hints and tips

Chat rooms are used quite a lot for flirting so you may get some unwanted (or wanted) attention in chat rooms. There is more on using the Internet for meeting new people in Chapter 25, including advice on keeping safe.

10 When you have finished chatting, you can click on the cross, or log out. In Yahoo!®, you need to click on 'Leave the Ship' as they have decided to theme the whole chat room around being on a ship!

Summary

In this chapter we have discussed:

- Downloading instant messaging software
- Using instant messaging software to send text and video messages
- Finding and using chat rooms

13 getting involved with online communities

In this chapter you will learn:

- **How to take part in ongoing discussions using a 'forum'**
- **How to pursue specialist interests via 'newsgroups'**
- **How to read and contribute to 'wikis'**
- **How to view 'social networking sites'**

Aims of this chapter

There are many ways of communicating with other people on the Internet. This chapter looks at ways in which you can take part in discussions with online communities. It will show you how you can join discussions with people who share your interests and specialisms through forums and newsgroups, and how you can add your own information to websites through wikis. Finally, it will show you how you can get to know other people through social networking websites.

13.1 Introduction

Millions of people now use the Internet on a daily basis. As well as using the Internet to find information, more and more people are now adding their own contributions. For example, as well as using the BBC **website** to read news articles, people are now **encouraged** to have their say about news items, to **post** comments and to get into discussions with other visitors to the website. Whole communities have developed on the Internet. For example, if you had a particular interest in gardening, you would be able to find **forums** where gardeners meet **online** to take part in discussions and share information.

Social networking sites like MySpace and bebo have become very popular. This is where people create an online profile of themselves for everyone to view. Finally, there is the phenomenon known as a **wiki**, an example being Wikipedia. This is an encyclopaedia that is written and constantly updated by anyone on the Internet who feels that they know enough to contribute to it.

13.2 Forums

A forum or message board is like an online notice board. Like a real notice board, users can post up messages for other people to read. Other users can then make comments about these messages and a discussion develops.

Hundreds of thousands of forums exist on the Internet covering every imaginable topic. Many websites carry forums to let people post messages about the website.

They are a bit like **chat rooms**, but the difference is that they are not in **real-time**. That means that you post your message, and then wait for responses to come back.

You can find forums by typing suitable search words into a **search engine**, for example: forum + genealogy. Alternatively, you will find forums on many of your favourite websites. For example, the BBC has a large number of forums covering all sorts of topics such as the news, gardening and money matters.

1 Type: www.bbc/co.uk/gardening into the **address bar** of **Internet Explorer®**.
2 To get into the gardening message board, click on 'Message board'.

3 The next page will show you some of the main discussion topics that are ongoing. You can click on any of these to take part in the discussion. For example, to get

involved in the discussion on 'Gardening on TV', click on the link.

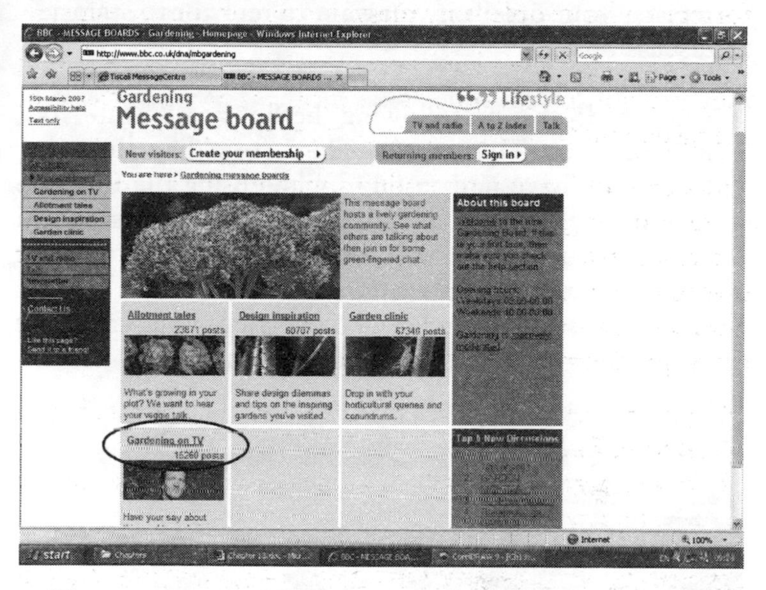

The next screen will show you all of the posts, which are messages that have been left by other people. This site has lots of posts that run over several pages.

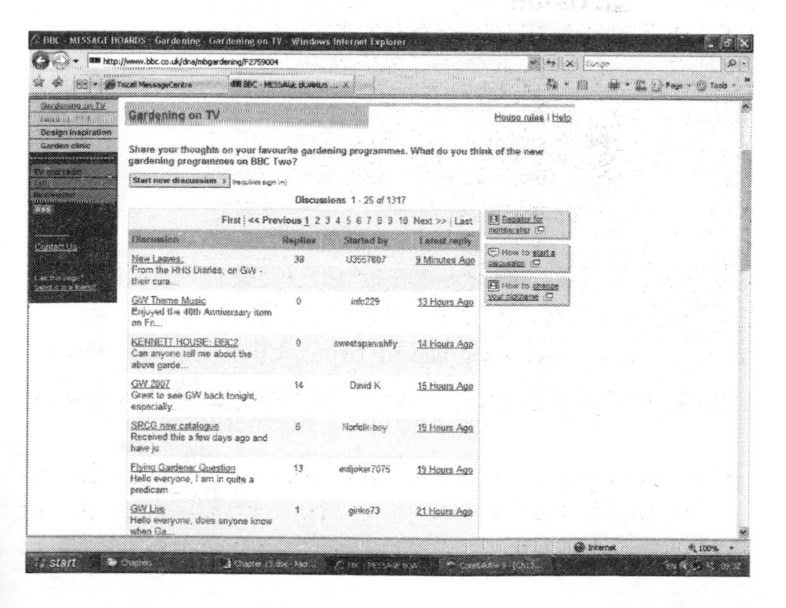

4 To read a post, click on it. Most forums let you read the messages without having to register, but ask you to register your details if you want to reply or to start new discussions.

5 You will need to register with the BBC website if you want to do this by following the links to 'Create your membership'. This is a standard form like the other forms you have had to fill in while using the Internet. You will need to put in your **email address**, as they will send you an email, which you must respond to in order to activate your membership.

6 Once your membership is activated you can post your own messages by clicking on 'Reply to this message'.

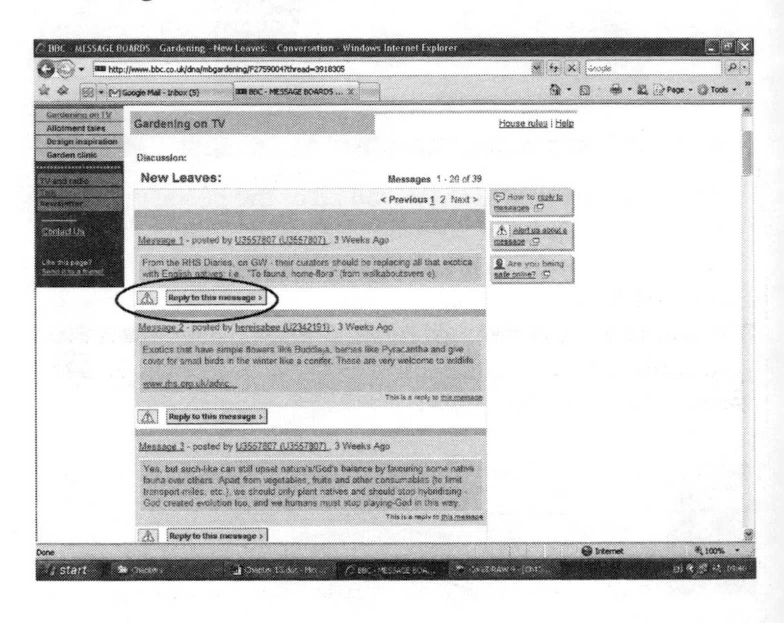

7 To start a new discussion topic, click on the general topic, for example 'Garden clinic'. Get back to this page by clicking the 'Back' button in Internet Explorer® or by typing: www.bbc.co.uk/gardening into the address bar and following the links to 'Message boards'.

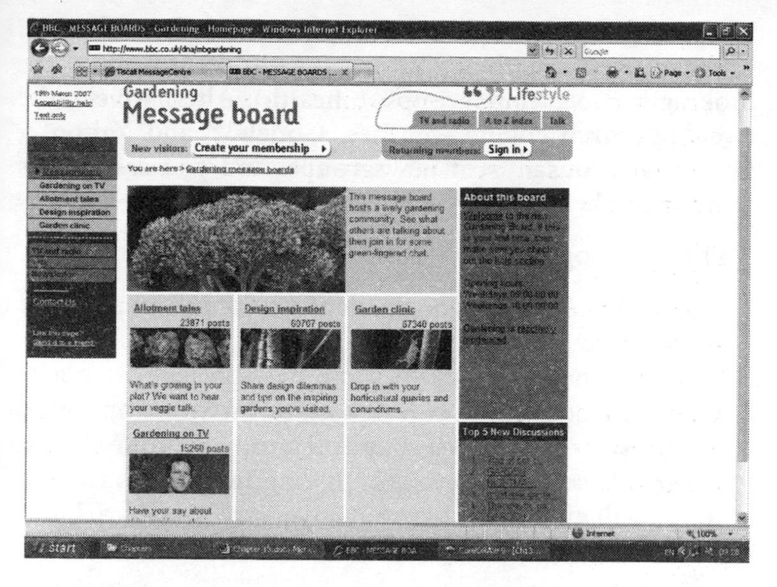

8 Click on the link to 'Garden clinic'.
9 Click on 'Start new discussion'.
10 Give your message a catchy title, type the message and click 'Post message'.

Hints and tips

There are so many discussions on the go, that you need to give yours a meaningful and interesting title to get people to take part in your discussion.

11 You can follow the replies by clicking on 'My discussions'.

13.3 Newsgroups

Newsgroups are very similar to forums in that they are electronic message boards. There are millions of newsgroups on the Internet covering every possible topic and subtopic that you can think of. Some of the topics are specific, so they are a way of finding people who share your interests, or finding advice on issues even if they are very specific.

You can get access to newsgroups in a number of ways. You can use a search engine and type in the topic you are looking for (e.g. newsgroups + health). Alternatively, the two big search engine websites, Google™ and Yahoo!®, both **host** thousands of newsgroups, and you can access them from their sites.

To find a Google™ newsgroup:

1 Type: http://groups.google.com/ into the address bar of Internet Explorer®.
2 You will now be shown some newsgroups categories and provided with a search box, or given the option to set up your own newsgroups on a topic of your choice. There are so many newsgroups that the chances are that there will already be one that covers what you are interested in.

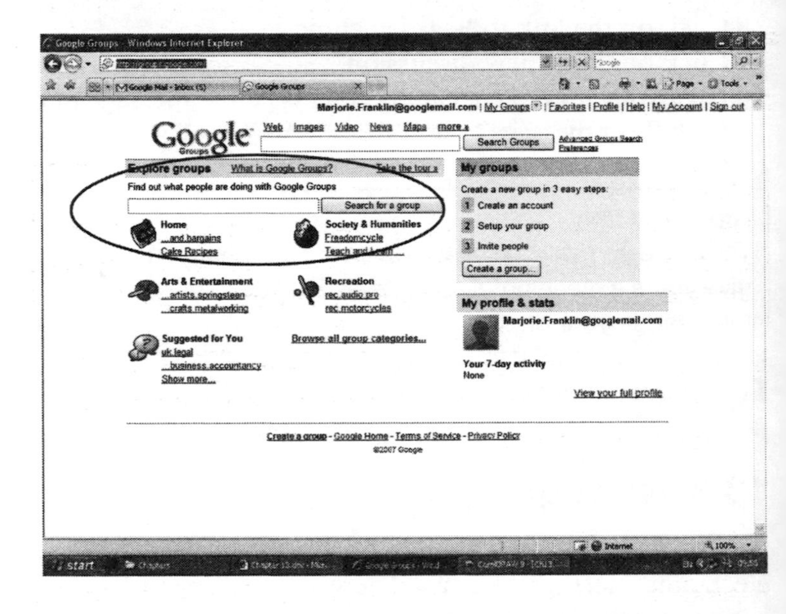

In this example, we will search for a newsgroup that covers the fairly specific topic of pension annuities.

3 Type: annuities into the search box and click on 'Search for a group'.

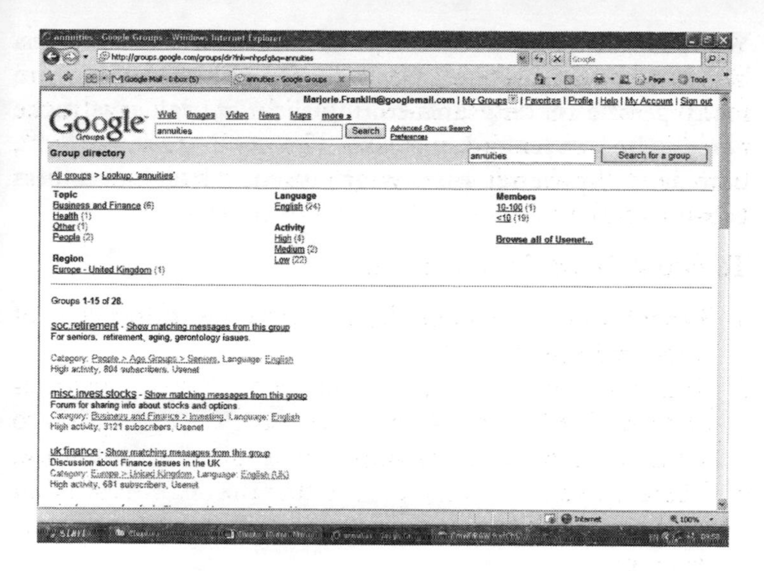

The results are now listed and you can see all the groups with a brief description as to what is covered.

4 Click on one of the links. The messages will now be shown.

> **Hints and tips**
> Remember that these are discussion groups, to which anyone can contribute. The opinions expressed in them are those of the person and should not be taken as fact.

5 You can read these messages, and reply to them by clicking on the 'Reply' link at the bottom of the message. You then type in your comment and click 'Send'.

13.4 Wikis

A wiki is a website that lets users read, add and edit the content of the website. These are becoming very popular as a way of collaboratively putting information on websites. The most well-known is Wikipedia which is an online encyclopaedia written and edited by anyone who wants to contribute.

Wikipedia employs people to check the information that is being put on the website. The logic of a wiki is that with so many people reading and editing the material, it is more likely to be correct and unbiased. The site is growing all the time as it gets better known. It currently has 1.7 million articles available covering all sorts of subjects.

To view Wikipedia:

1 Type: www.wikipedia.org into the address bar of Internet Explorer®.

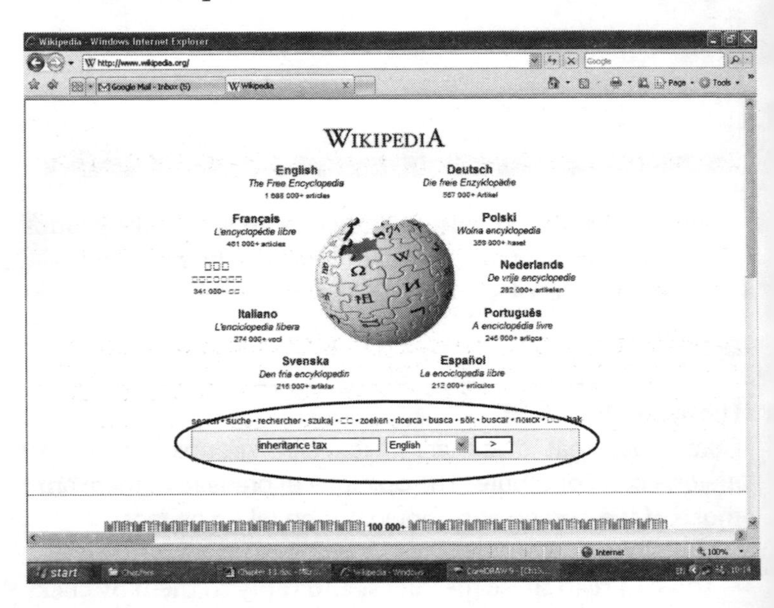

2 Type the topic you want to read or contribute to in the search box. In this example we are looking at 'inheritance tax'. The article on this subject is then displayed.

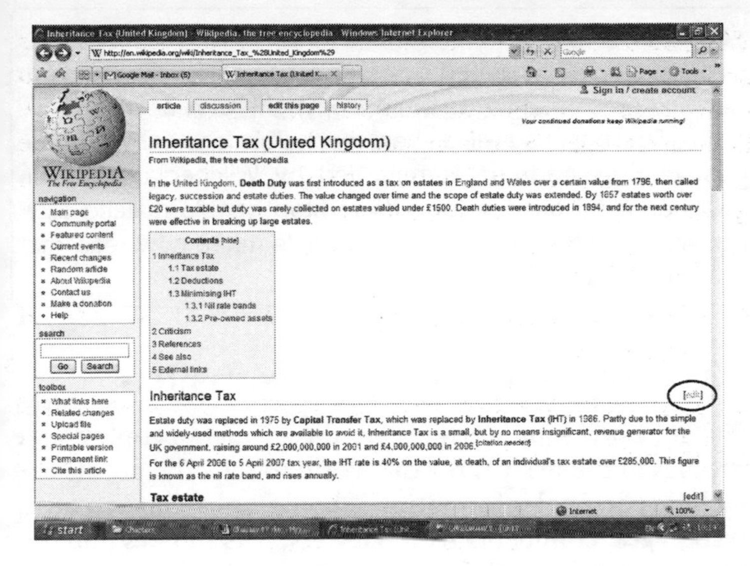

3 You can simply read this article, or because it is a wiki, you can edit it. To do this, click on the link to 'edit' on the section to which you want to make changes.

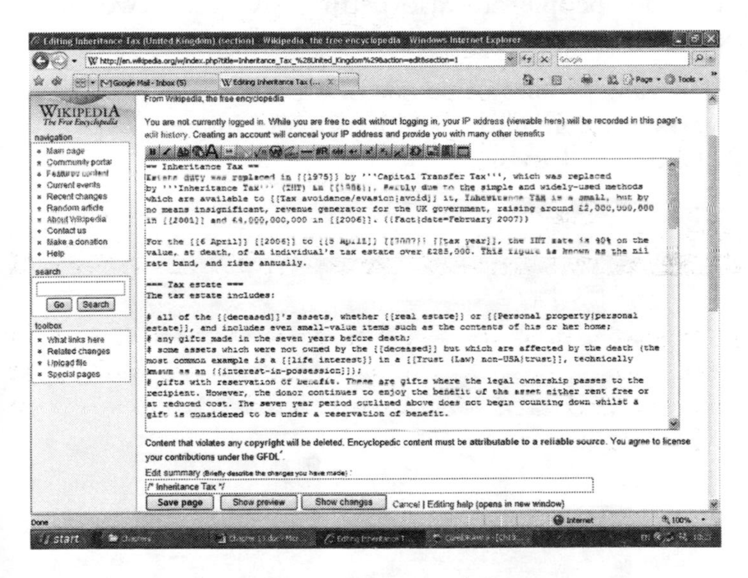

4 On this page, you can edit the text content of the article. When you have finished, click on 'Save page'. The changes you have made will be shown instantly.

> **Hints and tips**
> Your work will be edited by an editor at Wikipedia and you should be careful not to break copyright rules or write anything libellous. You will be held reponsible for what you write as your **IP address** is recorded by Wikipedia. That all sounds a bit serious, but it's to stop people making silly changes – after all, millions of people might now read the changes you have just made!

13.5 Social networking websites

Social networking websites are those where people create profiles of themselves for the world to see. The profile can include personal information, photographs, links to other **web pages**, comments from viewers, lists of likes and dislikes and information about relationships. As well as viewing other people's profiles, you can also create your own. These sites are very popular among young people, but older people are also getting involved. Two of the best-known sites are MySpace and bebo.

1 To view profiles of people of a similar age, type: www.myspace.com into the address bar of Internet Explorer®.
2 Click on '**Browse**'.

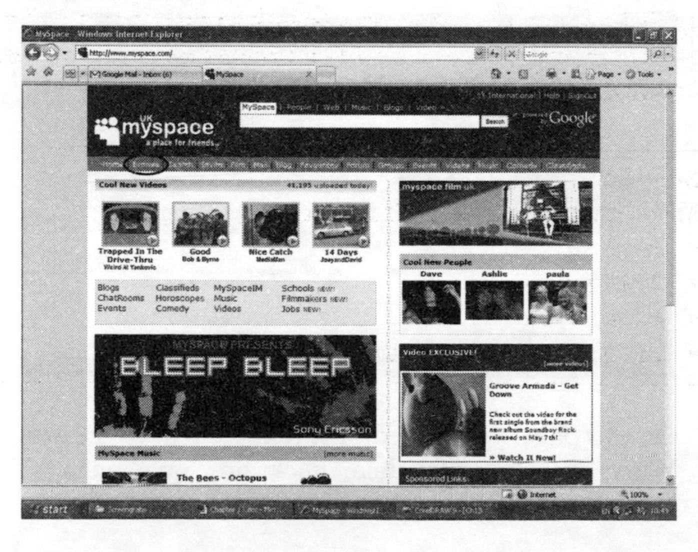

3 You can now filter out the thousands of profiles, so that you will be shown only those that meet the criteria you are interested in.

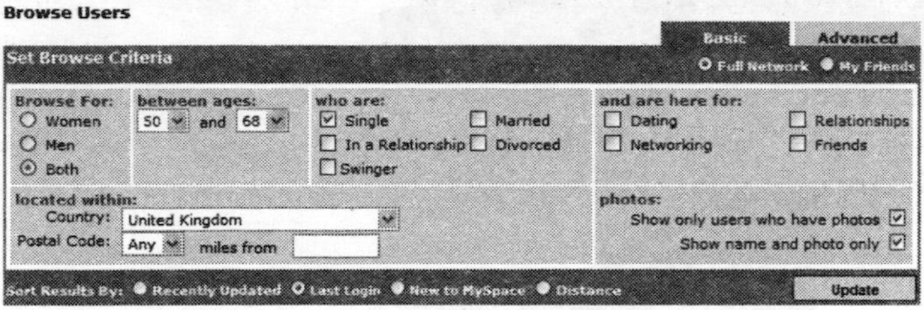

For example, you can just view profiles of people of a particular gender or age. As you can see, there is relationship information as well.

Hints and tips

Many people use social networking sites as a way of making contact with new people with a view to meeting up in the 'real world' as well as the '**virtual** world'.

4 Make your selections and click 'Update'. You will now be shown a list of profiles that meet your criteria.

5 Click on any of the pictures to link to their profile. Once in their profile you can add comments or send messages to the person.

Summary

In this chapter we have discussed:

- Forums
- Newsgroups
- Wikis
- Social networking websites

In this chapter you will learn:

- what a blog is
- how to find blogs that you might want to read
- how to read and comment on blogs
- how to set up a blogging site of your own
- how to write a blog

Aims of this chapter

This chapter focuses specifically on blogging as a way of communicating with others on the Internet. On the one hand, you may simply want to read other people's blogs as a source of information and entertainment. On the other hand, you may want to add your voice to the Internet by creating your own. This chapter will show you how to do both.

14.1 Introduction

A **blog** (short for web log) is a **web page** written by an individual or group of people, usually in the style of a journal that contains regular entries (like a diary). Each entry is called a **post**. Posts are dated and shown in reverse chronological order. The information in a blog could be anything from the day-to-day life of the **blogger**, through to information on particular topics and themes. Many blogs are text only, though they can contain images, movies and sounds. A blog usually reflects the personality of the blogger and may contain **links** to other **websites** that the blogger is interested in.

Some blogs have become extremely popular with millions of people reading them on a regular basis. Some people have become famous from writing blogs, and some famous people now have blogs.

14.2 Finding blogs to read

In common with anything else on the Internet, your start point could be to use a **search engine** to find blogs on themes that you are interested in. For example, typing: blog + "classical music" into a search engine will give you thousands of potential blogs to read. Many of your favourite websites may also carry blogs. For example, many leading newspapers and TV stations have blogs. This blog is from political journalist Nick Robinson:

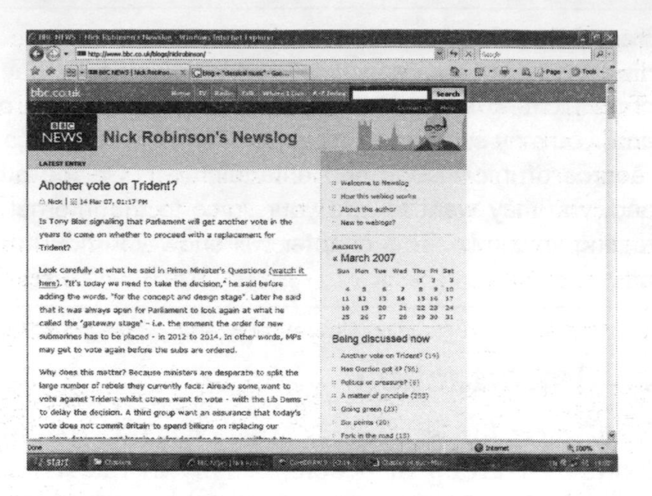

This is a fairly typical blog. It has the latest entry at the top and links down the sides to other blog entries, to topics being discussed, and to other websites that the blogger thinks you might be interested in.

Another way of finding a blog is to use a specialist bloggers' site. One of the most popular is www.blogger.com which is part of the Google™ network of websites.

1 Type: www.blogger.com into the **address bar** of **Internet Explorer®**.
2 The website will now open. From here you can set up your own blog (which we will do shortly) or search for blogs.

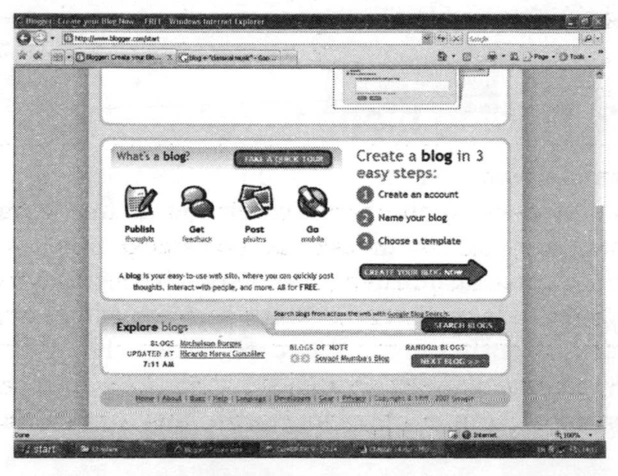

3 **Scroll down** to the bottom of the page where you will find a search facility.
4 Type in the subject that you are interested in (e.g. travel) and click on 'SEARCH BLOGS'.
As with any search, you should try to be as specific as possible with the search words to reduce the number of hits. In this example the search words were travel + Europe and it produced thousands of potential blogs to read.

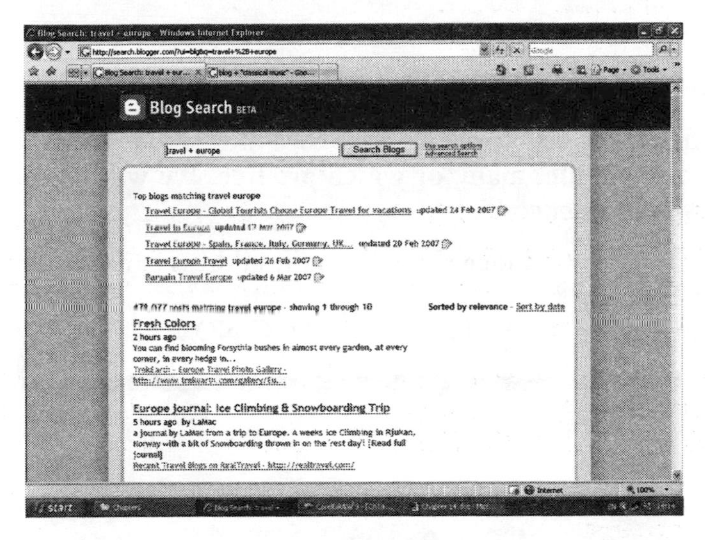

5 The search results shown give you a brief description of the contents of the blog. You can scroll through them, and move between the pages until you find one you want to read. Then click on it and the bloggers' web page will open.

> **Hints and tips**
> Many businesses now use blogs to link you to their websites so that they can try to sell you something. Look at the address of the blog before you click on it to decide whether this is the case, and whether you want to go to their site.

Depending on who has created the blog, the web page may either look very professional with lots of **multimedia** content, or it might be text heavy. Remember that blogs often reflect the personality of the blogger and some will be better than others. Once you are in the bloggers' website, it is just like being in any other website. You can read the text, look at photographs, play videos, etc. Bloggers also invite you to comment on their blogs. There will usually be a link to 'Comment' or 'Post comment' and you can type in what you think about the blog, or comments on the contents.

14.3 Creating your own blog

The easiest way to create your own blog is to register with a blogger site, many of which are free. We will be using www.blogger.com

1 Type: www.blogger.com into the address bar of Internet Explorer®.
2 Click on 'CREATE YOUR BLOG NOW'.

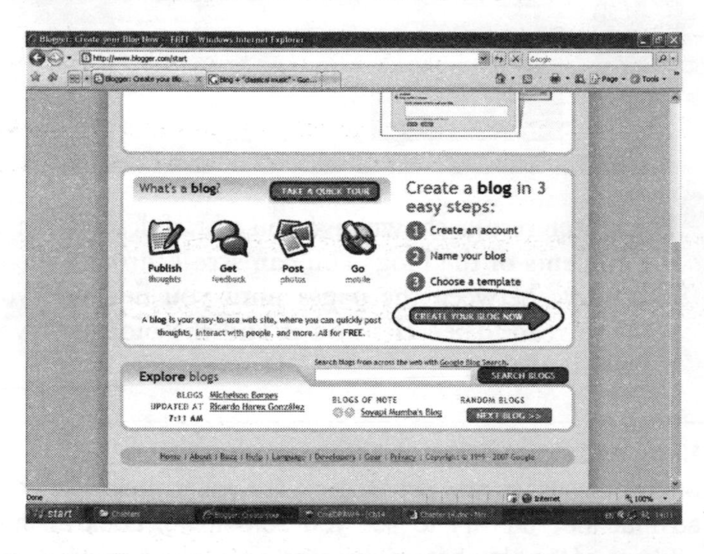

3 You will need to work through the registrations process by filling in a few forms. This is very similar to the registration for other websites we have looked at in this book. Blogger is a Google™-based website so it will use your Google™ identity. If you don't have a Google™ identity

(i.e. a googlemail address) you can set up one now, or revisit Chapter 5 to find out how to do this.

4 Choose a 'Display name' that will be shown on your blog. Tick the box to accept the terms and conditions and click 'CONTINUE'.

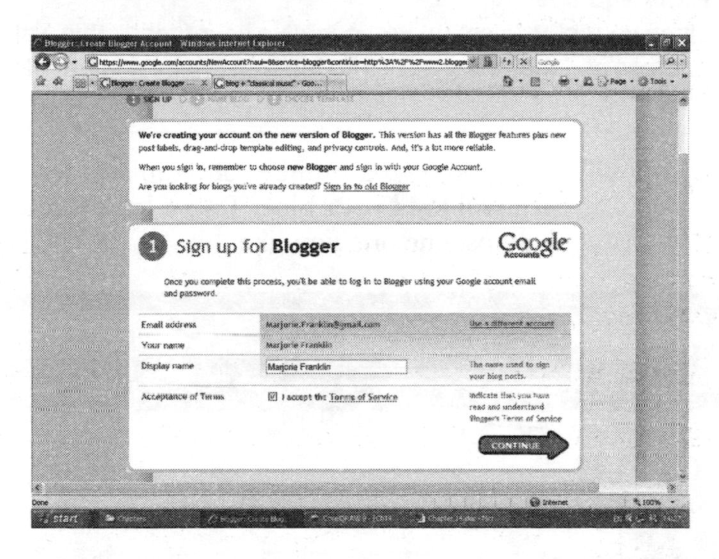

5 You now need to set up the title for your blog, and select a URL, which is the **web address** that will be allocated to your blog. Then click 'CONTINUE'.

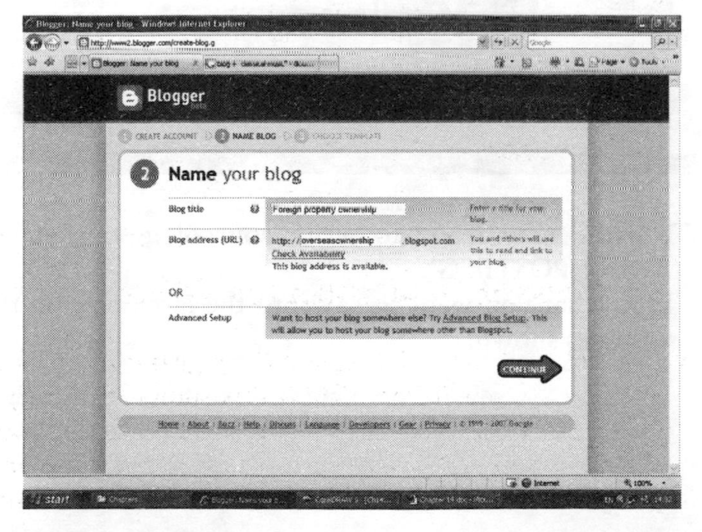

In this example the blog is going to be about owning overseas property and the URL will be http://overseasownership.blogspot.com

Hints and tips

Once your blog is set up you can give your friends this web address and they can type it into Internet Explorer® and read your blog.

6 You will now be shown a number of templates for the web page that will hold your blog. Take a look through the list and choose the one you like.

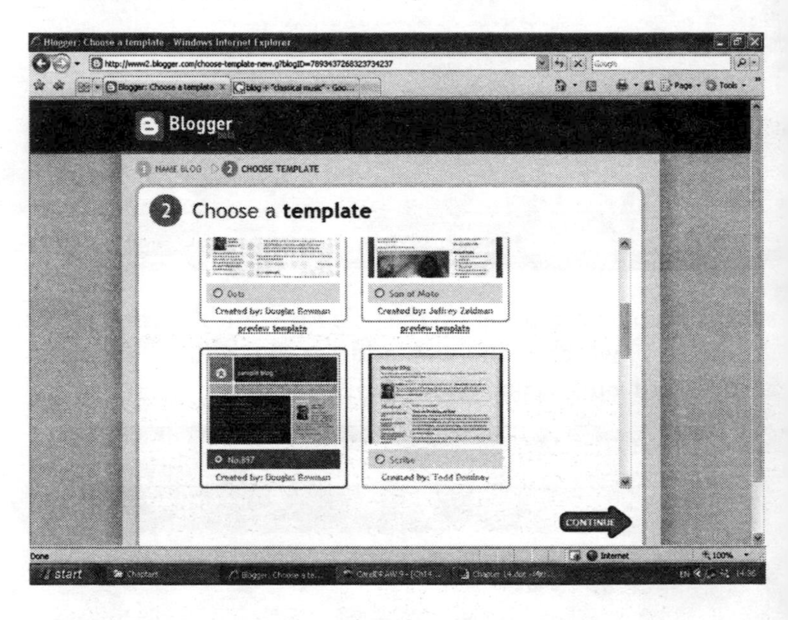

7 You are now ready to write your blog so click on 'START POSTING'.

8 Type what you want to say into the large box on the screen as shown.

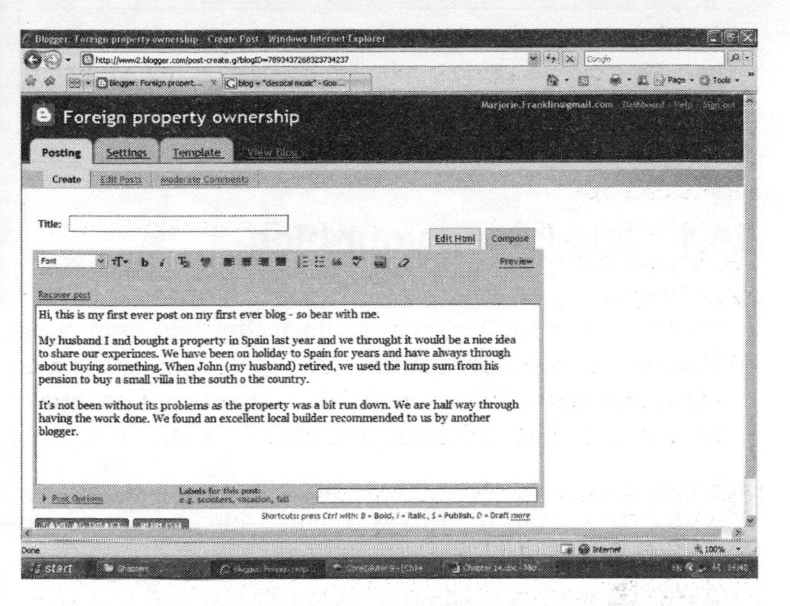

9 When you have finished typing, click on 'PUBLISH'.
10 Now click on 'View Blog'. Your blog is now published for the whole world to read and will look something like this:

> **Hints and tips**
> The advantage of using a site like Blogger is that you can create a professional looking web page without having to learn any specialist software.

14.4 Developing your blog

At the moment, we have created a fairly basic blog, which contains some text. You may want to develop your blog to include photographs, audio and video clips, and links to other websites. You might also want to put on more personal information about yourself to share with the world.

A useful start point for this is to edit your User Profile to let people know more about you.

1 Click on 'View my complete profile' from your blog web page.
2 Click on 'EDIT YOUR PROFILE'.

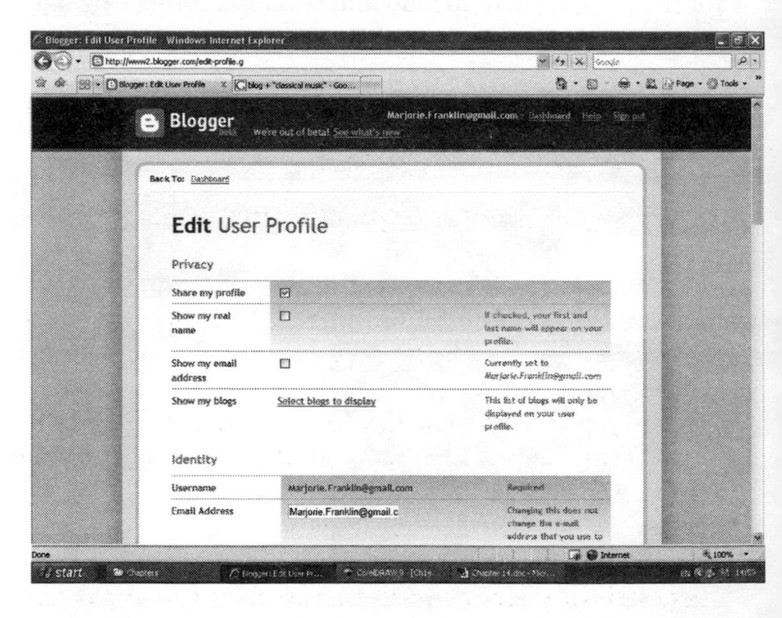

3 In here you can do things like add photographs of yourself, or video clips. You can also tell people more about yourself, your hobbies and interests. Remember that blogging is all about sharing your thoughts and ideas with the world, and being part of an **online community**.
4 When your profile is complete, click on 'Save Profile'.
5 Now click on 'Dashboard', which is in the top left-hand corner of this screen.
Your dashboard is where you can manage your blog.

You can view posts, add new posts, create new blogs, and get access to you user profile. You can also access the 'Help' screens from here to help you with other aspects of blogging.
6 When you have finished, make sure that you click on 'Sign Out' before you click on the cross to close the website.
7 When you want to get back to your blog, type: www.blogger.com into the address bar (or your could save it into your favourites), and then type your **user name** and password in as shown.

This will take you back to your dashboard.

Summary

In this chapter we have discussed:

- Finding and reading blogs
- Leaving comments on blogs
- Registering with a blogging website
- Creating your own blog

15 keeping your personal information safe online

In this chapter you will learn:

- **what risks are involved when using the Internet: identity theft and phishing, hacking, undesirable material, premium diallers**
- **how you can protect yourself against these risks**
- **advice on buying online**
- **advice on passwords**

Aim of the chapter

The aim of this chapter is to give some advice on what threats and risks there are to you and your personal information when you are on the Internet and how you can take steps to minimize or prevent any problems that might arise. There is a range of threats and the purpose of this chapter is to make you aware of them. Chapter 16 goes on to look at some of the threats to your computer system.

15.1 Introduction

The Internet is a global connection of computers with the connections being made by telephone cables and satellites. It works like the telephone system and logging on to the Internet is a bit like making a telephone call. In fact, your computer has its own number (called an **IP address**), which is transmitted whenever you are **online**. In the same way that a telephone call can be intercepted, so can any of the information that is transmitted when you are using the Internet.

The Internet is unregulated in this country, and pretty much anyone can get access to it. Unfortunately this means that it is open to abuse. This chapter lists the threats that exist and, in each case, explains what you can do about them.

15.2 Identity theft and phishing

Identify theft occurs when someone obtains personal information about you which means that they can pretend to be you, usually for fraudulent reasons. They could buy things from the Internet in your name, or perhaps borrow money or even clear out your bank account.

Phishing is where someone sends you an email claiming to be from your bank. They will ask for personal information including your bank account details, or direct you to a fake **website** that asks you for this information. These emails can look very convincing.

What to do about it:

- Banks will never email you to ask you for personal information such as PIN codes and **passwords**. If you are asked for it, don't give it.
- Make sure that when you are doing any banking over the Internet that the site is secure. **Secure sites** have https in the address and display a small padlock just to the right-hand side of the **address bar**:

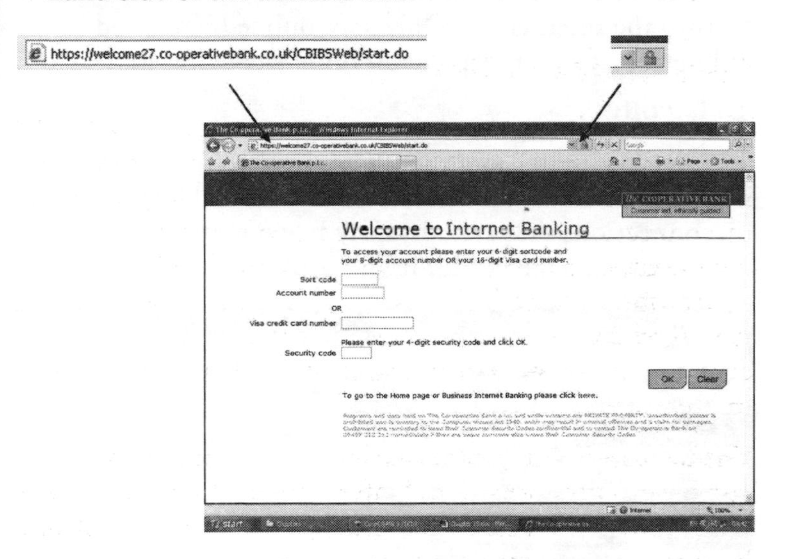

This is the **log on** page for the Co-operative Bank. Notice how the address has the https at the beginning and there is a padlock **icon**. Do not disclose any personal information unless the site has both of these showing.

15.3 Hacking

Hacking is when someone gains unauthorized access to your computer. They can do this any time you are connected to the Internet. You will not even know that it is happening. Hackers do it for various reasons. Often they are just bored teenagers, but some hackers do it with the intention of getting your personal information.

What to do about it:

- Install a **firewall**. This is **software** and **hardware** that examines information that is being passed to your computer while you are online. If it finds something it doesn't like, it will block it. If you are using Windows® you will already have a firewall. Many different makes of firewall software are available to buy. You can find these by searching for them on the Internet.
- Turn the Internet off. Only stay online (connected to the Internet) if you need to be. At other times, log yourself off.

To log off:

1 Click on 'Start', and then 'Connect to'.
2 Click on 'Show all connections'. You will be shown any connections that are currently being made between you and the outside world. It will look like this:

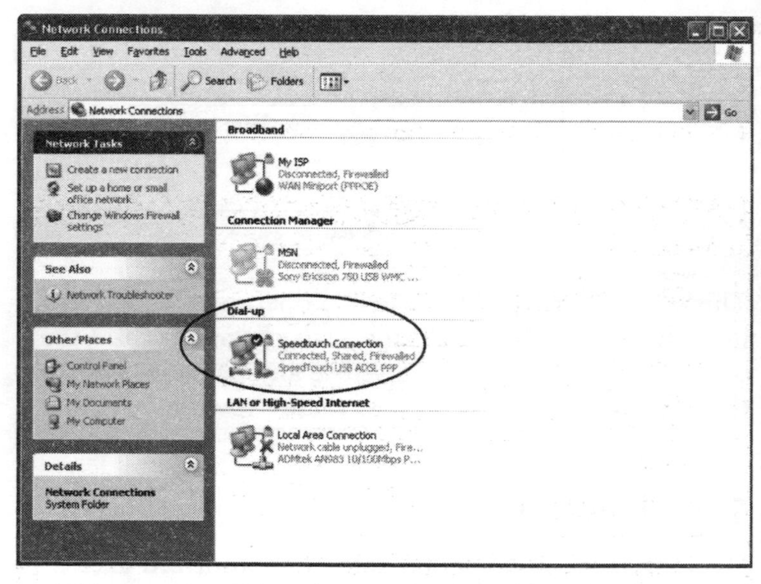

This computer has four connections but only one of them is actually connected. You can tell which are connected as the text next to the icon will read 'Connected'.

3 To disconnect, right click any connection that is connected and select 'Disconnect'.

15.4 Undesirable material

The unregulated nature of the Internet means that you can get access to plenty of undesirable material. Often you will click on a site that you think is perfectly innocent only to find that it contains undesirable content. This may be of particular concern if children have access to your computer.

What to do about it:

- Use your common sense. If you don't like what you see, click on the cross immediately to close the website.
- Install **filtering and blocking software**. This special software allows you to block access to sites that contain undesirable content.
- Set the 'Content Advisor rating' in Windows XP®. This is like the filtering/blocking software mentioned above but is already built in to Windows®.

1 To set the Content Advisor rating, click on 'Start'.
2 Right click in 'Internet Explorer'.
3 Select 'Internet Properties'.
4 Click on the 'Content' **tab** as shown.

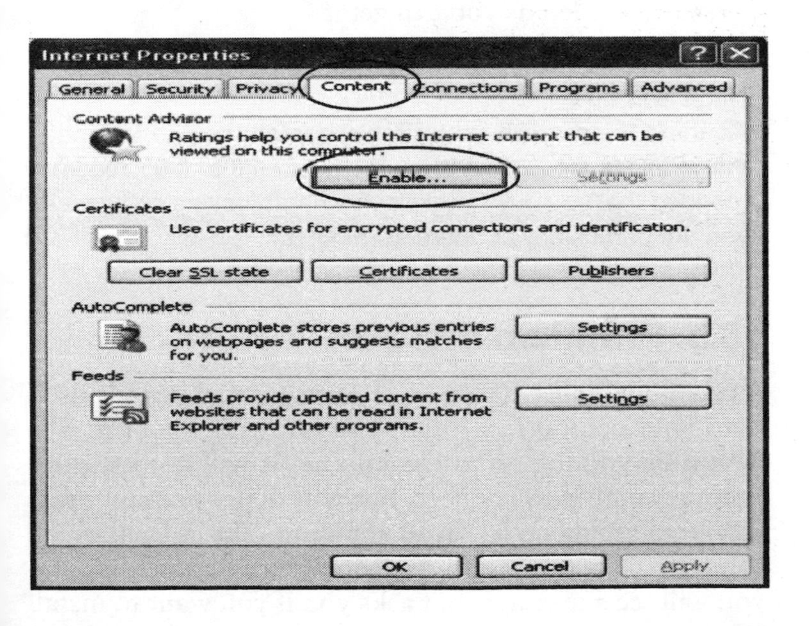

5 Click on 'Enable'. The following screen is displayed:

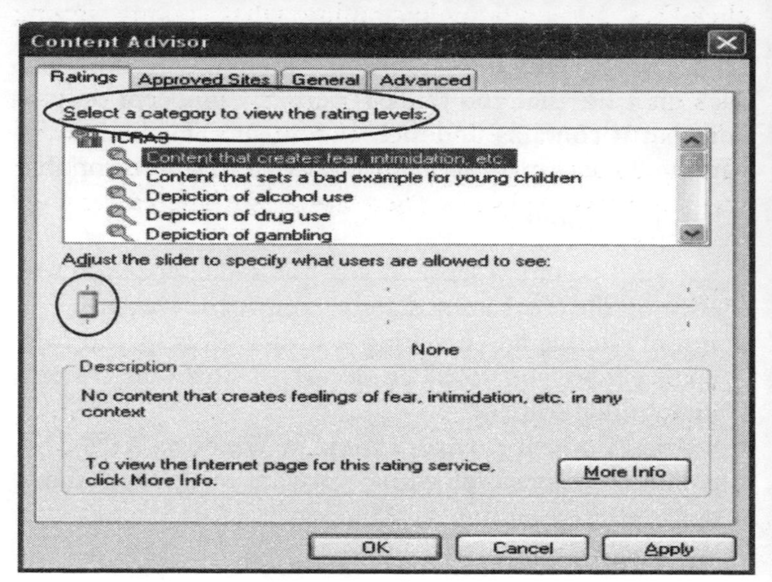

6 You can now select a rating for each category by moving the slider. In most cases, you will want the slider as far over to the left as you can get it.

Hints and tips
As there is so much undesirable content on the Internet, these filters are not 100 per cent effective. It is recommended that you buy specialist filtering/blocking software if you are particularly concerned about it.

15.5 Premium diallers

A **premium dialler** is a piece of software that **installs** itself onto your computer without you knowing about it. The next time you log on to the Internet it will not use your normal number to connect, but will dial a premium rate service charging up to £1.50 a minute. This is legal as the software does not install itself without you knowing it – you will see a message that asks you if you want to install it. However, the message is not clearly worded so you may click 'Yes' not really understanding what you are signing up to.

This is a tricky scam as you often see messages popping up when you are on the Internet, and most of them are fairly benign. You are most likely to encounter a premium dialler scam on **download** sites. These are sites where you can get free software.

What to do about it:

- Read all messages carefully before clicking in 'Yes' whenever you are on the Internet.
- Phone your telephone company (e.g. BT) and ask them to block all outgoing calls to premium rate numbers.
- Use only reputable sites.

15.6 Unreliable sites

Many of the problems described in this chapter come from unreliable sites. But how do you spot a dodgy site? It is not always easy as even bad websites can be made to look good.

What to do about it:

- Don't click on a link to a website that comes from an unsolicited email.
- Use your common sense. If it's too good to be true, then it's probably a scam.
- Look for a 'real world' presence, preferably an address.
- Use only sites of well-known businesses or sites that are recommended.
- Avoid sites that offer free downloads, free movies, free music, free games or **file-sharing**.
- Ensure the site is secure – look for the https and the padlock symbol.

15.7 Buying online

When you buy anything online there is always a danger that the goods will not be delivered, or that what is delivered, is not what you ordered.

What to do about it:

- Only buy from trusted websites. These could be the websites of large companies or those that have been recommended by a friend.
- Keep copies of all receipts. All decent online stores will provide a screen where you can print a copy of your order. Most will also send an email to confirm the order.
- Check for a real address so that you can contact them if something goes wrong. Preferably they should be located in the same country as you!
- Use your common sense. If a deal looks too good to be true – it probably is.
- Have a separate credit/debit card that you use for online transactions and have only a small credit limit on it.
- Use secure payment services such as **PayPal**. These provide insurance against non-delivery.

15.8 Passwords

Passwords usually in combination with a **user name** are required all over the place. Your computer itself will probably require a user name and password. Email sites, online auctions, **chat rooms**, etc. all require you to register with a user name and password.

Passwords are very important and keep you safe online. There are some rules that you should follow:

- Never give your password to anyone else ever.
- Change your password regularly and don't use the same password twice. (This one is tricky as it is difficult to remember them all.)

- Don't choose something obvious like names, dates of birth, etc. Use combinations of letters, numbers and other characters, as they are harder to guess.
- Don't write passwords down anywhere.

15.9 Don't have nightmares . . .

Internet crime is increasing and you are never immune to threats even if you take all of the precautions listed in this chapter. However, if you take precautions, the chances of becoming a victim are very small. Remember that millions of people now use the Internet regularly with no problems.

Summary

In this chapter we have discussed:

- What threats exist on the Internet
- How to protect yourself against them
- How to identify unreliable or undesirable websites
- Advice on buying online
- Advice on using passwords

In this chapter you will learn:

- what risks there are to your computer and the information stored on it: viruses, trojans and worms; spyware and adware; pop-ups
- how you can protect yourself against these risks
- what problems are caused by junk email (spam)
- how to create a back-up of important information in case of loss

Aim of the chapter
The aim of this chapter is to give some advice on what threats and risks there are to your computer when you are connected to the Internet and how you can take steps to minimize or prevent any problems that might arise. There is a range of threats and the purpose of this chapter is to make you aware of them. This chapter focuses on things that can damage your computer, whereas Chapter 15 focused on threats to your personal information and identity.

16.1 Introduction

Your computer is at risk every time you are connected to the Internet. It is virtually impossible to avoid picking up a few problems whenever you use the Internet. At one end of the scale, you might find that you get a lot of junk email (**spam**) or **pop-ups**, which are annoying, and clog up your computer, but do not actually damage your computer. At the other end of the scale, you could pick up a computer **virus**, which could destroy information and programs stored on your computer. Let's look at the annoying ones first.

16.2 Junk email

Junk email is affectionately known as spam. It is almost impossible to avoid. Junk emails appear in the **inbox** of your email **software**. You didn't ask for it and you don't know the person or organization that sent it. Most of the time, they are just advertising things.

Hints and tips
A lot of spam email is for Viagra, investments or pornographic material. A good rule of thumb is that if you don't know whom the email is from – delete it straight away.

What do to about it:

- Most email software will filter out spam emails for you and put them into a special folder called Spam. However, some will still come through.
- It is possible to minimize the amount of junk mail you get by blocking or reporting it when you get it. This means that you should not receive any more spam from these organizations again. For example, in Gmail™ you can click on the 'Report Spam' button when you get it:

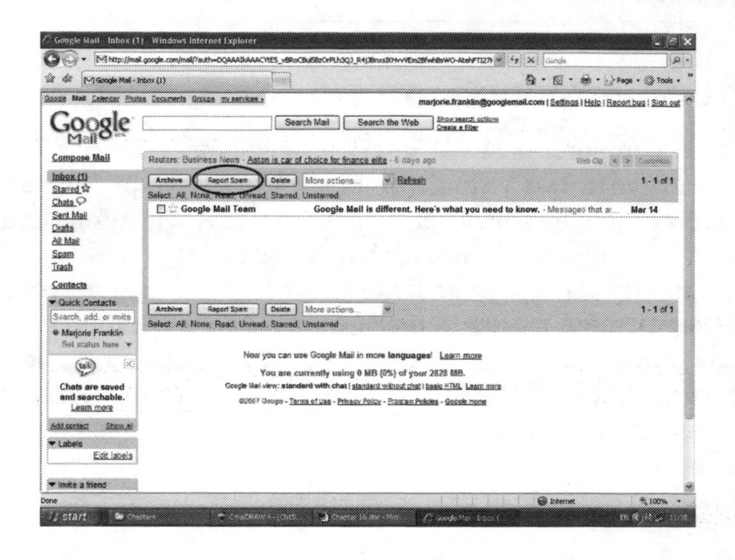

- If you do not know whom an email is from, delete it without opening it.

The real danger of spam is that email is a very common way to pick up a computer virus, and these can be quite serious, as we will see later on.

16.3 Pop-ups

Pop-ups are windows that just pop up (appear) when you are using the Internet. Like spam, they are not something that you asked for – they just appear. Most of these pop-ups are just advertising something. Some of them look quite enticing because they tell you that you have won something. This is usually just a trick to get you to visit their **website**.

Pop-ups are not necessarily bad, but they can be annoying if you get a lot of them. The simple solution to a pop-up is simply to click on the cross and get rid of them.

What to do about it:

- Read the pop-up, as it might be a genuine offer from a reputable company. If not, click on the cross.
- You can buy pop-up blocking software, which reduces the amount of pop-ups you will get.
- You can set up **Internet Explorer**® so that it stops most pop-ups:

1 Click on 'Start'.
2 Right click on 'Internet Explorer'.
3 Select 'Internet Properties'.
4 Click on the 'Privacy' **tab**.

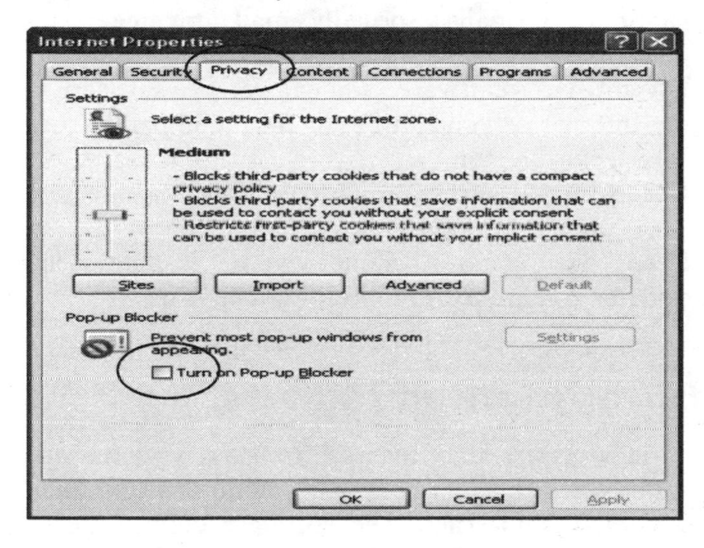

5 Tick the box to 'Turn on Pop-up Blocker'.
6 Click on 'OK'. This should now stop most pop-ups from appearing.

16.4 Viruses, trojans and worms

Viruses, **trojans** and **worms** are little programs that **install** themselves on your computer without you knowing about it. This normally happens when you **download** something from the Internet or when you open an email. Like human viruses, a computer virus will infect your computer causing all sorts of problems. Some are worse than others. Really bad ones will delete everything on your computer.

> **Hints and tips**
> Trojans are viruses that are hidden inside another **file** (as in Trojan horse). Worms are viruses that wriggle around inside your computer and may infect lots of different files, making them difficult to get rid of.

What to do about it:

- Download only from reputable sites or **secure sites** as explained in Chapter 15.
- Do not open emails (especially **email attachments**) if you do not know who they are from.
- Use anti-virus **software.** You can get free software from the Internet or you can buy it from companies such as McAfee or Norton.
- Keep your anti-virus software up to date as new viruses come out every day.
- Keep your version of Windows® up to date as many **updates** contain fixes for well-known viruses.

16.5 Spyware and adware

This is software that installs itself on your computer without you knowing about it. It can do this any time you are using the Internet. The software collects personal information that you fill in when online, and tracks which websites you visit. The information it gathers is usually used for marketing purposes.

What to do about it:

- You can download free software from the Internet that will check your computer for **spyware/adware**, or you can buy software that will do it for you. This type of software is called spyware or adware removal software.
- Keep your version of Windows® up to date. Once you have bought Windows® you are entitled to free updates from the Microsoft® website (www.microsoft.com).

16.6 Creating a back-up of your work

Most of these threats are relatively minor. The most dangerous of all these threats is that you get a virus. Viruses vary in seriousness. For example, some viruses just do annoying things like automatically redirect you from one website to another, or maybe it will close down Internet Explorer® automatically without warning.

In serious cases, viruses can destroy any of the information stored in your computer.

What to do about it:

- Keep in a safe place the original copies of all software (CDs/DVDs) that you bought.

Hints and tips

If your computer came with Windows® already installed on it, make sure that you ask your computer supplier for an original copy of the software on CD. This is proof that you have bought the software legally, and you can use it to set the computer up again if you get a bad virus.

- Make a **back-up** of anything that you have saved. The best way to do this is to copy it onto a CD or DVD.

Hints and tips

This will work only if your computer has a Rewritable CD or DVD drive.

1 Open the CD/DVD drawer on your computer by pressing the button.

2 Insert either a **CD-R, CD-RW, DVD-R** or **DVD-RW** shiny side down.

3 Click on 'Start'.

4 Click on 'My Documents'.
This is where anything that you have saved (e.g. music, films or other files made using other software) will be saved. You can create a copy of all the information in the My Documents folder on a CD/DVD.

5 Press CTRL and A at the same time. You will see that all the files and **folders** are **highlighted**.

6 Point the mouse at any one of the files and right click.

7 Select 'Copy'.

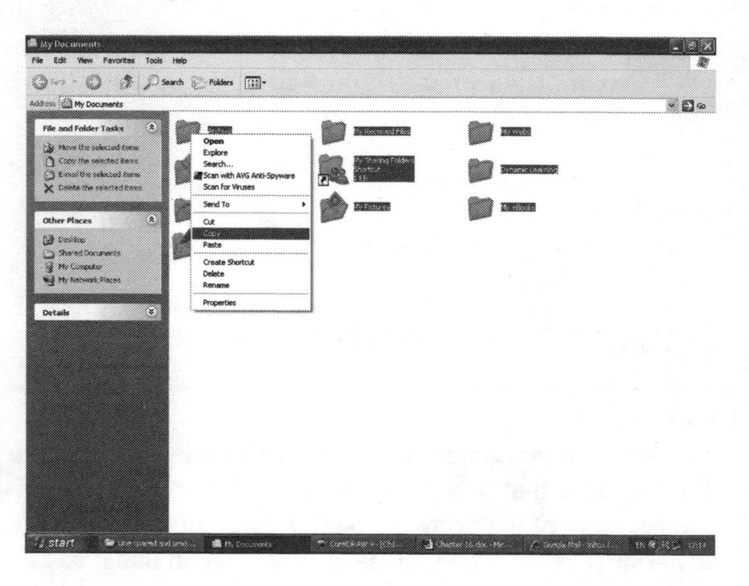

This image shows all the files and folders highlighted, and the menu that is displayed when you right click.

Hints and tips

If you have set up some folders of your own in addition to the My Documents folder, you will need to carry out this process on these folders too.

8 Click on the little arrow on the right-hand side of the **address bar** at the top of the screen.

This will display a list of all the different places where information can be stored on your computer.

Hints and tips

DVDs are more expensive to buy but can store much more data, so use DVD if you can.

9 Select the CD or DVD from the list. In this case it is called 'CD-RW Drive (E:)' but it might have a slightly different name on your computer. This will open up the CD/DVD ready to have files stored on it. A blank screen will be displayed:

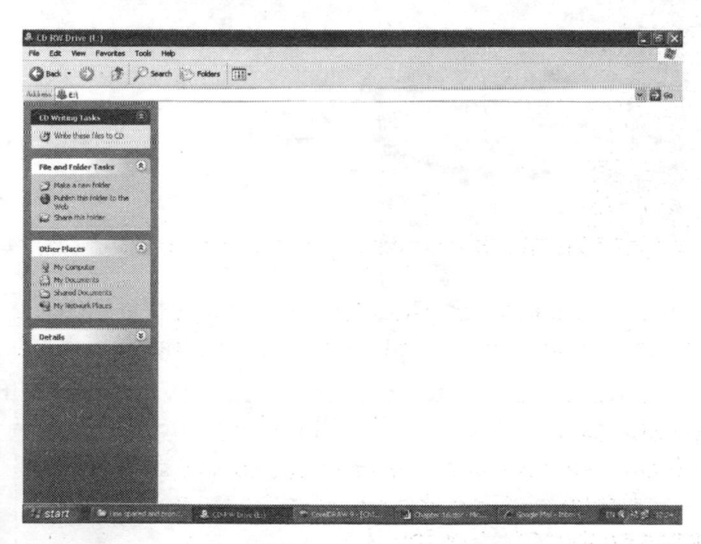

10 Right click anywhere in the white space.

11 Select 'Paste' from the list.
The computer will now start copying all the files and folders in your My Documents folder ready to put them on the CD or DVD. This could take a while. You will get a **progress bar** that gives you an idea of how long this will take.

> **Hints and tips**
> There is only so much information that you can physically store on the disk. If there is too much information you will get an error message at this point and you will have to go back to step 4 and choose individual files and folders within My Documents, instead of trying to do it all in one go.

12 If you get no error messages, when the process is complete click on 'Write these files to CD' in the top left-hand corner:

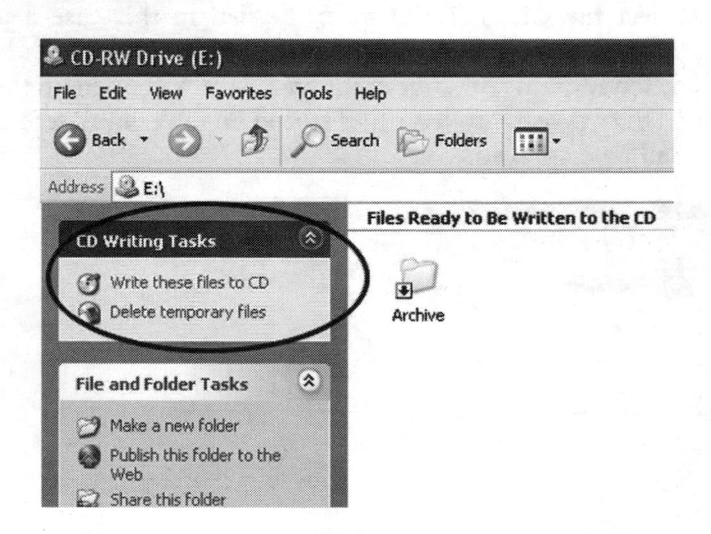

13 You are now prompted to give the CD/DVD a name (if you want to), otherwise it will use the date.

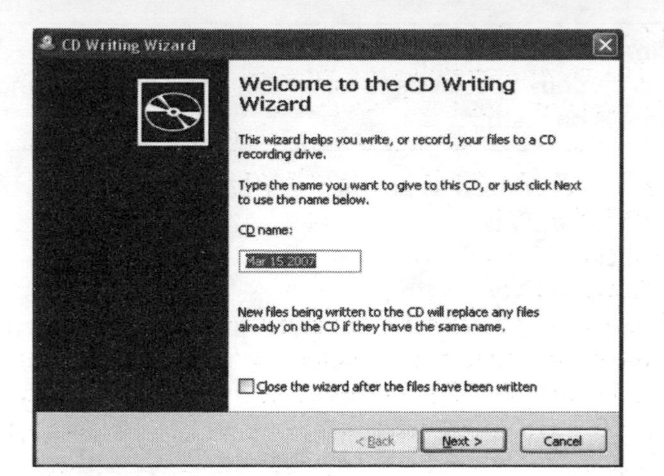

14 Click 'Next'.
It will now copy the files onto the CD or DVD. You will see a progress bar, which gives you an idea of how long it will take.

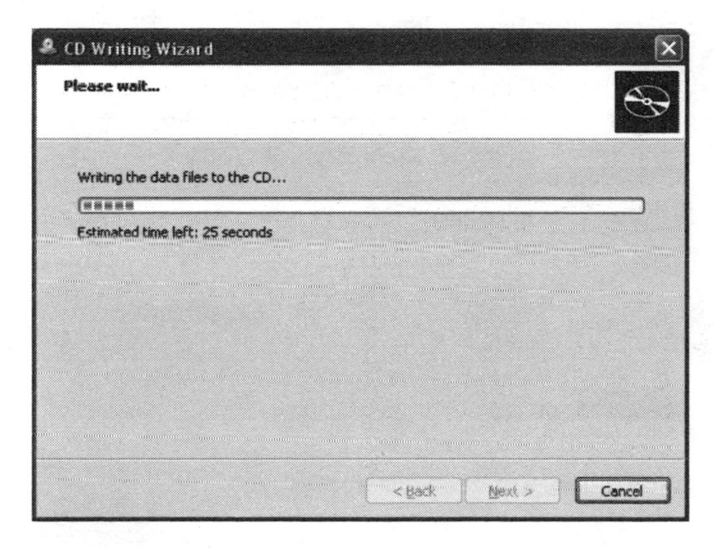

When it has finished, the CD/DVD will automatically eject.

15 You need to click 'Finish' on the screen.

16 Keep the CD/DVD somewhere safe.

Hints and tips
You can buy special pens for writing on CDs so you know what is on them.

If you ever need to get the information back again from this CD/DVD:

17 Click on 'Start'.

18 Click on 'My Computer'.

19 Select the CD/DVD and all the files it contains will be shown.

Summary

In this chapter we have discussed:

- What threats there are to your computer and data on the Internet
- Spam
- Pop-ups
- Viruses, trojans, worms, spyware and adware
- How to protect yourself against them
- How to back up important information

17 arranging and booking your travels

In this chapter you will learn

- **how to find suitable travel websites**
- **how to book a holiday/flight**
- **how to check train times and buy tickets**
- **how to use a route-finder for UK road travel**

Aim of the chapter

The aim of this chapter is to show you how to find out about and book different types of travel arrangements. It will tell you how to find suitable websites and then how to make the booking online. It covers everything from booking a holiday through to planning a route on UK roads.

17.1 Introduction

In Chapter 9 we looked at the basic skills required to **surf** the Internet. Once you have got to grips with using a **search engine** (such as Google™), you can use it to **search** for absolutely everything, including travel and holidays. The problem is that if you just type "holidays" into a search engine you will end up with millions of **hits** and it will be impossible to look through all of them.

One solution to this problem is to put more specific words into the search engine so that it finds only **websites** that are relevant to your requirements. Another solution to this problem is to find the **web address** of particular companies that you could use to arrange your travels. For example, Saga arranges holidays for the over 50s, so you could do a search specifically for this company.

17.2 Searching for travel and holiday websites

1 Open **Internet Explorer®**.
2 Type: www.google.co.uk into the address bar. The Google™ search engine will now load.

Hints and tips

You may prefer to use a different search engine from Google™. The instructions here will work for any search engine.

The trick now is to make the key words as specific as possible. For example, to find some cheap airline tickets to Melbourne in Australia:

3 In the search box, type: "cheap tickets" + Melbourne (exactly as shown here).
The use of speech marks means that the search engine will find only websites with that exact phrase in them. The use of the + means that the website must also have the word Melbourne in it. You can massively reduce the number of hits, if you think carefully about the search words that you want to use. If you know which company you want to use but you don't know its web address, then use the search engine to type in the name. It will then be displayed in the results page and you can link to it from there.
4 Click on the 'pages from the UK' button.
5 Click on 'Google Search'.
This search would bring up these results:

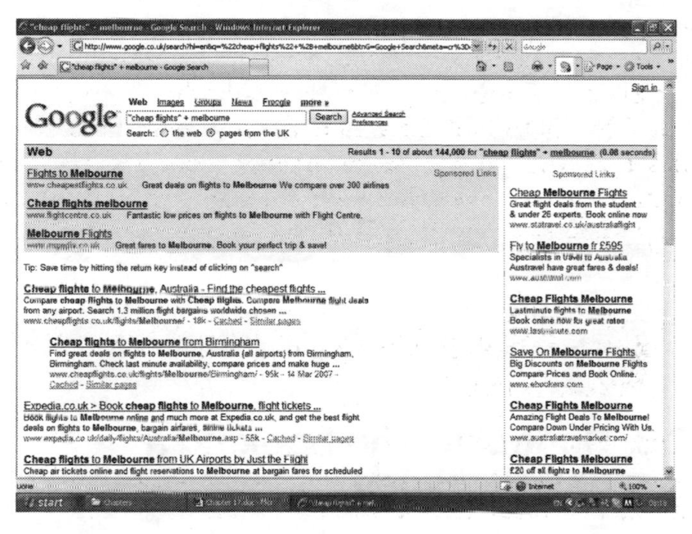

It has brought up 144,000 hits in this case, which is still too many to search through, but you should hopefully find what you are looking for within the first few pages of the results. Notice the first three results that have a grey background, and the results shown down the right-hand side of the page. These are all **sponsored links**, which means that the companies have paid Google™ to make sure that their websites appear on the first page.

You can now look at these results, read the text about each website and then decide which ones you want to look at. It is worth looking at a few different sites for comparison purposes.

To move onto the other pages:

6 Scroll to the bottom of the page.

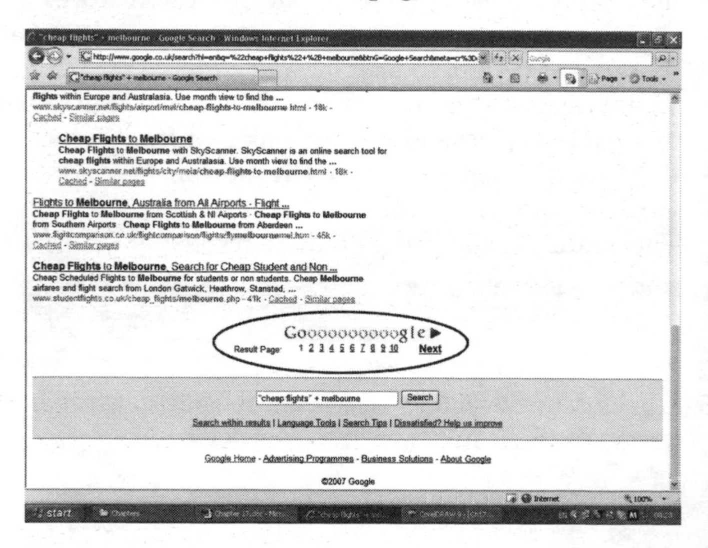

You can move through the pages of results using the 'Next' button, or by clicking on the numbers.

17.3 Choosing and booking a holiday/ticket

Once you have found the website you want to use, you then need to find the holiday or flight that you want, and book it. This process will be different depending on which company you use, as all of their websites are slightly different. However, the principle is the same in each case. You choose the holiday you want and then you have to fill in a form and make payment using your credit card.

We will use Saga Holidays as an example:

1 Type: www.saga.co.uk into the address bar of Internet Explorer®. The Saga opening page will now be displayed.

2 Click on the **links** to their travel pages.
3 The different holidays are shown and you can follow the links to find out more about individual types of holidays.

Every company's **web pages** are different so you need to take a bit of time to look around the site and find what you want. In this example, we will work through the process of booking a short break in Paris.

All holiday/flight booking sites use a search facility to check availability of whatever you are trying to book. You will be asked to type in your requirements in terms of dates, number of people travelling, etc. A typical search page will look like this:

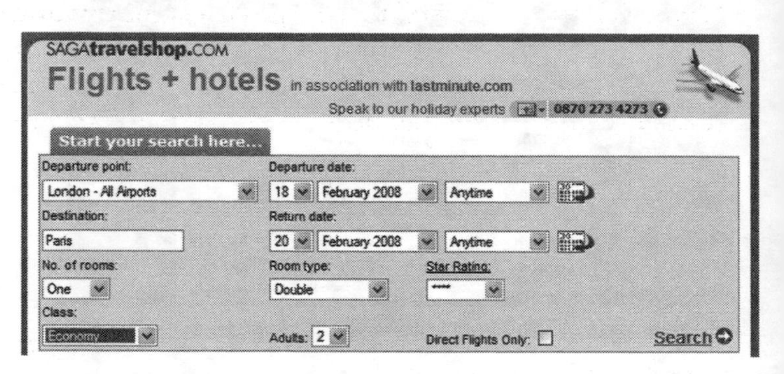

4 Fill in your details and click in 'Search'. A page of results will be shown from which you choose the deal that you want. Again this could take some time as you may not want to book the first one it offers you.

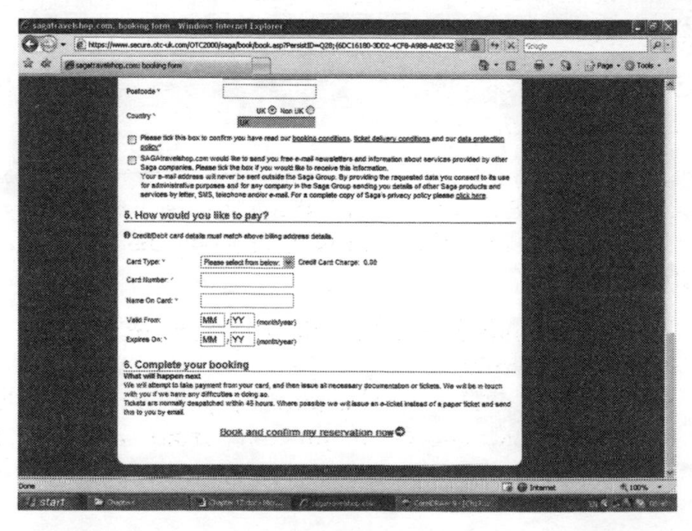

When you have found the deal you want, all holiday/travel websites will then take you through a few screens that you need to fill in. There will be a 'Next' or 'Proceed' button of some sort at the bottom of each page showing you where to go next. A typical example is shown at the foot of the previous page.
You are asked for lots of details including your credit card number.

5 When you have filled in everything, click on the 'Process' button. You will then be given a conformation of your booking, which you can print out as proof of purchase. Some websites will also send you an email to confirm the details, and post confirmation out to you as well.

17.4 Finding and booking train tickets

The process of finding and booking train tickets is similar to booking a holiday, although it is a bit easier as there are fewer options. In the UK, train routes are operated by specific companies, so you don't have any choice who you travel with in most cases.

There are two main websites that you can use to find and book train tickets:

- www.nationalrail.co.uk
- www.thetrainline.com

Both work in a similar way: you type in the route that you want to take, and it will show you what trains are available. You can then book them and pay for them online.

1 Type: www.nationalrail.co.uk into the address bar in Internet Explorer®.
2 Type in the details of the journey you want to take. This example shows a journey from London to Manchester.

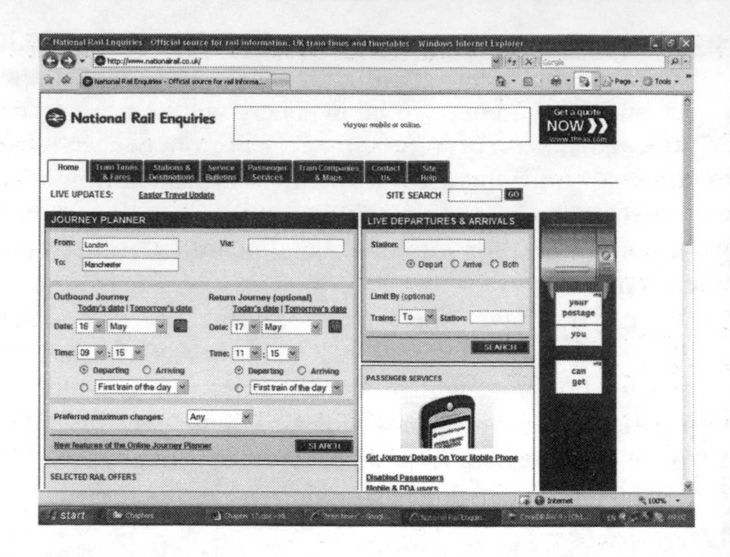

3 Click on 'Search'. Like the holiday booking, you are now taken through several screens where you finalize the details of your journey, type in your personal details and payment details. This website helpfully shows you where you are up to as you work through the stages:

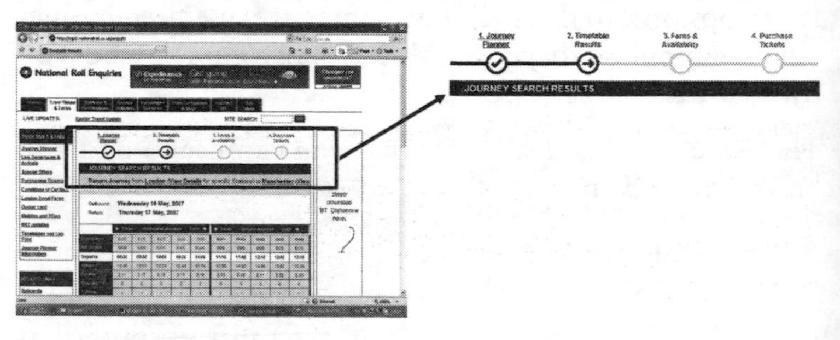

4 Complete all the details requested as you move through the screens.

Hints and tips

All websites are different, but they are all designed to be easy to use. It should be clear how to move from one screen to the next. The link to the next page is usually at the bottom of the page.

17.5 Using a route planner for a road journey

If you are planning a road trip, you can get detailed instructions and maps free on the Internet. All you have to do is type in the start point and your destination. A few websites offer this service. Two of the main sites are provided by motoring organizations:

- www.theaa.com
- www.rac.co.uk

Both have the route-planner facility on their **home page**, which makes them very easy to find. In this example, we will use the RAC website.

1 Type 'www.rac.co.uk' into the address bar.
  The route-planner is near the top of the page as shown.
2 Type where you want to start your journey from and where you want to go to in the two boxes. This can be a place name or postcode and click 'Go'.
3 You may get another screen asking you to confirm the two locations. Click 'Go' on screen. After a few seconds, a map will be displayed showing the route.

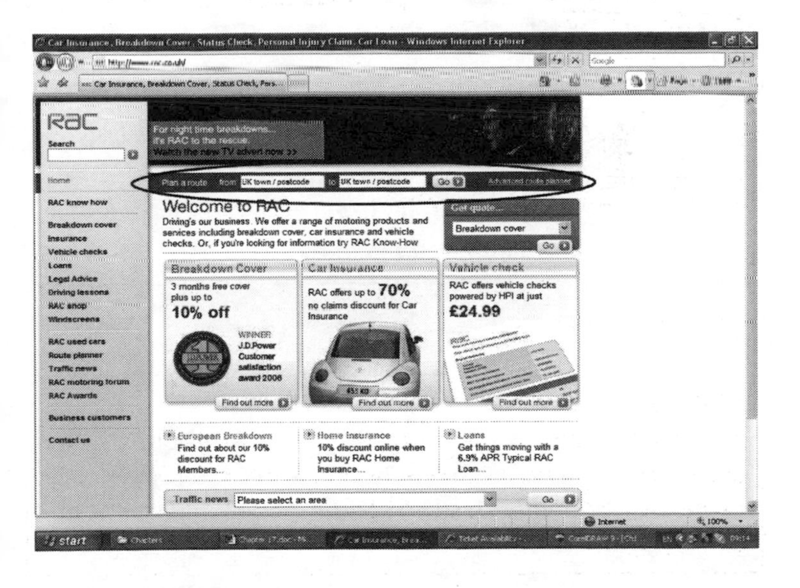

4 **Scroll down** the page and you will find detailed instructions on the route, including distances and approximate timings.
5 At the bottom of the instructions you will find a button called 'Printable version'.
6 Click on this if you want to print out the map and instructions.

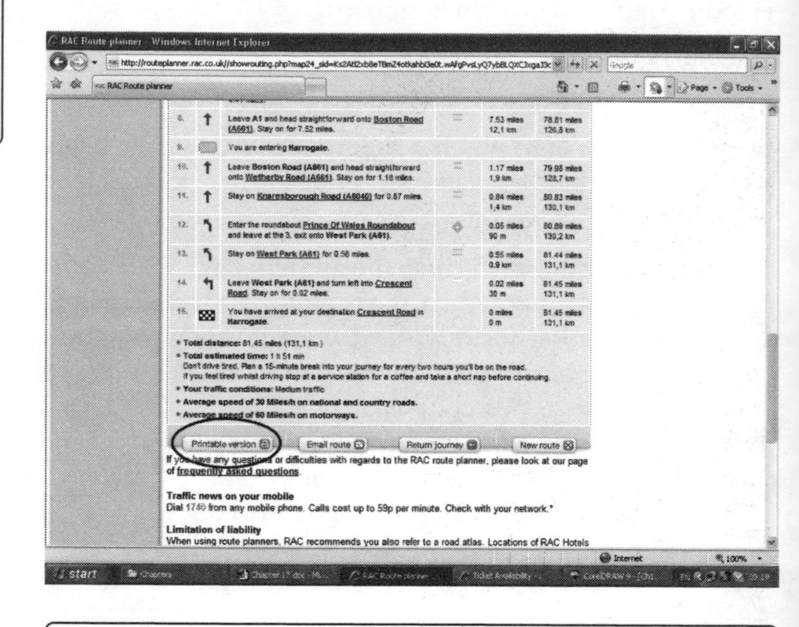

Summary
In this chapter we have discussed:
- Finding and booking a holiday/flight
- Finding and booking a train ticket
- Planning a route for a road journey

8 banking online and other financial services

In this chapter you will learn:

- **how to access your bank online**
- **how to run your current account**
- **how to carry out typical banking transactions**
- **how to access other financial services**
- **about price comparison sites**

Aim of the chapter

The aim of this chapter is to show you how to do your banking online. It covers how to set up and operate a current account using one of the main high-street banking websites as an example. It will also show you how you can access other financial services and looks at how to use price comparison websites.

18.1 Introduction

All of the main high-street banks now offer an **online banking** service. It is possible to carry out most banking transactions online without having to visit your branch or use the telephone, including:

- checking your balance
- viewing statements
- paying bills
- changing or cancelling standing orders and direct debits
- transferring money.

You can also access a range of other financial services including arranging loans, mortgages, life insurance, ISAs and investments. You might want to do this through your existing bank, or you can use the Internet to shop around.

18.2 Getting started with online banking

Before you start online banking, you have to register your details with the bank for security purposes. Depending on the bank, you may need to do this over the phone or in the branch. Some banks allow you to do it using the Internet. If you want to do online banking with your existing bank, you will find details of how to register on their **website**.

Part of the registration process is to choose a security code (like a PIN) and answers to security questions (for example, mother's maiden name or first school). Once registered you will have to type in your sort code, account number and then you will be asked for the PIN and for the answer to the security question.

> **Hints and tips**
> All banks use slightly different security methods. Some ask for selected digits of the PIN, others ask you to choose dates as the security question.

Once registered, you can **log on** to your account. This example shows you the procedure for the Co-operative Bank. Other banks' websites will look different from this, but the basic processes will be the same regardless of the bank.

1 Open Internet Explorer® and load the website of the bank. In this case, it is www.co-operativebank.co.uk. This is the bank's log-on screen, which is typical of any bank. It asks you for the account numbers and security details.

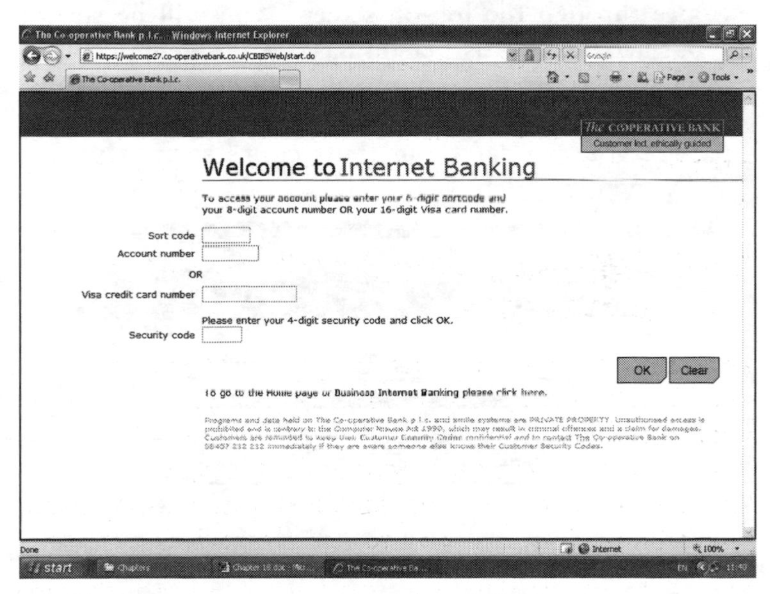

2 Click in each box and type in the details.
3 Click on 'OK' to move on to the next screen.

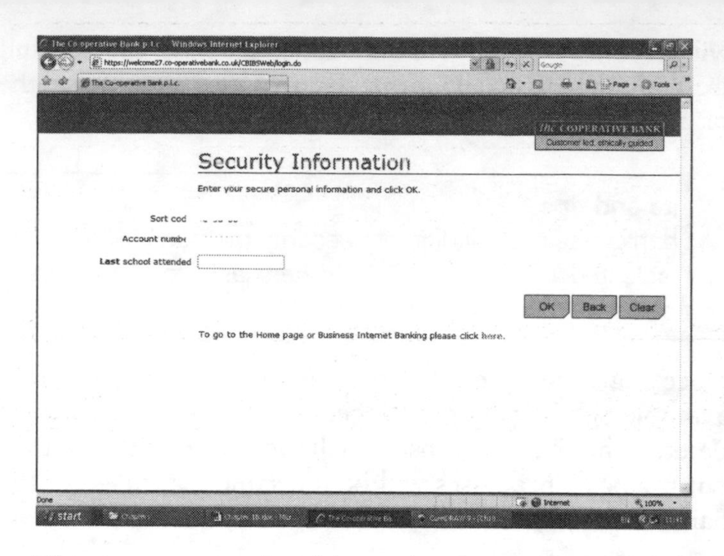

This is an example of how the security questions are used. This bank asks for several security questions when you register. Every time you log on, it will ask you just one of these questions.

Once through the log-on screens, you will be shown your accounts. This person has five different accounts including a current account, savings accounts and loans. Also notice the list of options on the left-hand side, where you can carry out transactions such as paying bills and direct debits.

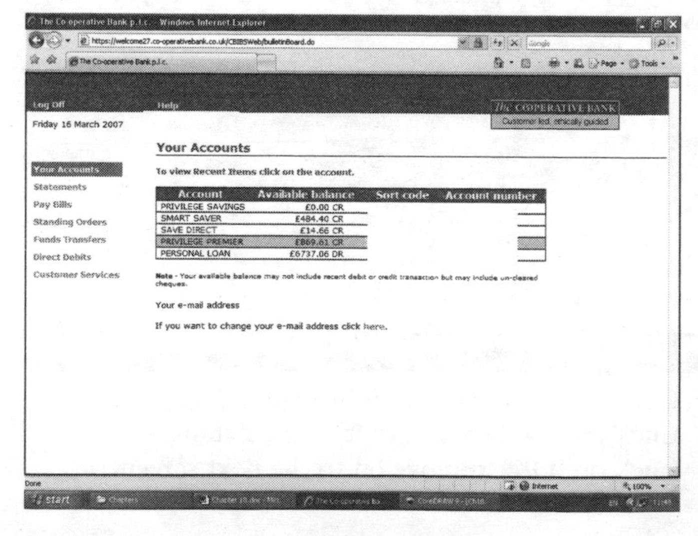

Hints and tips

Note that for security reasons, we have blanked out some of the details on the screen images used in this chapter.

4 To view one of the accounts, click on the account you want to look at. In this example we will look at the 'Privilege Premier' account.

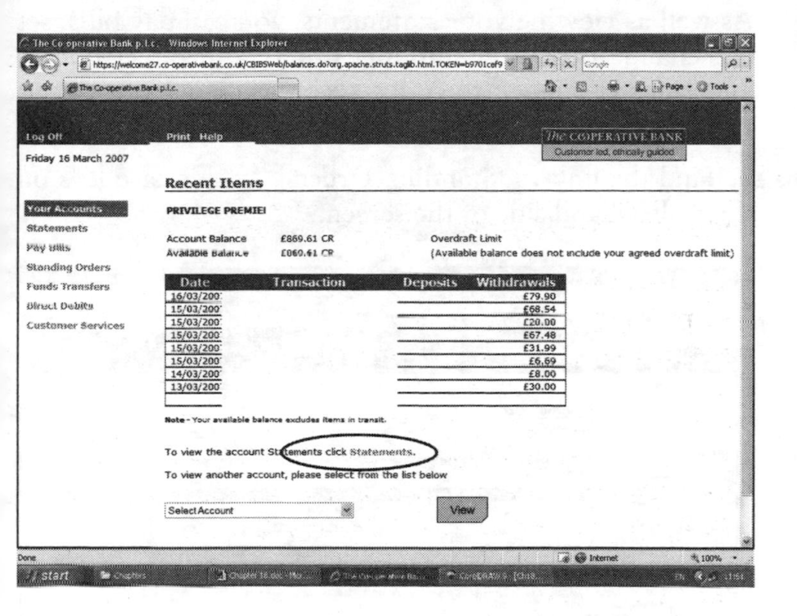

A list of recent transactions is shown in the table. This will include cheques, cash withdrawals, direct debits and standing orders. You can view a whole statement by finding and clicking on the link to 'Statements'. These are the electronic equivalent of the statements that you get through the post. Most banks will let you view statements from up to a year ago.

You can still ask the bank to send you paper copies of your statements, or you can print them out from here. To print:

5 Click on the 'Print' **icon** in Internet Explorer®:

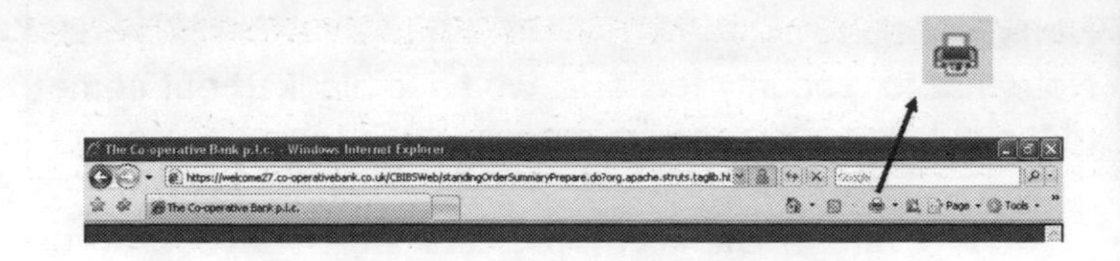

18.3 Carrying out transactions

As well as viewing your statements, you can pay bills, set up, change or cancel standing orders and direct debits, and transfer money to other accounts. For example, to change or cancel a standing order:

1 Find the link to 'Standing Orders'. In this case it is on the left-hand side of the screen.

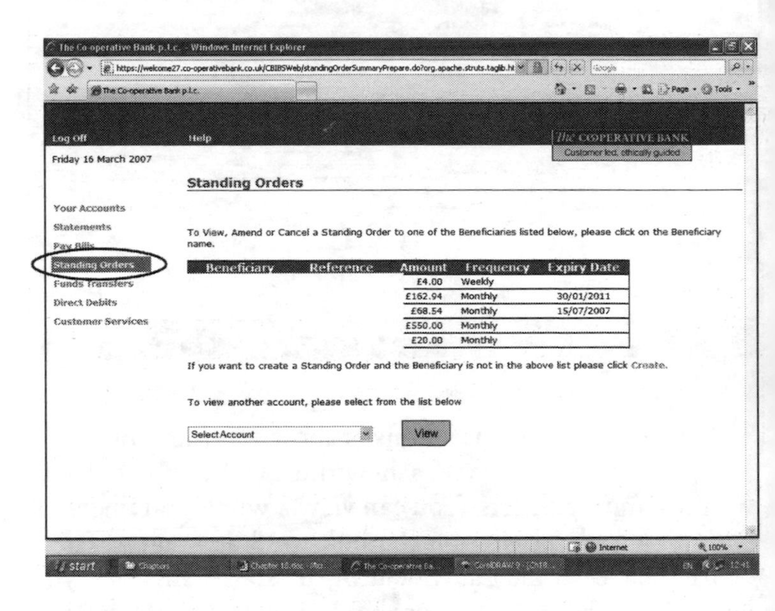

All of your existing standing orders will now be displayed.

2 To change or cancel a standing order, double click on the name of the person or organization who is receiving the money from you. The individual details of the standing order are now shown and you can amend or cancel it by clicking on the appropriate link.

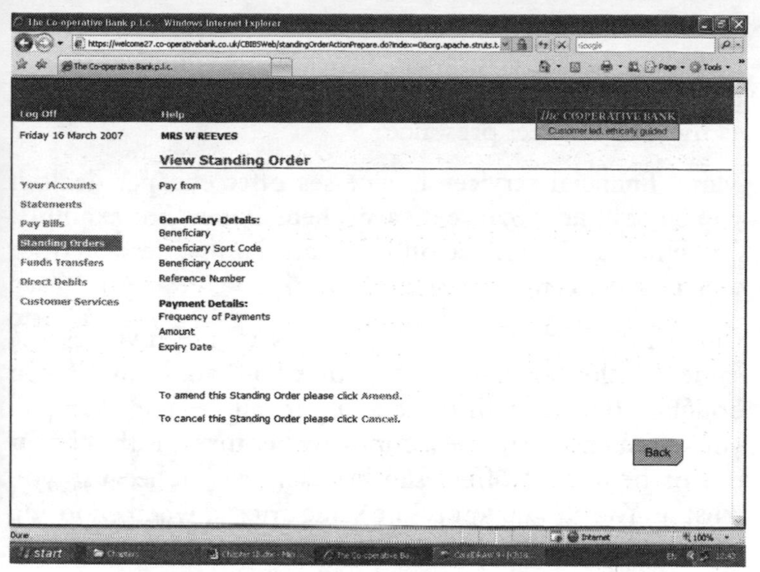

Once you are familiar with one transaction, all of the others arc very similar. For example, managing your direct debits and bill payments is very similar to sorting out your standing orders.

Hints and tips

All the banks have customer helpline services, so if you get stuck, you can phone the helpline and someone will talk you through the problem. This will cost you only the price of a phone call.

When you have finished banking, it is important that you log off from the website, rather than just clicking on the cross. There will bc a link to 'Log Off' or it might be called 'Sign Out'. This guarantees that the connection between your computer and the bank's is closed, which makes you safe from hackers.

18.4 Other financial services

The Internet has become an important factor for all financial services businesses. In addition to the banks, there are lots of other financial services available over the Internet including loans, insurance, investments, mortgages and pensions. All the big companies now have websites as well as their high-street presence.

Many financial services businesses offer cheaper deals if you buy online, because it saves them money. For example, if you buy car insurance online, many companies will offer you a 10 per cent discount.

Choosing which of these businesses to use involves the same decision-making process that you would use if you bought from them without doing it online. For example, you might choose to use a company because it is the cheapest, or because it offers the best service, or because you trust it. You should apply the same criteria when choosing whom to deal with online.

To access the websites of these businesses you either need to know the **web address**, which you can type straight into Internet Explorer®, or you can use a **search engine** to find them.

18.5 Price comparison sites and money search engines

A relatively new phenomenon on the Internet is the price comparison site. These are websites that are set up to collate information about all sorts of products and services (including financial services) from lots of different companies and then compare them. The idea is that they do the shopping around for you, so that you need to use only one website. Information is collated from most of the major companies in the UK.

There are also websites that call themselves 'money search engines'. These are like normal search engines (e.g. Google™) but the results are focused on financial topics.

There are lots to choose from. Some popular sites at the moment are:

- www.moneysupermarket.com
- www.moneyfacts.co.uk
- www.confused.com
- www.kelkoo.co.uk
- www.pricerunner.co.uk

This is not an exhaustive list and if you type: "price comparison site" + finance into a search engine, you will find others to choose from.

They all work in the same basic way. For example, using Kelkoo:

1 Type: www.kelkoo.co.uk into the address bar of Internet Explorer®.
2 Click on the link to 'Finance'.

You can now click on the links to look at certain types of financial services (e.g. Loans, Credit Cards, etc.), or you can use the **search** facility.

Hints and tips

Many websites have their own search engines, which you can use to search for something just on their website. They work like a normal search engine, but rather than searching the whole Internet, they search only the one website.

To use the search facility:

3 Type the key words into the search box and click on 'Search'. In this example, the site will be searched for details on ISAs. The results page lists the first 20 of 100 hits.

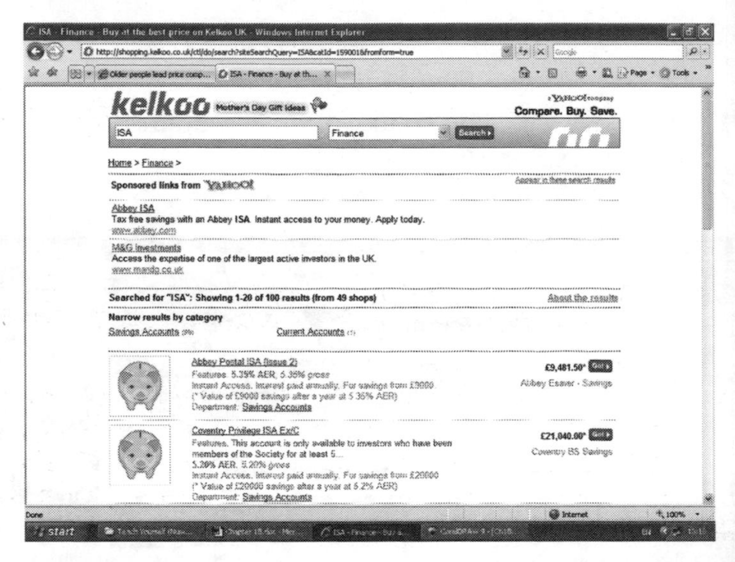

You can look through the results as you would with any search engine results. There is a small amount of text about each ISA and a link to the website of the company that is offering it. There are also some **sponsored links** at the top. Once you have linked to the website, you will be able to apply to buy financial services online in the same way that you can buy anything else online.

Another example is www.moneysupermarket.com

4 Type: www.moneysupermarket.co.uk into the address bar of Internet Explorer®. You can see that their site is organized slightly differently and looks different, but basically it does the same thing as Kelkoo. In this example, we will compare the cost of personal loans.

5 Click on 'Money'.

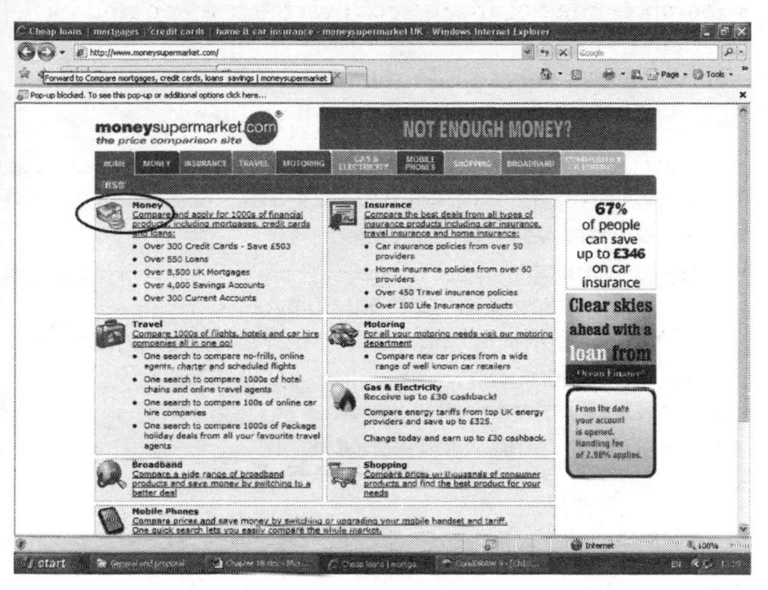

6 In the section on Loans, click on 'Compare Now'. You can now type in the amount you want to borrow and it will compare the cost of borrowing from several different companies, and then provide you with a ranked list of results like the one shown here.

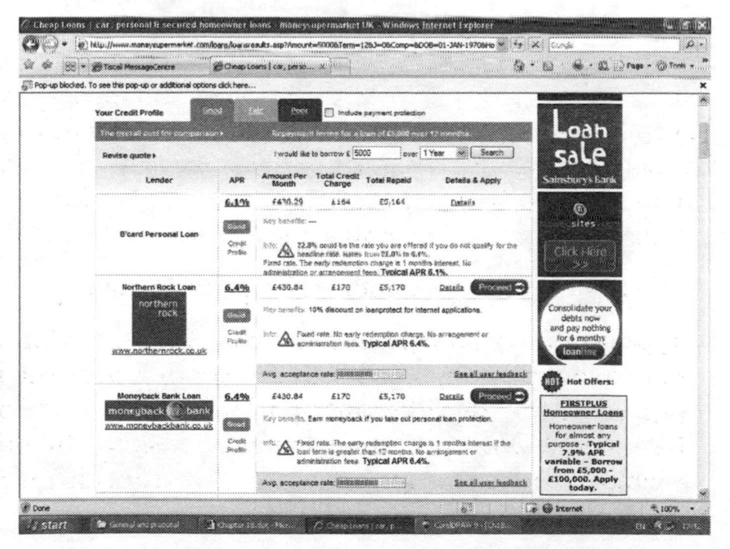

Again, think of this like the list of results that you get from a search engine. You can scroll through them, and click on them to go to the website of the company offering the loan. You can then apply online, or phone them up, or enter your details and they will call you back.

Summary

In this chapter we have discussed:

- Online banking
- Managing your current account online
- Common banking transactions such as standing orders and direct debits
- Accessing other financial services
- Using price comparison websites

9 buying from an online auction

In this chapter you will learn:

- **how to set up an eBay™ account**
- **how to search and browse for products**
- **how to place a bid**
- **how to pay for your product**
- **things to watch out for when using eBay™**

Aim of the chapter
This chapter will show you how to use the eBay™ auction site. It assumes that you have never used an online auction before and will show you how to register, how to find what you want and how to bid for it, and eventually pay for it. The final section includes some tips on buying successfully from eBay™.

19.1 Introduction

eBay™ is currently the world's biggest online auction site boasting more than 180 million users worldwide with at least 3 million items for sale at any one time.

It works in much the same way as a traditional auction in that items are offered for sale, you look at them and read the description, and then decide whether you want to bid for the item or not. Many other people will be doing the same thing and bidding against you. The big difference with a real auction is the period of time over which the bidding takes place, as it can be several days. At the end of this period, if your bid is the highest, you win. You then pay for the product and the seller sends it to you, or you go and pick it up.

Although eBay™ was originally intended for items of relatively low value, it is now possible to buy virtually anything including cars, holidays and even houses.

19.2 Getting started

First, you need to register. To do this, you MUST already have an **email address**. If you do not have one, refer to Chapter 5.

1 Open Internet Explorer® either from the **desktop** or from the 'Start' menu.
2 In the **address bar**, type: www.ebay.co.uk.

Hints and tips
eBay™ operates in more than 30 countries, so make sure that you use the .co.uk version (assuming you are in the UK, of course).

The opening page is displayed and will look something like this.

3 Click on the 'Register Now' button. You will have to fill in a form (something you will be getting used to by now). This will ask you for your personal details and email contact details. You will also be asked to think of a **user name** and **password,** which you will need to use every time you **log on** to eBay™.
4 Complete the form. This may take a few minutes. Make sure you type in the phone number correctly, as you will get an automated phone call to activate your account.

Hints and tips
When you are filling in forms, you can use the TAB key on the keyboard to move from one box to another. This is sometimes quicker than using the mouse to click into each new box.

This shows how Marjorie Franklin would fill in the form. You will need to **scroll down** as the form is quite long and takes up more than a screen-full.

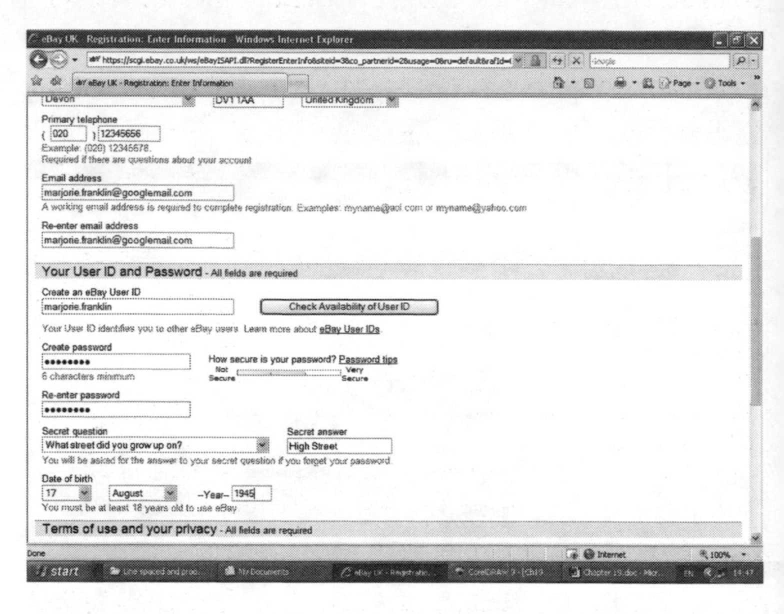

5 Make a note of your user ID and remember your password.

6 Scroll to the bottom of the form and tick the boxes that say you have read and agree to the terms and conditions. Click 'Continue'.

7 On the next screen, tick the box for 'Phone verification' and request a phone call straight away. As if by magic your phone will ring and you will be given a 4-digit number. Write this down.

8 On the next screen you have to type in this number.

9 When you have completed the form, you will be sent an email from eBay™. This is an automatic process and should be instant.

10 Go to your email account and open the email from eBay™. You could do this by opening your email in a new **tab** in Internet Explorer®.

11 In the email, you are asked to click on a **link** that will activate your eBay™ account. Click on the link. It will

take you back to the page on the eBay™ website where you can now start bidding for products.

To make sure you are in the 'Buy' section, click on the link to 'Buy' in the top left-hand corner of the page:

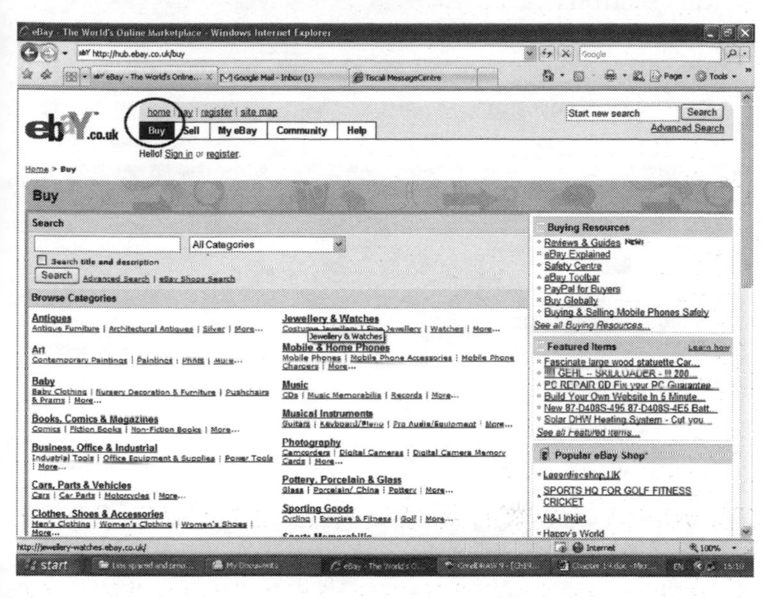

19.3 Finding what you want

There are two ways to find the items you are looking for:

- You can '**browse**', which means you can look through a wide range of products under certain categories.
- You can '**search**', which means you type in a few key words that describe the item you want and it will search through all the items and display only those items that match the description you have typed in. This is like using a **search engine**, but it will search only the eBay™ site.

Browsing for an item

If you do not specifically know what you want, then **browsing** is the best option. For example, if you want to look at pottery, but do not have a specific item in mind:

1 Look through the categories until you find the one you want. In this case, it will be under 'Pottery, Porcelain & Glass' so click on this link. You are now presented with a more detailed list of categories within this section.
2 Under Pottery click on 'Clarice Cliff'. You are now at the screen that lists all of the items that are for sale under this category.

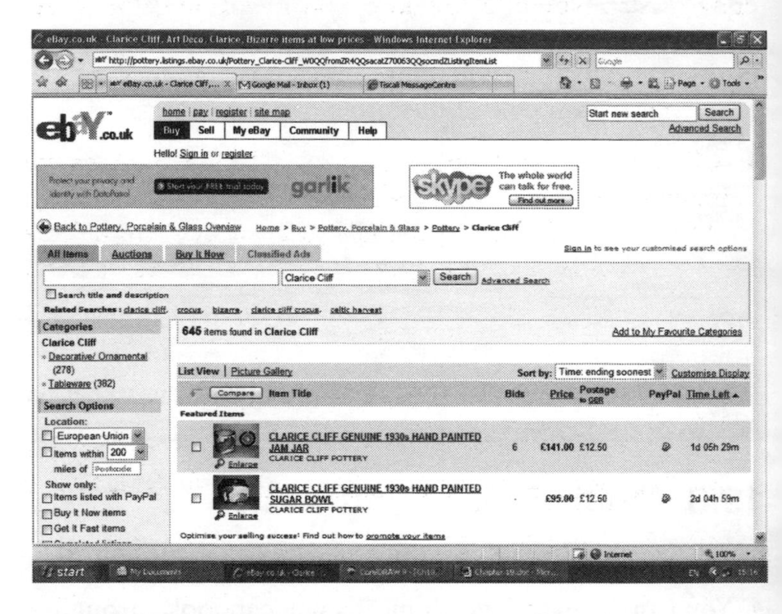

In this example, there are 645 items for sale.
3 To view the entire list of items for sale, you need to scroll down. This is very much like looking at the results produced by a search engine. It is not possible to show all 645 items on one page, so at the bottom of the first page, there are links to several other pages.

On the left-hand side of each page, you will see that there are further subcategories. In this case, there are categories for 'Decorative/ Ornamental' and 'Tableware'. This will help you to narrow down your search, reducing the number of items listed.

Hints and tips
It would take you hours to view all 645 items in this example so it would be better to try to narrow down the search, if you can, using the subcategories.

Searching for an item

The preferred method of finding what you want on eBay™ is to type in a few key words that describe it. As you saw in the previous section, browsing through categories can be very time consuming as there are often so many items for sale.

1 Click on the 'Buy' button again to take you back to the main buying page where all the categories are listed.
   At the top of this page, there is a 'Search' box. This example will show you how to search for a specific item, a Clarice Cliff vase.
2 Click in the 'Search' box and type: "Clarice Cliff Vase".

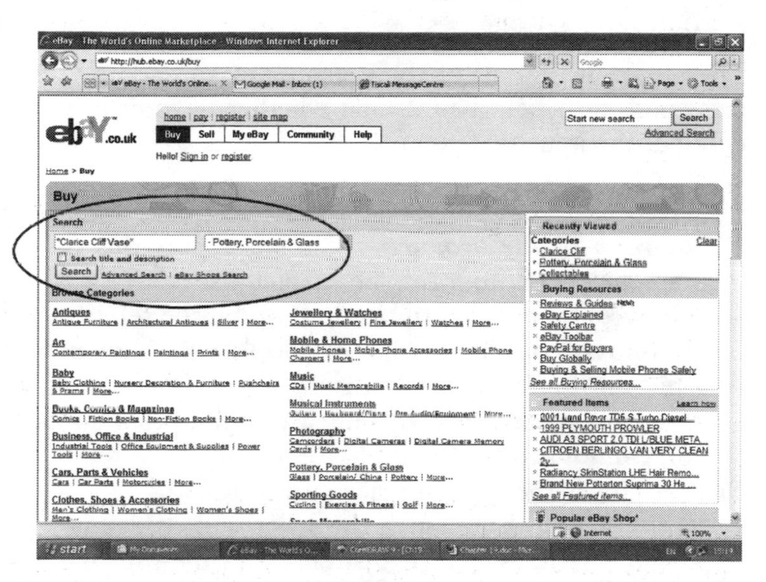

You can narrow down the search by only searching within a category using the box to the right of the 'Search' box.

3 In the 'Category' box, which currently reads 'All categories', select 'Pottery, Porcelain & Glass'.

> **Hints and tips**
> If you do not know into which category something fits, you can just leave this box set to 'All categories'.

4 Click on 'Search'. After a few seconds, you will be presented with a list of all the Clarice Cliff vases that are currently for sale.

19.4 Selecting your item

Once you have located an item in which you are interested, you need to get a few more details about it and the seller. In the first instance you need to know the price, how many bids there are on it, and how long there is left on the auction.

The screen listing all of the items gives you some useful information to help you decide whether to look in more detail at the item.

These are:

Photograph of the product – The seller puts this on. If there isn't a photograph, be suspicious.

Item Title – A brief description put on by the seller.

Bids – Shows you the number of people who have put in a bid on this item. If it is displaying the 'Buy It Now' symbol it means that you must pay the price quoted, you cannot bid for it.

Price – This is the highest price currently bid.

Postage – This is how much the seller will charge you to send the item. Keep an eye out for over-the-top charges.

PayPal – This is a method of online payment where you pay for the item via email using a credit/debit card. This can make the transaction easier as you don't have to wait for cheques to clear.

Time Left – This is how many days or hours there are left until the auction closes. When the auction closes, the highest bidder at that point wins.

This information is displayed for every item that is for sale. If you are still interested in the item you can now find out more about it and the seller.

19.5 Finding out more about the item and the seller

To view more details about any specific item:

Click on the photograph or on the item title.

This then displays a further page that gives you details about the product, usually some more photographs and the seller rating, which gives you an idea of how reliable the seller is.

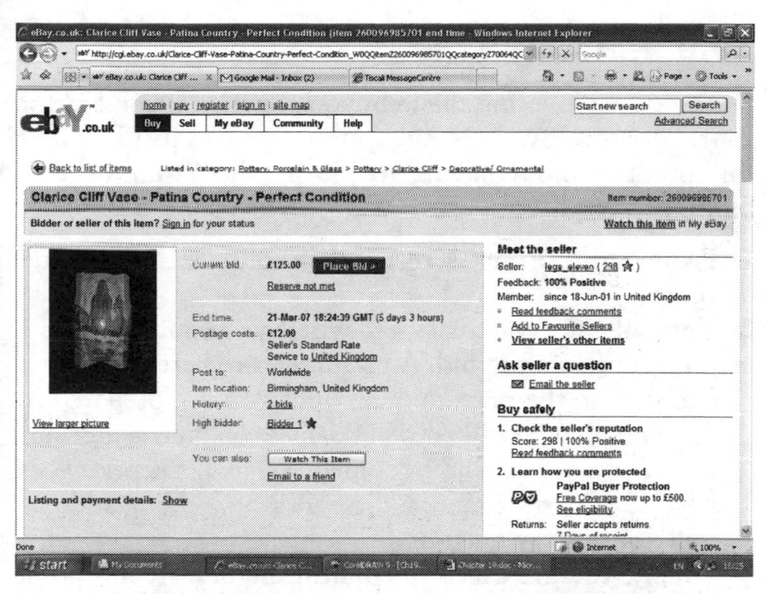

A fuller description of the product can be obtained by scrolling down the page.

On the right-hand side is a seller rating. When people buy items from eBay™ they are asked to rate the seller and make comments about them. You can view these comments and read the ratings by following the links. It will show you the number of people who have commented and provides an overall rating. In this example, the seller has 298 comments and they are all positive giving a 100 per cent rating.

You can contact the seller direct to ask questions about the product or delivery arrangements. This is advisable on items of greater value in particular.

Hints and tips

eBay™ provides useful hints and tips about trading on the site. For example, the page shown has a link to a section on safe buying tips.

19.6 Making a bid

Once you have found the item you want, you can bid for it. If there is a 'Buy It Now' option, you can just buy it at this point without having to bid at all. **Assuming that bidding is required:**

1 From the current screen, click on the 'Place Bid' button.
2 This will take you to a screen where you can type in how much you want to bid. A useful feature here is that you can type in the maximum amount you are prepared to pay and eBay™ will automatically keep increasing your bid, if you are out-bid by someone else. If the price goes beyond your maximum bid, it will stop bidding and you will not win the auction.
3 Finally, you are asked to confirm the bid. At this point you are entering a legal contract to buy the item. So if you win, you *must* buy it. Only confirm the bid if you want to buy the item!

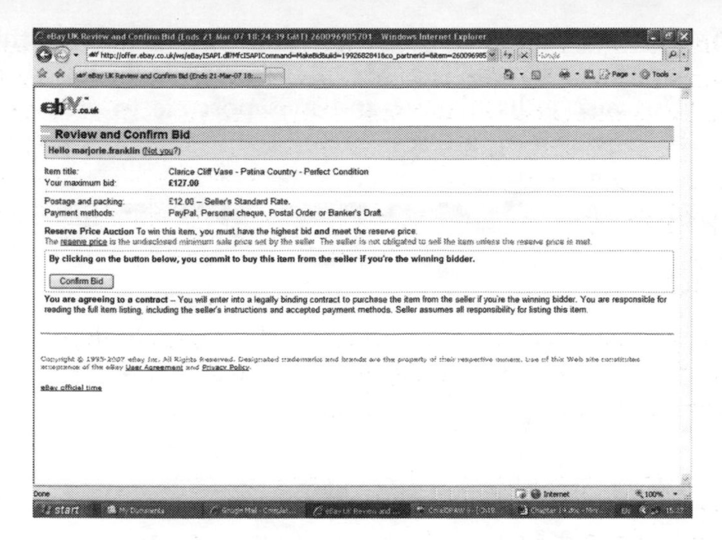

4 The next step is to keep an eye on the bidding from time to time, or just wait until the time runs out and see whether you have won.
eBay™ has a feature called 'My eBay'. You can opt to 'Watch This Item', which means that it will put this item into a list for you, where you can watch the progress of the bidding.
5 To do this, from the item's description screen like the one shown, click on 'Watch This Item'.

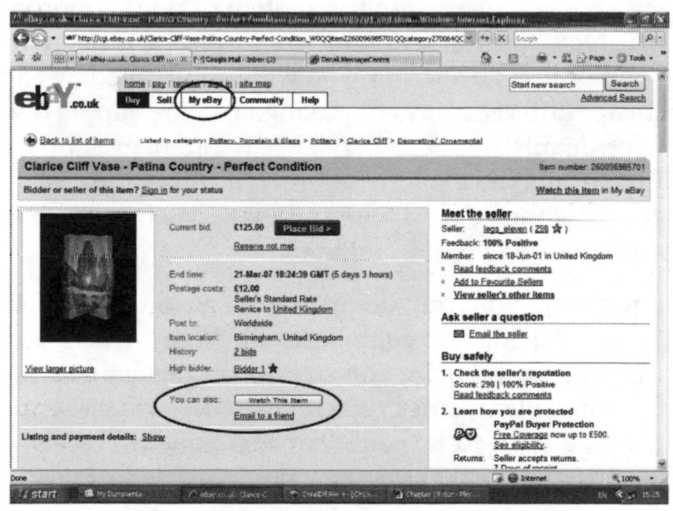

6 To view the 'My eBay' area, click on 'My eBay' near the top of the screen. The 'My eBay' screen looks like this. The vase is listed here and it is possible to view the bidding as it progresses.

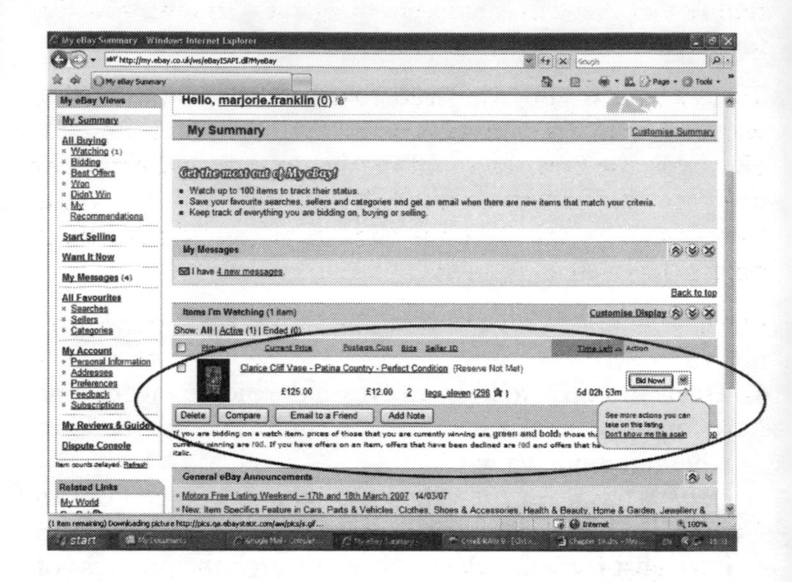

19.7 Winning and paying

When you win an auction for an item or if you opt for the 'Buy It Now' option you now need to pay for the item. If you win or lose an auction, you will be informed by email. There are different ways of paying. You are supplied with contact details of the seller. This is often just an email address or maybe a phone number. If this is the case, you could just contact the seller and make arrangements like any other buying/selling arrangement.

Alternatively, you can do it all online or via the post with no need for any contact at all. Many sellers accept cheques but will require you to post the cheque and allow time for it to clear. This is where the seller rating is important, as you need to be confident that you will receive the item.

The other option is **PayPal**. This is a free and secure service where you pay using your credit or debit card via email. This is quicker than a cheque as the money will transfer much more quickly. It also provides protection in the eventuality that the item is not sent, or that it is significantly different from the way it was described.

To use PayPal you will need to register with the PayPal website first. This process is similar to registering for eBay™ in the first place and can be done by following the links to PayPal from the eBay™ site or by typing 'www.paypal.co.uk' into the address bar and then clicking on the 'Sign Up Now' link.

Once you have done this you will be able to use this method wherever the seller accepts PayPal. You will receive an email confirming your order, and you click on the 'Pay Now' option.

19.8 Things to watch out for using eBay™

In common with anything else on the Internet, there are plenty of dodgy people out there who might try to rip you off. The anonymous nature of the Internet perhaps makes this a bit easier for these people. The best advice is to use the seller ratings to make a judgement about how reliable someone might be.

Decide how much you want to spend and stick to it. In common with traditional auctions, it can be very tempting to keep upping the price that you are willing to pay, only to regret it later. Many bidders leave it until the last minute to make their bids; so don't get caught up in a bidding war.

Make sure you are aware of all the charges that will be added. Keep an eye on postage costs and VAT. Many businesses now use eBay™ as their main way of selling products, and they will have to add on VAT. Also, make sure that the item is for sale in your country, or you may have to pay additional shipping costs and tax.

Finally, eBay™ has become an international phenomenon and, as a result, there is a lot of information written about it. A good starting point is the site's own Help centre, which can be accessed from the Help tab on the **home page**.

Summary

In this chapter we have discussed:

- How to register with eBay™
- How to browse and search for items
- How to make a bid
- How to make a payment
- Things to watch out for when using eBay™

20 selling using an online auction

In this chapter you will learn:

- **how to add a listing to sell an item on eBay™**
- **how to categorize and describe your item**
- **how to add a photograph**
- **how to work out how much it will cost to sell on eBay™**
- **how to register as an eBay™ seller**

Aim of the chapter
This chapter will show you how to use the eBay™ auction site to set up a listing of an item that you want to sell. It assumes that you have read Chapter 19 and that you are familiar with the basics of using eBay™ and that you have a **user name** and **password** for the eBay website.

20.1 Getting started

1 Open Internet Explorer® either from the desktop or from the 'Start' menu.
2 In the address bar, type: www.ebay.co.uk

The opening page is displayed. In the previous chapter you registered yourself with the eBay™ site, which you only have to do once. From now on when you use eBay™, you need to sign in using your user name and password:

1 Click on 'Sign in'.

2 Now type in your user name and password and click on 'Sign in Securely'.

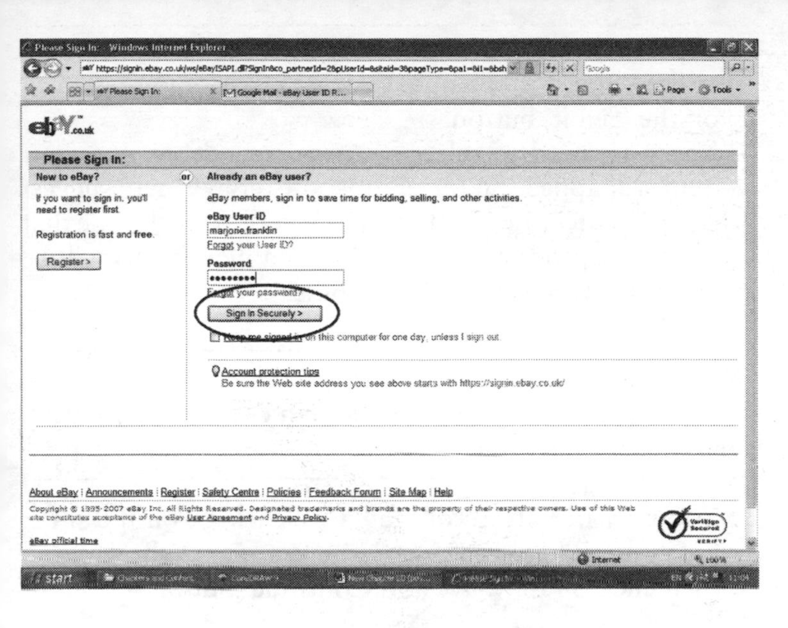

20.2 Setting up the listing for your item

1 The main eBay™ page will now load. Click on 'Sell' at the top of the screen and you will then be prompted to complete some details on the item that you are selling.

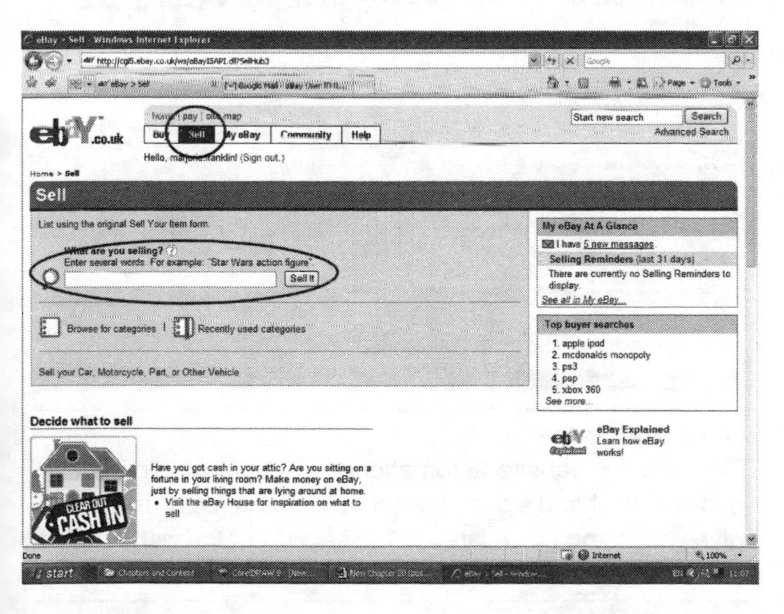

2 Type a description of the item into the 'What are you selling' box, for example Gent's bicycle, and then click on the 'Sell it' button.

3 You now need to select a category under which your item will appear on the eBay™ site. eBay™ will suggest suitable categories, and you need to click on the one that is most appropriate. In the case of a bicycle this will be 'Sporting Goods > Cycling > Bikes'.

> **Hints and tips**
> You can place your item in more than one category if you think it is appropriate.

4 You now need to **scroll down** by clicking on the small arrow in the bottom right-hand corner (as shown) and then click on the 'Save and Continue' button.

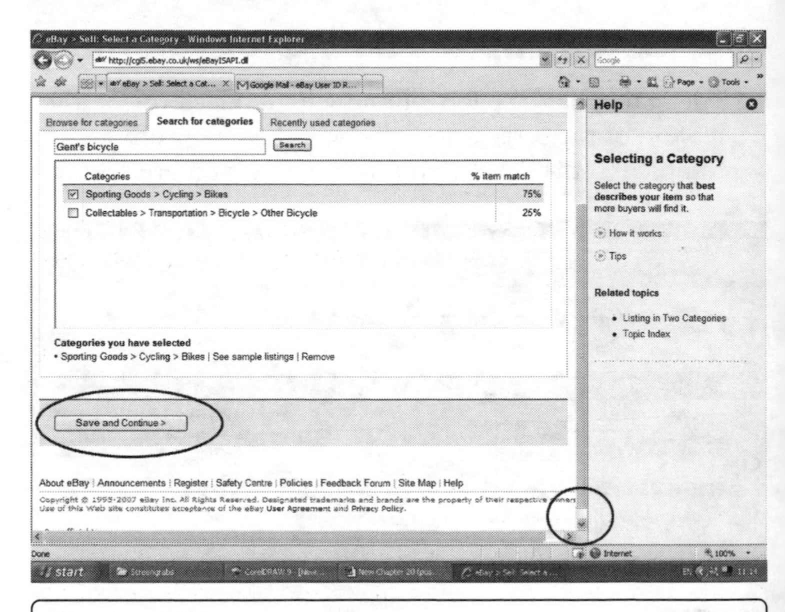

> **Hints and tips**
> The eBay™ website automatically displays a help section on the right-hand side of the screen. This is really useful and gives hints and tips related to the section of the website that you are on at the time.

You are now asked for more details about the item, and to add a photograph (or photographs). This chapter assumes that you already have a photo of the item on your computer and that you know which folder it is in and what the name of the file is.

5 Type a more detailed description of the item into the box labelled 'Title'.

6 Now click on 'Add Pictures'.

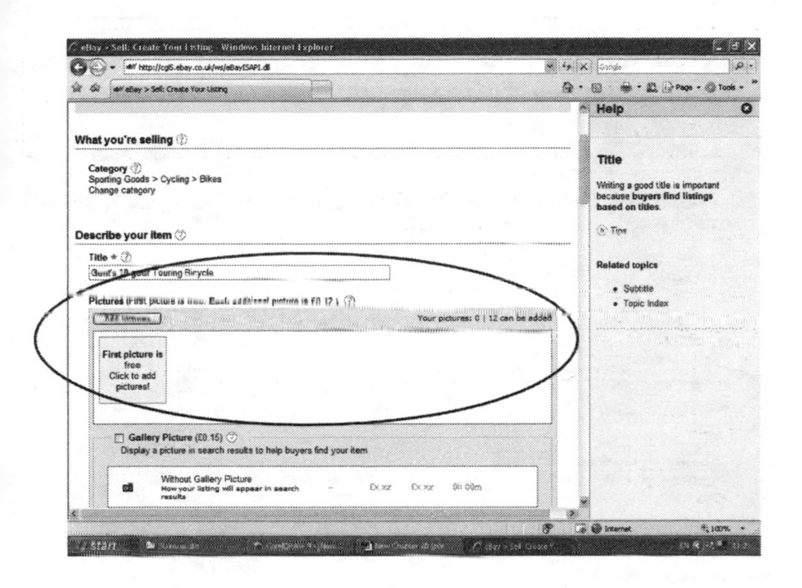

7 A new window will open. Click on 'Browse' and find the photograph of the item. Your photos will probably be in the folder called 'My Pictures' unless you have set up a new folder yourself.

8 Find the photo and double click on it.

9 Now click on 'Upload'.

10 You are now taken back to the main screen where you need to scroll down and fill in more details about the item for sale (you have to fill in quite a lot of information so you need to keep scrolling until it is all complete). In this case, we are asked to fill in details such as the age, colour and number of gears. If you were selling a different type of item, for example, an antique vase, it

would ask for details that were relevant to that category of item. There is also a large white box where you can type in extra information about the item.

Hints and tips
The more information you give people, the more likely you are to get bidders on your item. You might consider adding more photographs too, although there is an additional cost for this.

11 Scroll down further and you are asked to complete information on the selling price.

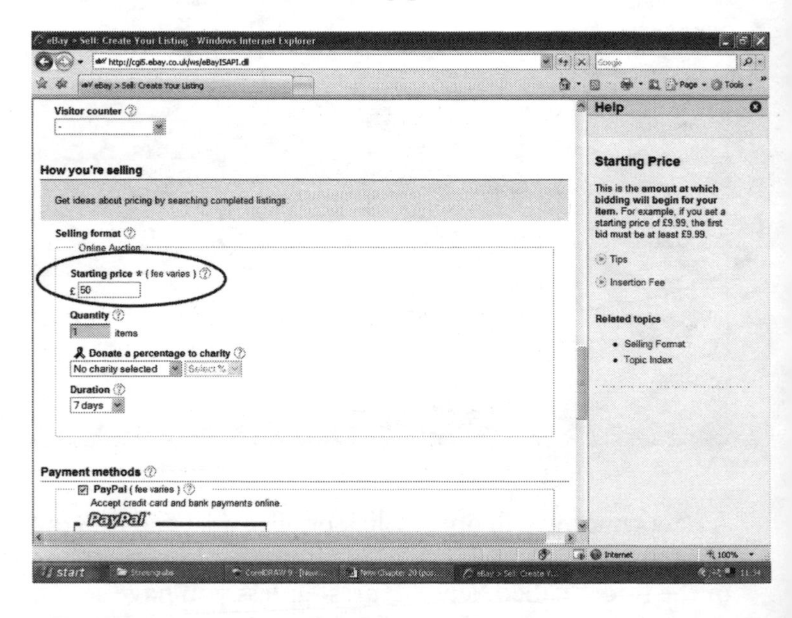

12 Fill in the details in the boxes. At this stage it is worth clicking on the 'fee varies' link that will open a new window where the eBay™ fees are shown. You pay eBay™ a one-off insertion fee and then a percentage of the final price. Fees vary depending on the price and the type of item. So you should check this carefully before you go any further.

13 Continue to scroll down completing the sections on payment methods, postage costs, location and the

end-date for the auction. Use the 'Help' screen on the right if you do not know what any of these sections mean.

14 When you have finished this (quite long) form, click on the 'Save and Continue' button.

The next screen allows you to check all of the details and change them if necessary. It will also give you lots of other options of ways in which you can make your item stand out to give you more chance of selling it for a higher price. These cost more money, so it's up to you whether you go for these options or not.

20.3 Setting up a seller's account and listing your item

1 You will now be prompted to set up a 'Seller's account'. This will take you to a screen where you will have to type in your credit cards details, which eBay™ will use to collect their fees.
2 You have a final chance to review and edit your listing. Scroll to the bottom of this page and click on 'List your item'.

You can now wait for the bids to come in. At the end of the auction period, the highest bidder wins (assuming your reserve price has been met) and you then make arrangements to take payment and deliver the item to them.

As mentioned in the previous chapter, eBay™ has become an international phenomenon and there is lots of help and advice out there that will help you improve your chances of selling. There are whole books and websites dedicated to it. Some people have even become 'eBay millionaires' by using eBay™ as a way of selling. The eBay™ help screens are a useful start point, and you could use the web searching skills you have learnt in previous chapters to surf the Internet for more help and guidance.

Summary

In this chapter we have discussed:

- Setting up a listing for an item that you want to sell
- Categorizing and describing the item
- Adding a photo
- Working out the cost of selling
- Registering as a seller
- Adding the listing

doing your grocery shopping

In this chapter you will learn:

- **how to check who delivers in your area**
- **how to register for online shopping**
- **how to find and select the products you want to buy**
- **how to book a delivery slot**
- **how to pay**

Aim of the chapter
This chapter will show you how to do your grocery shopping online. It will show you how to select which shop you are going to use, and then select the products you want to buy, add them to your basket and pay. It also covers the selection of a delivery time and redeeming money-off vouchers.

21.1 Introduction

Many, but not all of the big grocery retailers now offer an **online** shopping service. Lots of smaller, local shops also offer a home delivery service. The first stage of the process is to check that the retailer you want to use does deliver to your area. For example, Tesco, Sainsbury's, Asda and Waitrose all offer delivery services, but you do have to check that they will deliver in your locality. You also need to consider the cost of delivery, which is usually around £5. You can then order your products by filling up a **virtual basket**. You book your delivery slot, pay online and then wait for the van. Generally speaking, you need to book a day or two in advance and then wait in for a delivery slot, which are normally given within a two-hour time period (e.g. 9am–11am).

The first time you shop online it might take quite a while, but it will be quicker when you do it subsequently, because the **websites** use the 'favourites' idea that we looked at in Chapter 10, to remember the things that you bought last time.

21.2 Choosing an online grocery store

If you are lucky, you might have a choice of grocery shops where you live, and they might all offer online shopping. In other areas you might find that there is only one option. To check you will need to go to the websites of the shops and type in your postcode. To find the **web address** of the grocery shops you can either use a **search** engine, or you can type the address straight in to the address bar.

> **Hints and tips**
> The website addresses of big companies are usually quite predictable (e.g. www.tesco.com; www.asda.com; www.waitrose.co.uk and www.sainsburys.co.uk). Even if you get the .co.uk or .com wrong at the end it will still take you to their website.

As an example:

1 Open **Internet Explorer®** and type: www.asda.com into the address bar.

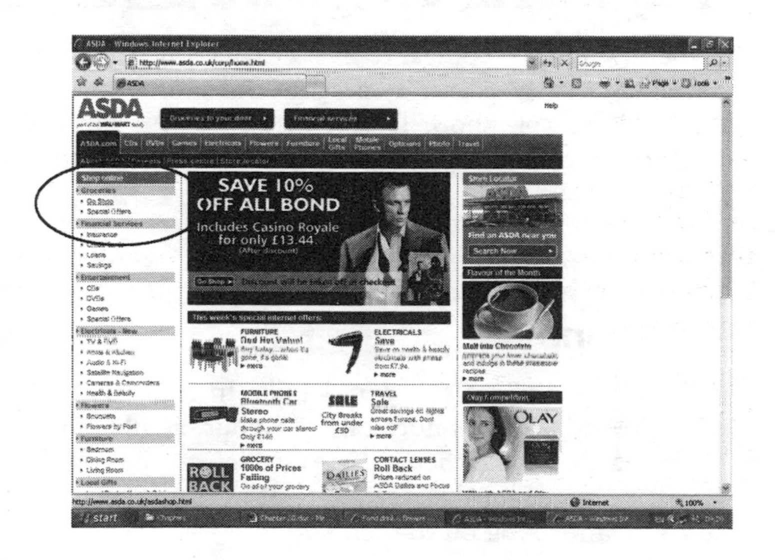

2 Click on the link to 'Groceries' shopping, which on this site is in the top left-hand corner. The first thing it will do is ask you for your postcode so that it can check whether they deliver in your area.

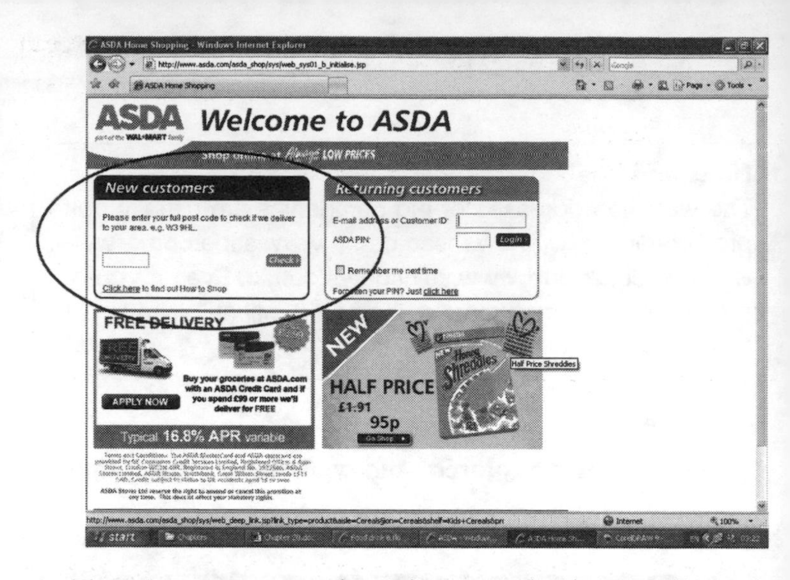

3 Type in your postcode and press 'Check'. It will check instantly and give you a message indicating whether or not you can shop. If you can, you can proceed with the shopping. If not, you will have to try another shop.

21.3 Registering for online shopping

The next step is to register you details. In common with most websites, you will normally use your **email address** as your **user name** and then be asked to select a **password.** You will be asked for these two bits of information every time you want to **log on** to their site.

This is the log-on screen for Tesco:

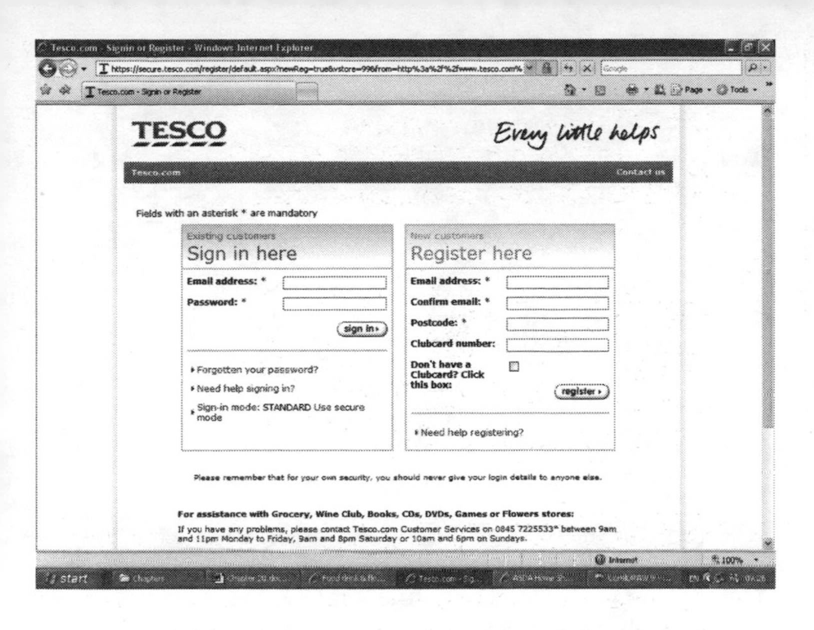

If you were already registered you would fill in the details on the left ('Sign in here'). If not, you need to register by filling in the section on the right ('Register here').

To register, you have to fill in a form with all of your personal details (something you will be getting used to by now). Obviously, they will need your home address and phone number as they are delivering to your house, and your credit/debit cards details so that you can make payment. Once you have filled in the form you are ready to shop.

21.4 Filling up your basket

This is the main **web page** on the Tesco website where you choose what you want to buy. Notice on the right-hand side that there is a basket and a checkout. These are the virtual equivalent of the real thing. In a real shop you fill up your basket and then take it to the checkout when you have finished. It works the same way here.

You will also notice that, like real shops, you are bombarded with special offers, trying to entice you to add a few more items to your basket. It's up to you whether or not you are enticed!

There are three main ways of finding the products you want to buy. If you look at the top of the page you will see the options:

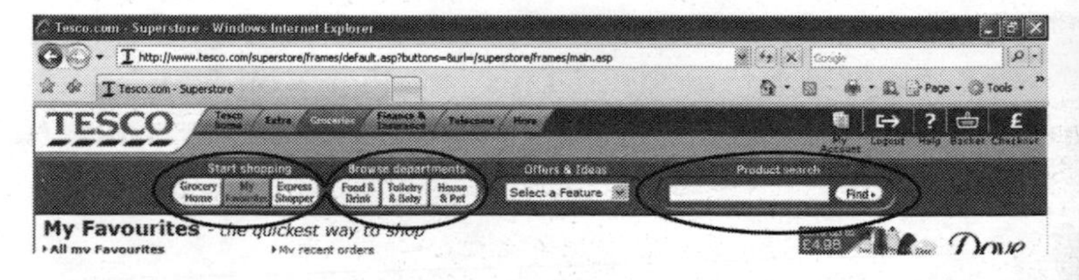

- If you have shopped before, you can look in 'My Favourites' in the 'Start shopping' section so that you can re-select the same products.
- Alternatively you can use the 'Browse departments' options, which will show you a range of products in each section.
- Or you can use the 'Product search' option where you type in the name of a specific product.

> **Hints and tips**
> You will notice that many websites have things in common. For example, the '**browse**' and '**search**' options are a common feature of many websites, and they work in the same way on each site.

Once you have found the product you want, you add it to your basket, and then move on to the next product. When you have finished, you go to the 'Checkout', book your delivery slot and pay.

Let's work through three examples using each of the three methods.

Browsing

In this example, we will buy a bottle of wine.

1 Click on 'Browse departments'.
2 Click on 'Food & Drink'.
3 There are further categories on the left-hand side – click on 'Wines'.
4 More categories are displayed – click on 'Red Wine' and then on 'French Red Wine'. All the French red wines are now displayed, and you can **scroll down** and look through the list.

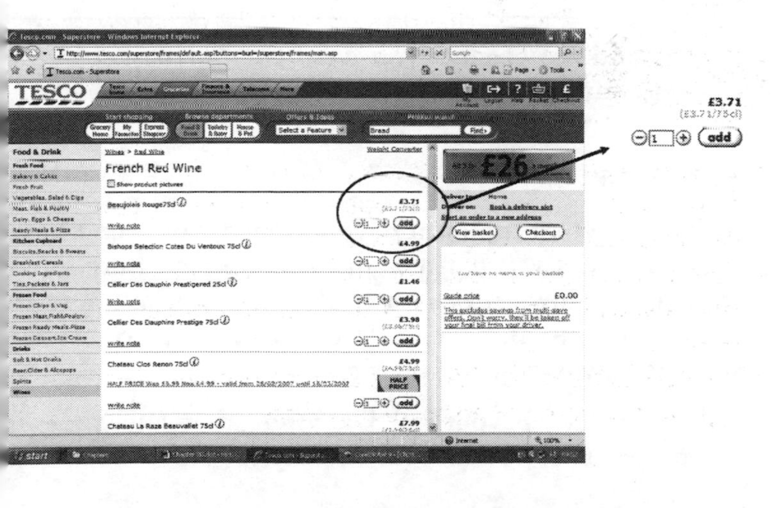

5 When you have found the one you want, select how many you want, and click on 'add'. This is now added to your basket and you can continue with your shopping. You can view the contents of your basket at any time by clicking on the 'View basket' button. At the moment, it will have just one bottle of wine in it.

Searching

In this example, we will buy some olive oil.

1 Click in the 'Product search' box and type: Olive oil

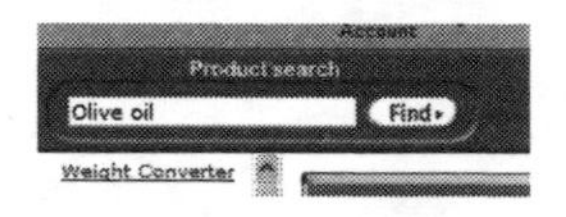

2 Click on 'Find'. All the olive oils are now displayed, and you can scroll down and look through the list.

> **Hints and tips**
> The 'search' option is much quicker than browsing, providing you know what you are looking for. You can be quite specific with your search words. For example, if you want Tesco own-brand olive oil then type in 'Tesco olive oil' to reduce the number of **hits**.

3 You add the product you want to your basket in the same way as described before.

Favourites

If this is the first time you have shopped, you won't have any favourites yet, but it is shown here for future reference. Using favourites is probably the quickest way to shop, but you will have to do one shop first, so that the site knows what your favourites are.

1 Click on 'My Favourites'. Everything that you have ever ordered is stored in your favourites. This means that

you can look for it in your favourites rather than having to search the whole shop.

2 You can look at 'All my Favourites' which lists everything you have ever bought. Alternatively, you can look in particular categories, or select 'My recent orders' which will show you your last shopping list.

Hints and tips

If you buy pretty much the same things every week, you can click on 'My recent orders' and select last week's shopping order. You can then just go through and add and remove from this list. This is much quicker than building the list from scratch every week.

21.5 Booking a time slot and paying

Once you are happy that you have got everything you want, it's time to book your delivery slot and make payment.

1 On the right-hand side, click on the link to 'Book delivery slot'.

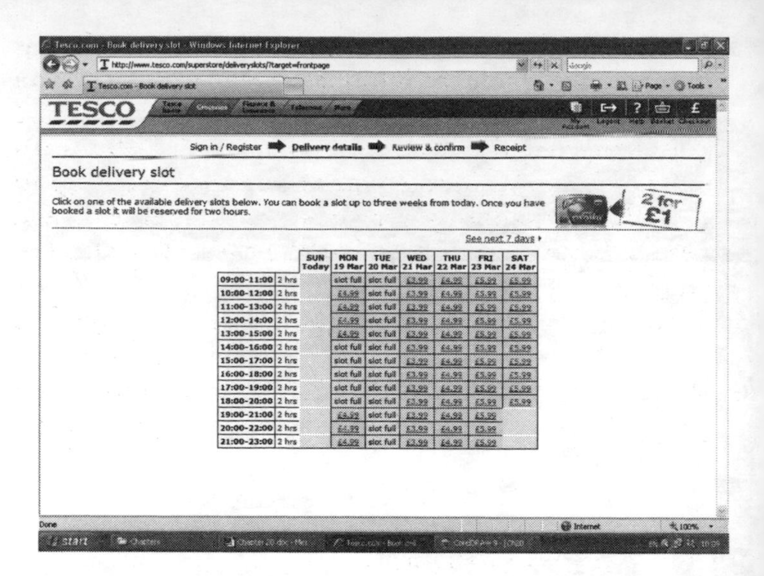

		SUN Today	MON 19 Mar	TUE 20 Mar	WED 21 Mar	THU 22 Mar	FRI 23 Mar	SAT 24 Mar
09:00-11:00	2 hrs		slot full	slot full	£3.99	£4.99	£5.99	£5.99
10:00-12:00	2 hrs		£4.99	slot full	£3.99	£4.99	£5.99	£5.99
11:00-13:00	2 hrs		£4.99	slot full	£3.99	£4.99	£5.99	£5.99
12:00-14:00	2 hrs		£4.99	slot full	£3.99	£4.99	£5.99	£5.99
13:00-15:00	2 hrs		£4.99	slot full	£3.99	£4.99	£5.99	£5.99
14:00-16:00	2 hrs		slot full	slot full	£3.99	£4.99	£5.99	£5.99
15:00-17:00	2 hrs		slot full	slot full	£3.99	£4.99	£5.99	£5.99
16:00-18:00	2 hrs		slot full	slot full	£3.99	£4.99	£5.99	£5.99
17:00-19:00	2 hrs		slot full	slot full	£3.99	£4.99	£5.99	£5.99
18:00-20:00	2 hrs		slot full	slot full	£3.99	£4.99	£5.99	£5.99
19:00-21:00	2 hrs		£4.99	slot full	£3.99	£4.99	£5.99	
20:00-22:00	2 hrs		£4.99	slot full	£3.99	£4.99	£5.99	
21:00-23:00	2 hrs		£4.99	slot full	£3.99	£4.99	£5.99	

2 Find the delivery slot you want, and click on it. Notice that some times are more popular than others and will already have been taken.
3 Go back to 'View basket'.
4 Click on 'Checkout'. At the checkout you can redeem any money-off vouchers by clicking on the link. If you have vouchers they will have a code on them, which you have to type in at this point.

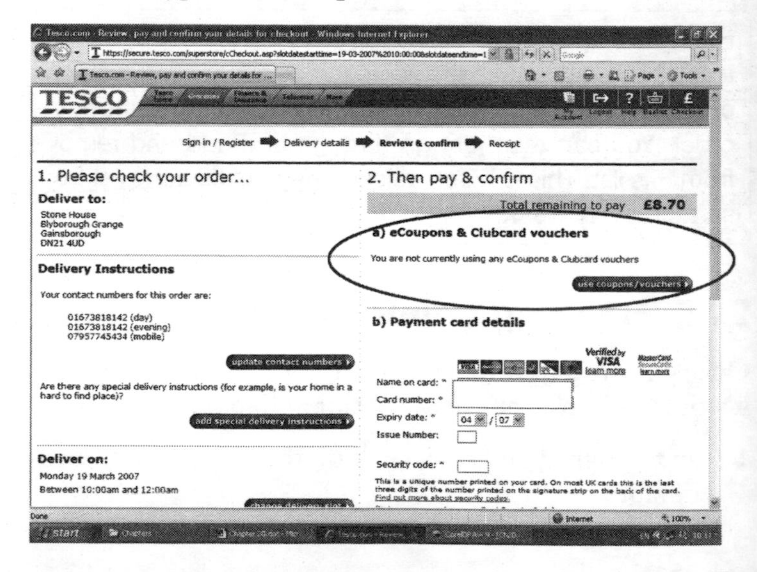

Most of the details on this page are already complete as they are taken from the information you gave when you registered. You can check and change them from here if you need to. For example, your credit/debit card number is shown here, so make sure that this is up to date. If you suddenly remember something else you need to buy, you can go back to the basket from here to add items.

5 Scroll to the bottom of this page and click 'Confirm order'.
6 You can now print out your order if you want to so that you have the list to check off the items when they are delivered.

21.6 Taking delivery

All shops operate their deliveries in time slots, so it is important that you are able to stay at home for the duration of that period. If there are any products that were not available in the shop, they will have been substituted for something similar. The delivery driver will tell you about these and they will be listed on the copy of your order. You don't have to accept the substitutions if you don't want them.

The driver will hand you a copy of your order with the final price on it. It may vary slightly from the price you were originally given because the substitutions may have been a different price. The driver will then give you a hand-held computer device, and you sign on the screen to confirm receipt. Job done.

Summary
In this chapter we have discussed:

- Choosing a grocery retailer and checking they deliver in your area
- Browsing and searching for products and adding them to your basket
- Using 'Favourites' to speed up the process
- Booking a delivery time
- Redeeming vouchers and paying
- Taking delivery

22 working and learning

In this chapter you will learn:

- **how to find help and guidance on employment and pension issues**
- **how to find a new job**
- **how to find advice and information on starting your own business**
- **how to find voluntary work**
- **how to find training courses**

Aim of the chapter

This chapter will show you how to find help and advice on all matters relating to employment, training and education for the over 50s. There are now more than 20 million over 50s in the UK, the majority of whom are still working and taking part in ongoing education. There are some issues that affect the age group specifically, and this chapter aims to highlight these issues and show the help and advice that is available.

22.1 Introduction

Patterns of employment are constantly changing. It's hard to find a job for life these days, and the idea that you are on the scrapheap when you are over 50 is outdated. Many businesses value the experience that more mature employees bring to their work. It is also easier then ever to start your own business and capitalize on all that experience for yourself.

Patterns of education have changed too, with more and more older people taking part in courses, either for pleasure or to gain qualifications. For example, recent research by Age Concern suggests that more than half of the 60–69 year olds in the UK are taking part in some form of education.

A mass of information is available on the Internet, and this chapter will point you in the direction of some of the most useful **websites**. The **web address** is given for every site mentioned, so all you have to do is type this address into the **address bar** in **Internet Explorer®**.

22.2 Help and guidance on employment and pension issues

Older workers face some issues specifically related to their age. For example, there have been recent changes to the legislation on age discrimination. One very useful site provided by the government is: www.direct.gov.uk

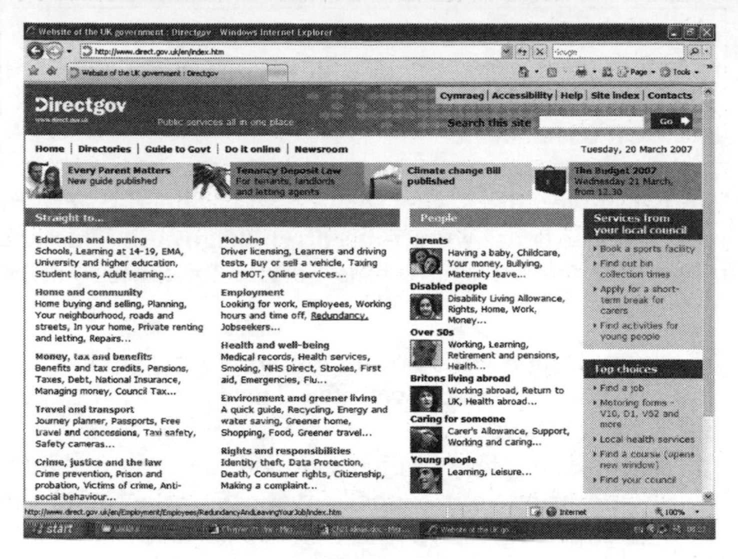

This is a really useful site for all kinds of government information, not just employment. To find the employment information, follow the **link** to 'Employment' and then the link (on the left-hand side) to 'Over 50s'. You can now follow the various links depending on what you are interested in, for example 'Looking for work' or 'Planning for retirement'.

More specific advice about pensions can be found at: www.thepensionservice.gov.uk

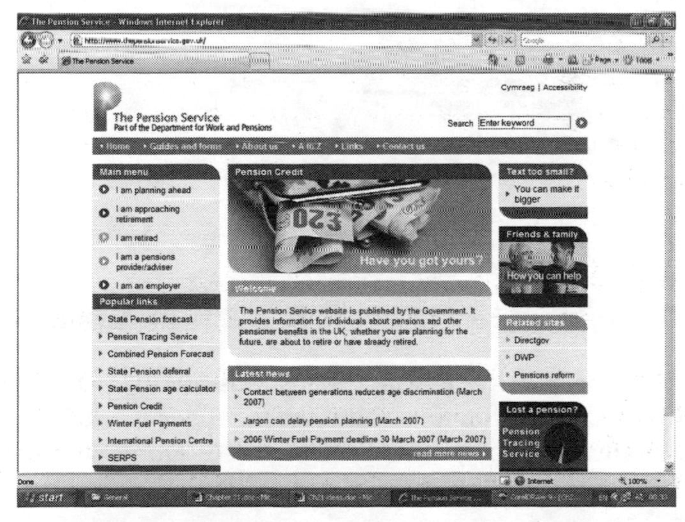

> **Hints and tips**
> Note that these sites have .gov at the end of the address. This means that the site has been created by a department of the UK government.

Another government site that covers other aspects of finding work is at: www.jobcentreplus.gov.uk. This has links to the 'New Deal 50 plus' service for those looking for work.

Other good sources of information are your local government and county council websites. The easiest way to find your local authority site is to use a **search engine** and type in, for example: "County Council" + Leicestershire. This should bring your council's website to the top of the list. You can then follow the links to local employment information.

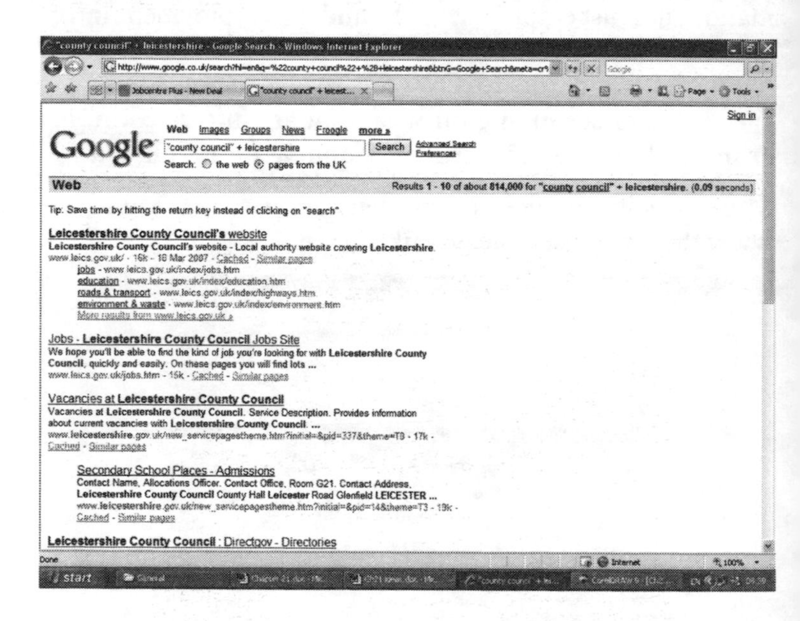

At www.agepositive.gov.uk the Age Positive campaign provides lots of information and links for older workers. This site focuses on the particular benefits of employing older workers, and the experience and skills that they offer, as well as providing information on age discrimination, pensions and other issues.

22.3 How to find a job

If you are looking for work, there are thousands of jobs advertised on the Internet every day. There are so many **online** jobs websites now that it is difficult to know which one to choose. As ever, you could start by using a search engine to find the websites on offer. Typing 'Jobs' will bring back millions of **hits**, so you might want to be more specific with your search words.

Most of the jobs websites offer a facility to search for jobs by type and by area. When you find a job you are interested in, you can apply for it and send your CV online.

One of the biggest job sites in the UK is: www.monster.co.uk. The site works like a search engine, listing jobs that match your search words. In this example, the search is for banking jobs in Leicestershire.

The results are also listed like search engine results and you can work your way through them, clicking on the links to find out more about each job.

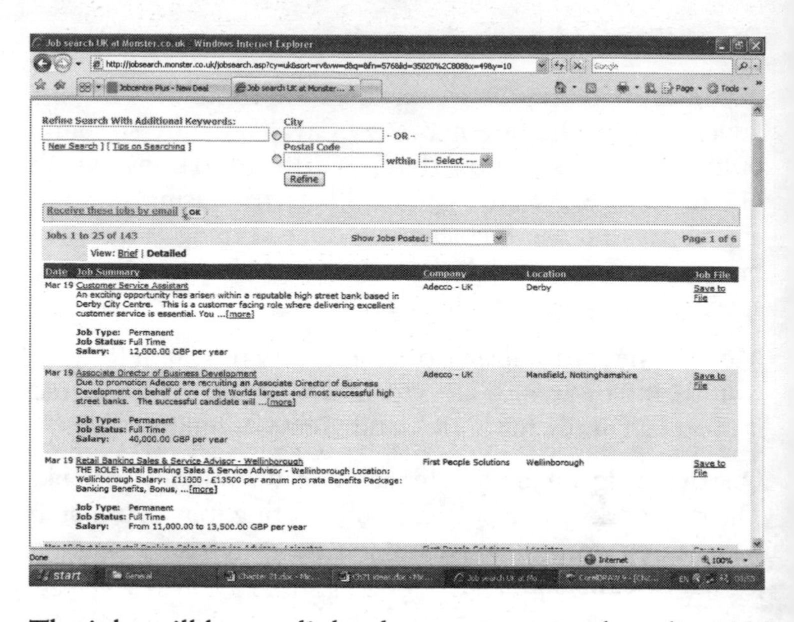

The jobs will have a link where you can apply online. To do this you will need to register with the website, completing all your personal details. This site also has a facility to complete a detailed CV.

22.4 Starting your own business

As you get older you are more likely to want to start and run your own business. Around 25 per cent of people aged over 56 are self-employed. There is a lot of help and guidance available in the Internet.

Some of the sites we have looked at already feature sections on self-employment (e.g. www.direct.gov.uk). Further help can be found at www.businesslink.gov.uk

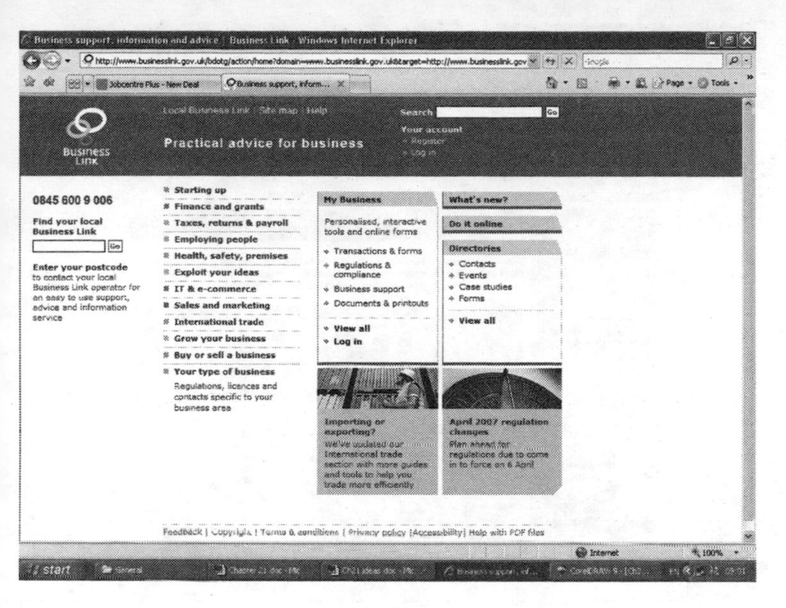

Follow the links to 'Starting up'.

The Citizens Advice Bureau also has lots of useful information and links for the self-employed at http://www.adviceguide.org.uk/. Follow the links on the left-hand side to 'Employment' and then the 'Self-employment: checklist'.

Hints and tips

Notice that this site is useful for lots of other information too, not just about employment.

22.5 Volunteering

If you want to volunteer, there are a number of useful sites that will give you further information, and enable you to offer your services.

Go to www.volunteeringengland.org.uk and click on 'I want to volunteer'. You can then look for volunteering opportunities in your area.

Hints and tips

Notice that this address ends in .org unlike the others we have looked at so far in this chapter. Org means organization and usually means that the website is run by a charity or other not-for-profit organization.

Other volunteering websites can be found at:

- www.do-it.org.uk
- www.timebank.org.uk
- www.csv.org.uk
- www.vso.org.uk

If you would like to offer your services to a particular charity, use a search engine to find their website and then follow the links to volunteering. For example, the National Trust encourages volunteers at: www.nationaltrust.org.uk. Follow the link to 'Volunteering'.

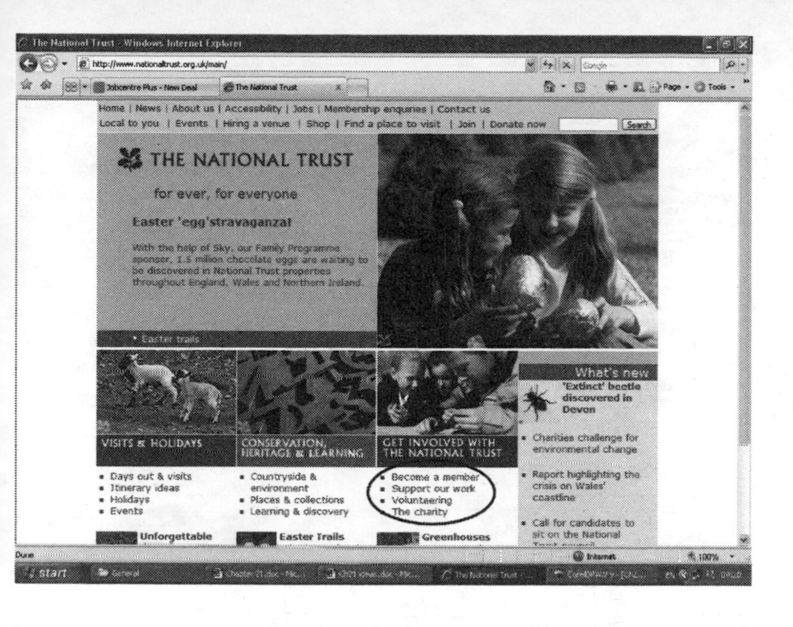

22.6 Training and education

There are two main ways of using the Internet here. You can use it to search for courses that are running in your local area, or you can take an online course.

There are so many courses available throughout the country that it can be difficult to find the one you want. The government has a commitment to ongoing education and they will fund free places on courses for older people. These courses are run through the Adult Education departments of the local authorities. Therefore, a good place to start is your local authority website.

For example, to find all the courses running in Devon you would type: "county council" + "adult education" + devon. This is a very specific search and should bring exactly what you want to the top of the list:

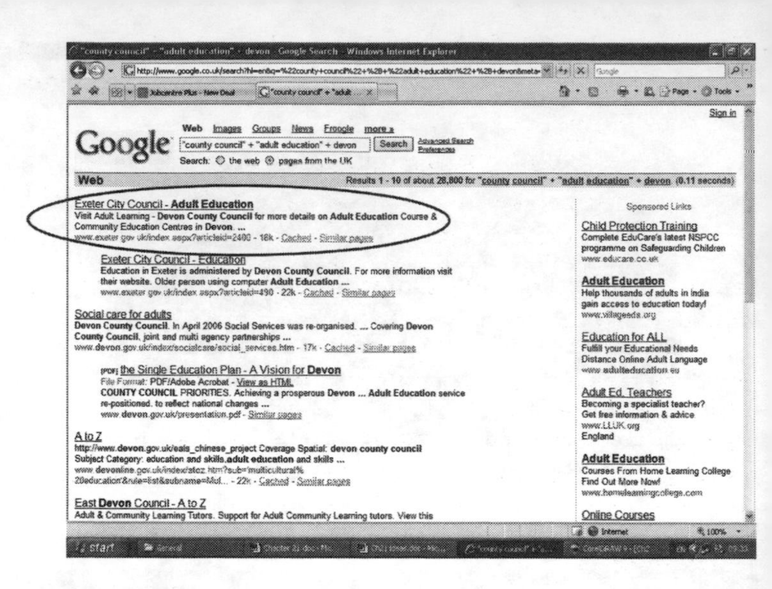

Once you have linked to the site, you can look for further links to the colleges and they will list the courses that are available. Some sites will have a search facility to make this quicker.

You may find links to free courses in some of the other websites we have mentioned in this chapter already, for example the over 50s section of the direct.gov.uk site.

You can also take **online courses** over the Internet. These are the modern version of what used to be called correspondence courses, where you may never actually meet your tutor, or fellow students. You carry out research and complete assignments and then send them over the Internet to your tutor to be marked.

You will communicate with your tutor using email and sometimes you may have an online conversation using the techniques explained in Chapter 12. Some courses do have a residential aspect where you all meet up somewhere, usually during the summer. You can follow courses like this purely for pleasure, or it is possible to study for academic qualifications using this method.

The first task is to find an online college. Again, you can use the Internet to search for one. Some of the better known sites are:

- www.bbc.co.uk/learning/onlinecourses/
- www.open.ac.uk
- www.learndirect.co.uk

Many of the main universities now also offer online versions of their courses.

Hints and tips

Notice that some of the websites end in .ac. This means that they are an academic institution i.e. a university or college.

Summary

In this chapter we have discussed:

- Help and guidance on employment and pension issues
- How to find a new job
- Advice and information on starting your own business
- How to find voluntary work
- How to find training courses

23 accessing radio, TV and games

In this chapter you will learn:

- **how to find radio, TV and games websites**
- **how to listen to live radio**
- **how to listen again to radio programmes**
- **how to watch TV programmes**
- **how to play online games**

Aim of the chapter
This chapter will introduce you to some of the ways in which you can use the Internet for entertainment purposes. There are different ways of doing this, but this chapter will focus on using the Internet to listen to the radio, watch TV and play online games.

23.1 Introduction

Multimedia (the mixture of text, sounds and images) is what the Internet is all about. The Internet lets us access multimedia content (music, videos, games, etc.) whenever we want it. There are two main ways of doing this. The first, which is covered in this chapter, is going onto **websites** where we can watch TV, listen to radio and play games. The second, which is covered in the next chapter is **downloading** music and video to your computer so that you can view and listen to it without having to be **online**.

You do need to exercise a bit of caution with the websites that you use. The law of copyright covers music, film and computer games, among other things. The website that is providing these things must have permission to do so. Many sites are legal and do have permission to do this, and this chapter will show you some of these. Most websites have links to pages that explain the legal issues, and you should check that the sites you are using are legal.

Hints and tips
There is a big debate at the moment about copyright material and how it applies to the Internet. At the moment you can be fined for downloading material without the permission of the copyright holder.

23.2 Listening to the radio

There are two main ways of doing this. The first is that you can listen to live radio as it is being broadcast. The other is that you can use the 'listen again' feature to listen to programmes that you missed the first time round.

There are hundreds of online radio stations and a quick **search** with a **search engine** will give you plenty to choose from. The beauty of the Internet is the range of different stations which you can access. For example, you will find radio stations that cover very specific musical tastes. Some of these radio stations and free, and some are paid-for.

We will look at the BBC stations, as they are provided free, there is a good selection of stations to choose from, and you can be sure that they are legal in terms of copyright issues.

1 Type: www.bbc.co.uk/radio into the **address bar** of **Internet Explorer**®.

There are 11 main stations that you can listen to, plus you have access to all of the local radio stations as well, even if you are not in the area normally served by that station. Some of these stations are available on your normal radio, but some are available only as **digital channels**.

> **Hints and tips**
> Digital stations can be accessed through the Internet, or through digital TV, or through a DAB radio, but you cannot get digital radio stations on a normal radio.

If you know what station you want to listen to:

2 Click on the link to the station. In this example we will go to Five Live.

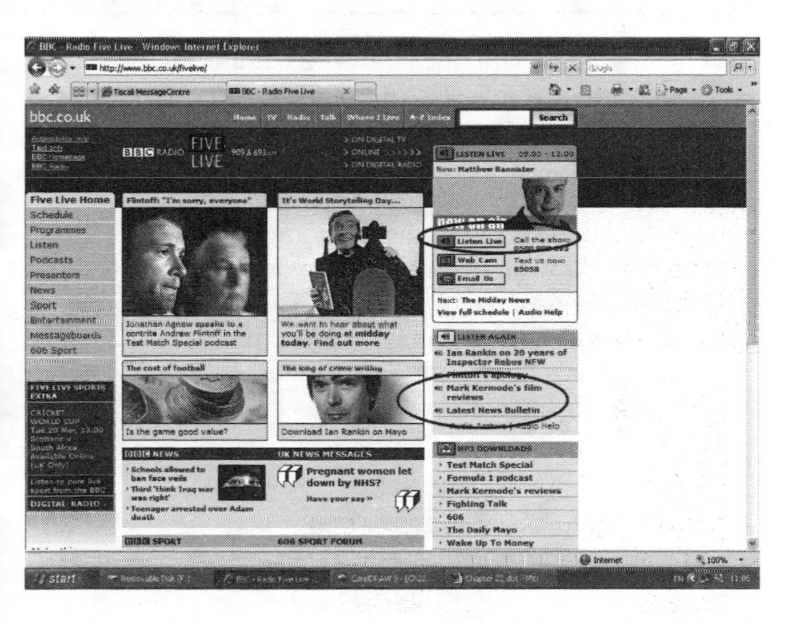

3 From this page you can either listen live, which means you can hear what is being broadcast right now, or you can listen again to a programme that you missed.

4 To listen live, click on the 'Listen Live' link.

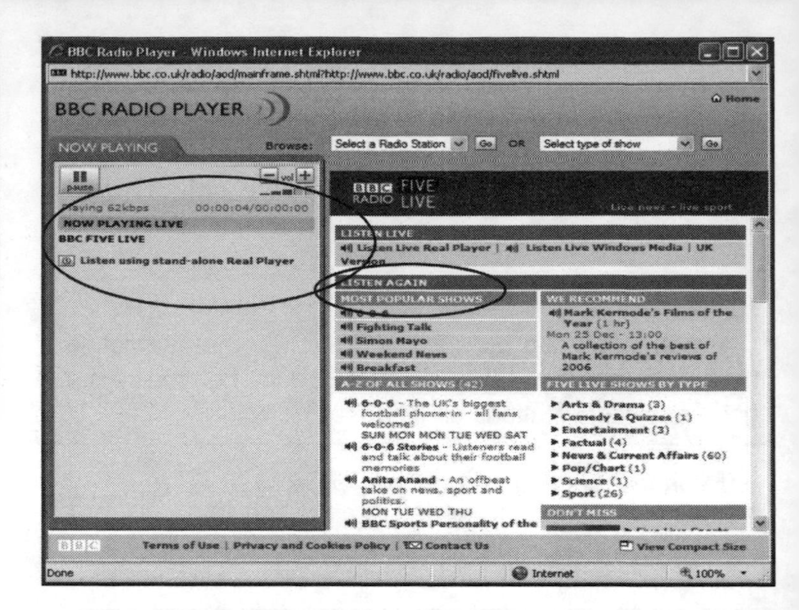

A new window will open and you should hear the radio programme coming out of your speakers. On the left-hand side of the screen, you will be shown what is currently playing.

5 You can access the 'listen again' feature from this screen as well. All the programmes that are available are listed, and you click on the one you want to listen to. The current programme will stop and the one you have selected will start to play. Notice that you have the option of fast forwarding or rewinding when you are using the 'listen again' feature.

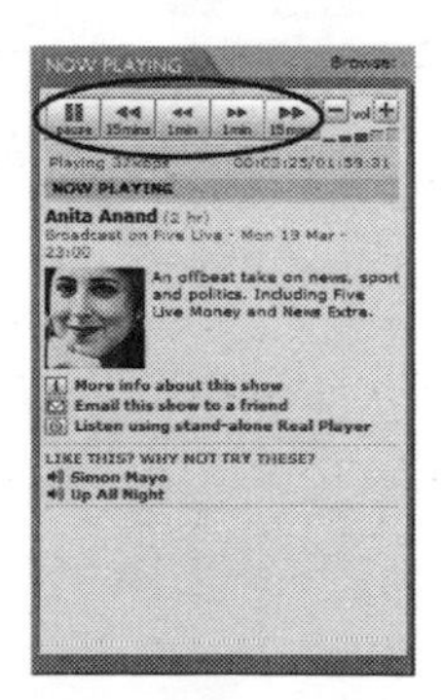

6 You can leave the radio station playing and now go off and do other things on the Internet by opening a new **tab** in Internet Explorer®.

7 When you have finished, click on the cross to close the website. You will get a message asking you to confirm that you want to close down.

8 Another useful feature of Internet radio, which the BBC uses, is to categorize by musical taste. For example, if you like jazz music, you might find programmes you want to listen to on Radio 2, Radio 3 and local radio stations. You can **browse** for individual programmes you might want to listen to regardless of what station they are on. To do this return to the main BBC radio page at: www.bbc.co/radio

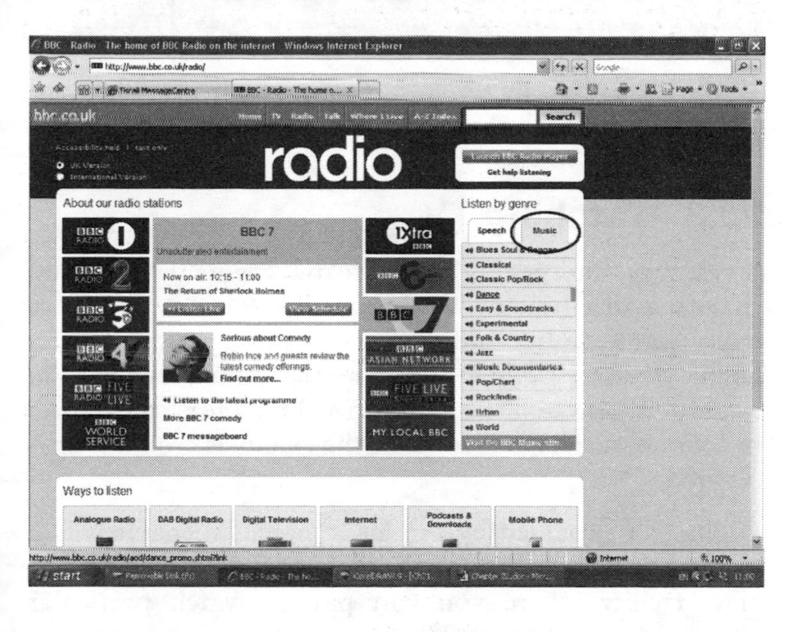

9 Select the music or speech type that you are interested in, for example Jazz. A new window will open that lists all the BBC programmes that feature jazz music.

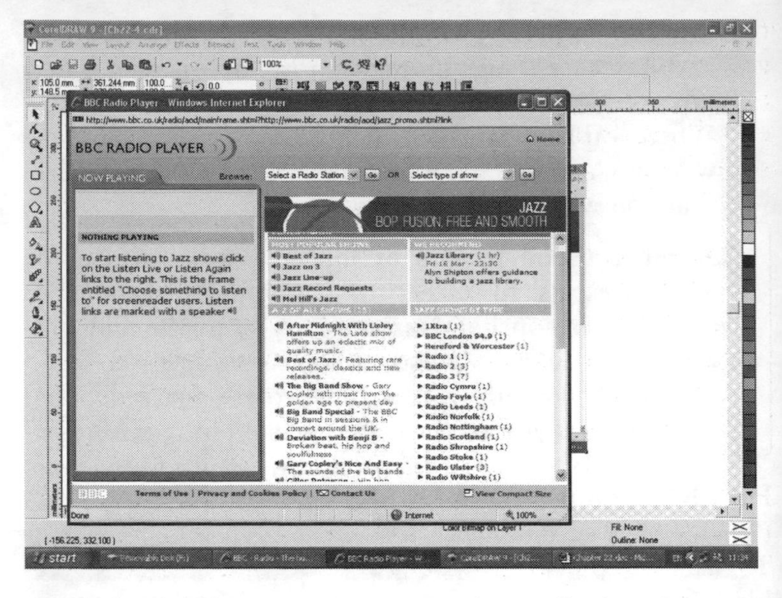

10 Click on the one you want and it will play the programme using the 'listen again' feature described earlier.

23.3 Watching TV

If you type 'Internet TV' into a search engine you will find that there are thousands of online TV stations to choose from. Some are free and some are a pay-per-view service. Many of these TV stations are the same stations you might find on satellite or cable TV. Like radio, the nature of Internet means that some of the channels are quite specialized.

Online TV provided by the UK's main TV channels is a mixed bag. Some channels, like Channel 4 have a pay-per-view facility where you can pay to watch particular Channel 4 programmes. This is called 'TV on demand' and is being offered by other companies as well, like Virgin Media and Sky.

Other websites offer a 'watch again' feature for some of their programmes, but usually only for a week after the programme was shown on normal TV. More commonly, the websites will offer snippets or trailers for TV programmes rather than the whole thing. The BBC, for example, offers a wide range of short video clips, including everything from news articles to exclusive behind-the-scenes videos.

> **Hints and tips**
> Internet TV is one of the fastest changing areas on the Internet. For example, at the time this book was written, Channel 4 was trialling a system that shows Channel 4 programmes live over the Internet. Other channels may offer this service.

However you access Internet TV you will watch it through a special piece of **software** called a **media player.** To see how this works, we will look at a free video clip on the BBC News site.

1 Type: www.bbc.co.uk/news into the address bar of Internet Explorer®.

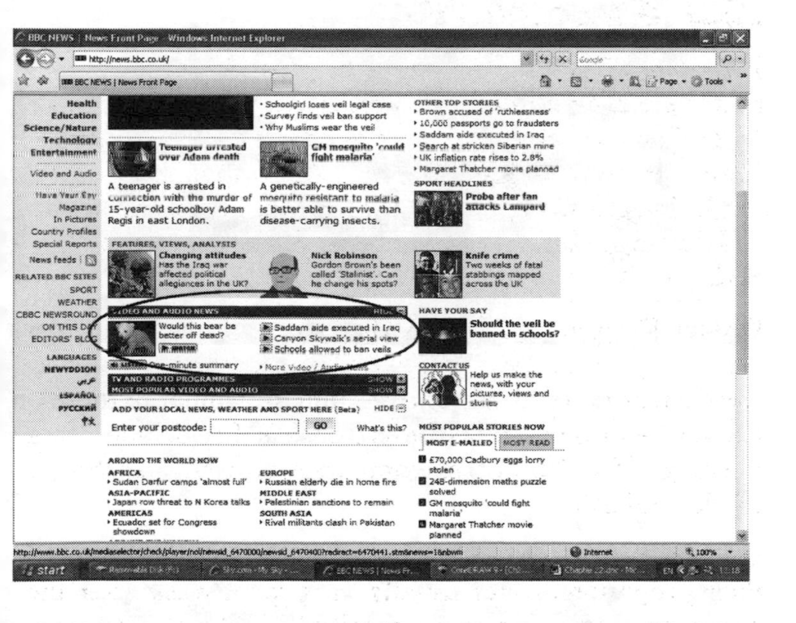

2 Wherever you see the 'Play' **icon**, [play icon] it means that there is a video clip that you can watch.
3 Click on the 'Play' icon. A new window will open. If you are asked to choose a 'player' then choose 'RealPlayer'. The video will then start to play.

Hints and tips
If this is the first time you have viewed a video on this computer, you may need to **install** the media player software. If this is the case, follow the on-screen instructions.

4 You can control the video you are watching using the media player controls underneath the picture.

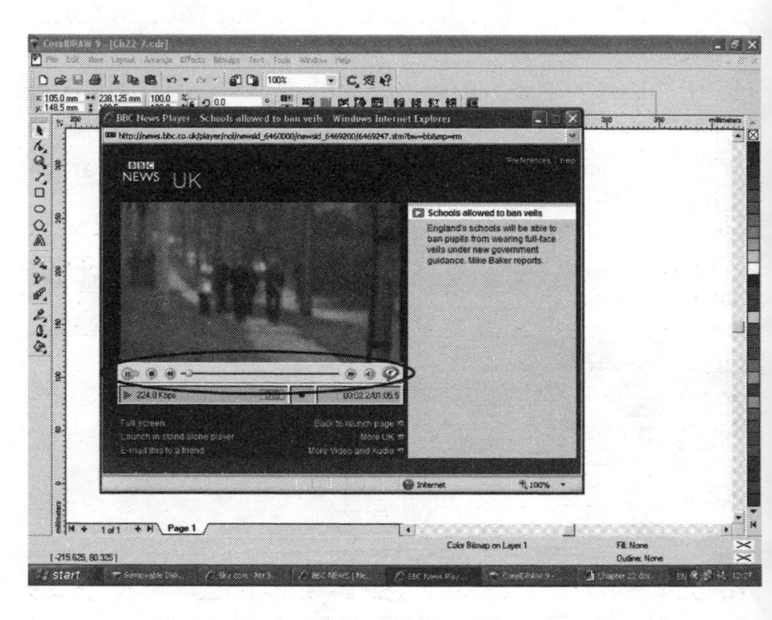

These are standard controls, and are similar to those on your video or DVD player. These are:

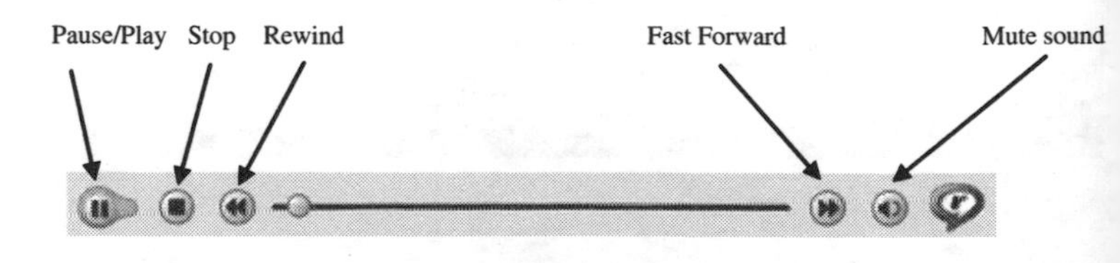

23.4 Online games

The intention of this section is not to show you any specific games, but to give some general advice on online gaming.

There is a range of options for playing games online. Some games sites are just for fun. Most computer games fall into this category: for example, you can play cards, Scrabble, dominos or chess. You can either play online against other players or download the game from the Internet onto your computer. Many of these games are free, but you may have to buy some of them. You may need to register with the website before they let you play.

> **Hints and tips**
> You need to be careful when downloading free games. It is possible to pick up **viruses** this way. If in doubt, get your games from a reputable and legal site.

There are also sites where you can play traditional gambling games like cards, roulette and bingo either against the computer or against other online players. You can potentially win (or lose) lots of money on these websites. These sites require you to register and you will also need to put in your credit/debit card details as you are playing for real money. Most sites ask you to deposit funds where you put a set amount of money in before you start playing. This way you can gamble only up to a certain limit.

To find games sites use a search engine and type in the games that you are looking for. Alternatively, many well-known companies, such as the national bingo clubs, have websites where you can play gambling games online.

Summary

In this chapter we have discussed:

- Listening to live radio
- Using the 'listen again' feature to listen to radio programmes
- Watching live TV and video clips
- Online games

In this chapter you will learn:

- how to download and listen to music
- how to download and listen to podcasts
- how to use the Internet to buy CDs and DVDs
- how to rent films over the Internet

Aim of the chapter
This chapter will show you how to find and then download music and podcasts and other audio/visual content from the Internet. It will also cover how you can use the Internet to buy traditional CDs and DVDs from online stores.

24.1 Introduction

The Internet has roughly 1 billion users throughout the world. Anyone with a computer and an Internet connection can become part of the network. This represents a massive market for businesses and one of the big areas for them is music, audio and video. What this means is that however obscure your musical or film tastes, you will be able to find it somewhere on the Internet.

Another advantage is that you can get access to the music that you want almost instantly as you can **download** it straight onto your computer. You don't have to go to the shops and you don't have to wait for delivery.

Hints and tips
Downloading blockbuster films is possible over the Internet but, like TV shows that we discussed earlier, it is a rapidly changing area. Make sure if you are doing this that it is a legal site.

A disadvantage is that a lot of the music and films that can be downloaded is on **websites** which are not legally entitled to do so, because the websites in question do not have copyright permissions. The difficulty is knowing which sites are legal and which are illegal. You do usually have to pay to download music and films and this is often a good sign that the site you are downloading from is legal.

One other factor we will cover in this chapter is that you can also use the Internet to buy traditional CDs and DVDs from **online** stores. We will also look at DVD rental sites, which are the modern equivalent of a video shop, with the added advantage that you don't have to leave the house.

24.2 Downloading music

Some music is available for free over the Internet, but most legal sites will charge you to download. There are hundreds of download sites to choose from and a quick Internet **search** will list these for you. We will be using one of the biggest music download sites called **iTunes™**.

> **Hints and tips**
> You may have already heard of iTunes™, which is run by Apple, the same company that makes the **iPod™** music player. iPods are very popular among younger people but are used increasingly by older people too, as is iTunes™ which features music of all genres.

1 Type: www.apple.com into the **address bar** of **Internet Explorer®**.
2 Click on the link to 'iPod + iTunes'.

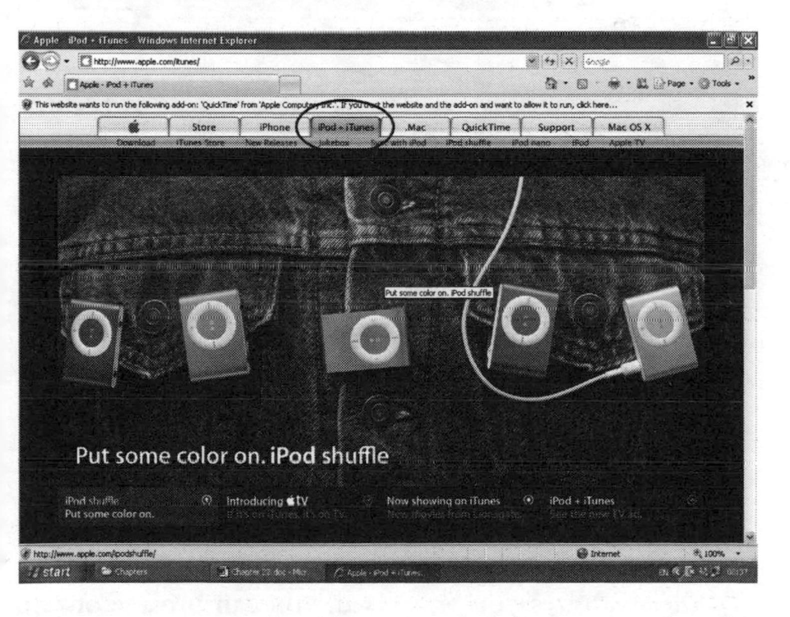

3 Click on the link to 'Download'.

You are now going to download the iTunes™ **software** to your computer. This may take a few minutes to load. You need to put in your **email address** and they will ask you for some other personal details. Work your way through the screens, and click 'Run'.

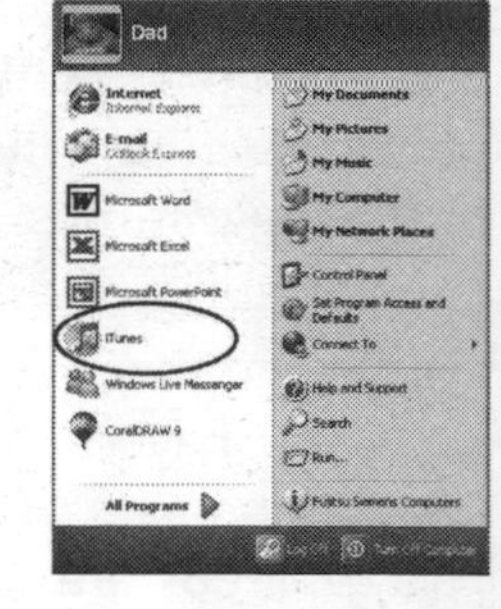

When the software is installed, you can run it from the 'iTunes' **icon** on the **desktop**, or you will find that 'iTunes' is now listed when you click 'Start' and 'All Programs'.

4 Open the iTunes™ software.
  The iTunes™ software looks like this:

5 Click on 'iTunes Store' on the left-hand side.
  Because a lot of younger people use iTunes™, the first thing you see is lots of adverts for noisy music. Don't worry, there are many different types of music available. You've got two options for finding it: in common with other websites you have used, you can **browse** or you can search.

6 If you know the exact piece of music you are looking for, type the track name or artist into the search box in the

top right-hand corner and press the ENTER key. This example shows a search for Cole Porter:

At the bottom the screen, all tracks matching the search words are shown.

7 To hear a 30-second snippet, double click on the song title.

8 To buy the track, click on 'BUY SONG'.

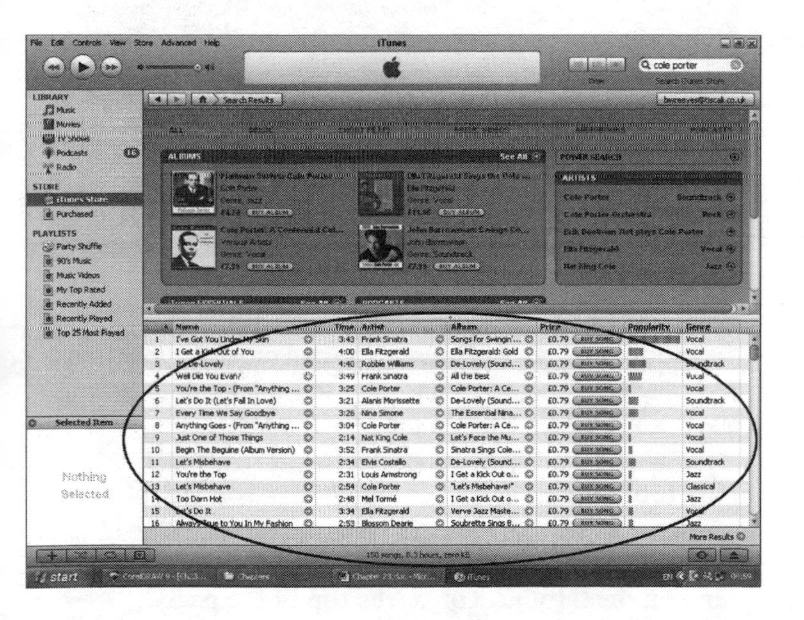

9 If you do buy a track, it will take a short while to download. You can then double click on it to hear the whole song.

10 You will now be asked for your **user name** and **password**. If you have not set up this yet you can do it now. You will need to enter your personal details and credit/debit card number.

All songs that you buy are stored in what is called a **playlist**. This playlist is called 'Purchased' and you can access it at any time by clicking on 'Purchased' on the left-hand side, and then double clicking on the track you want to hear.

Hints and tips

If you download a lot of music, you can organize your tracks into playlists, and you can copy the tracks onto an mp3 player so you can listen to them on the move.

11 To browse through everything that is available in the iTunes Store, go back to the main screen, by clicking on 'iTunes Store' again and then clicking on the 'Home' icon at the top of the page.

If you **scroll down** a bit on this page you will see the 'Genres' under which you can browse.

12 You can now follow these **links** and see what is available. Notice just above the Genres, that there are other things available from iTunes™ such as audio books, games, films and **podcasts**. You can download these in exactly the same way that you download music. We are going to look specifically at podcasts now.

24.3 Podcasts

Podcasts are self-contained media (audio and video) **files** that are distributed by subscription. This means that you subscribe to a particular podcast site and it will download the latest instalment (called an episode) every time you **log on**. Podcasts are available from lots of different sites. Some are free subscriptions and you have to pay for others. Examples of popular podcasts might be those produced by radio DJs or TV presenters, who put together podcasts purely for entertainment purposes. Another use is for learning a language, where each episode is a short lesson.

As with anything else on the Internet, a quick Internet search will throw up thousands of sites that you can look at. In this example, we will use iTunes™ again, which distributes podcasts from a range of different providers.

1 Go to the 'iTunes Store' main page and click on 'Podcasts'.

2 You can now browse the categories or use a search if you know what you are looking for.

3 The process of subscribing to the podcast is the same as buying a track.

4 In this example, we have followed the links to 'Education' and clicked on the link to the Times Online Mandarin Chinese Conversation language course.

5 You can now click on the 'GET EPISODE' button to download a single episode. Or click on 'SUBSCRIBE'. This will then automatically download the next episode when it becomes available.

6 All podcasts to which you subscribe are stored in the playlist called 'Podcasts' and you can access them at any time by clicking on this link.

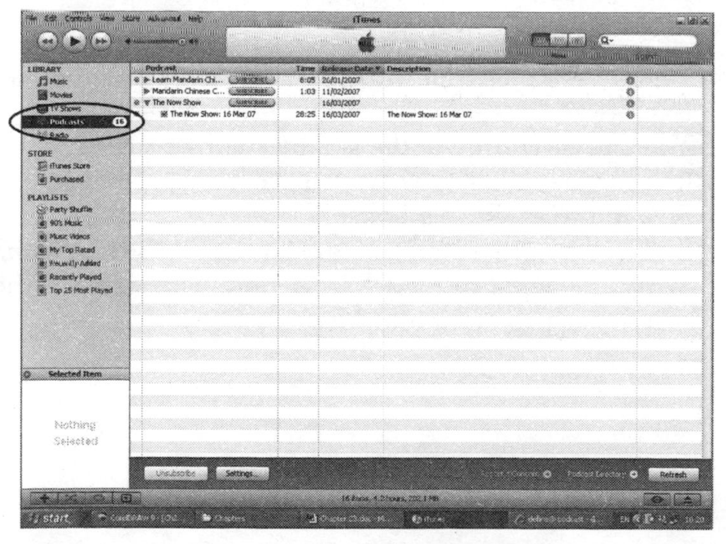

24.4 Buying CDs and DVDs from online stores

One disadvantage of downloading music and video onto your computer is that you have to sit in front of your computer to watch it, or copy it onto a CD or DVD so that you can play it in your conventional equipment. Also, many people still like to buy a CD or DVD as they like to own the physical product, with the sleeve notes and all the extras.

If you are one of those people, the Internet can help you here, too, as there are lots of sites where you can buy CDs and DVDs and then have them delivered. Many of the businesses that do this are Internet-only and are able to offer lower prices. You will also be able to find an enormous selection of music and films, even if they are obscure or old.

The process of buying online is the same here as it would be for any other online purchase – you find what you want, order it and put in your delivery address and credit/debit card number. This example will use a website called Play.com although there are lots to choose from, including websites run by well-known high-street music retailers.

1 Type: www.play.com into the address bar of Internet Explorer®.
2 You can now browse the site by following the various links or, if you know what you are looking for, you can type it into the search box.
3 In this example, a search is carried out for the film *Gone With The Wind* in the DVD section. The result of the search has produced four **hits**.

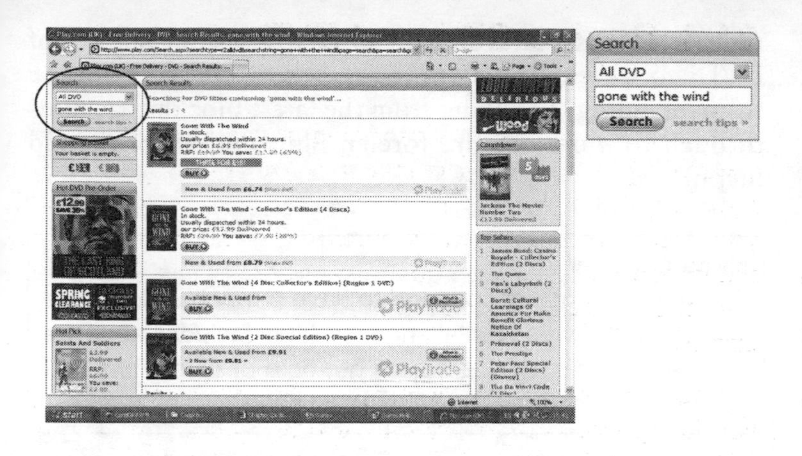

4 You can now click on any of the links to find out more about the DVD. When you have chosen the one you want, click on 'BUY'.
5 If you want to buy more CDs or DVDs you can carry on searching and adding things to your **basket**. When you have finished shopping, click on 'Checkout' and you can pay.
6 As with all online shops, you need to register with the site. Most sites now use your email address as the user name and you then choose a password. Registering may take a few minutes, but once you have done it, it will remember your details for next time you buy something.

24.5 DVD rental

A fairly new Internet idea is the online DVD rental website. Once registered you create a wish list of films that you would like to watch. The DVD rental company then sends you them one by one using the good old-fashioned postal system. You watch them and send them back by post. When the company gets the DVD back, it sends you the next one on the list, and so on.

You pay a monthly fee for this that varies depending on how many videos you want at any one time. If you work it right it means that you will have a constant supply of DVDs to watch. There are thousands of DVDs to choose from including everything from the latest blockbuster films through to more obscure foreign films and all of the old favourites.

Hints and tips
Online DVD rental shops tend to have a much wider range than a normal video rental shop, and this includes all of the old classics. It's a great way to get hold of older films that you wouldn't normally find in a video shop.

There are a few sites to choose from and many large companies have got involved including Tesco, Blockbuster, Amazon, EasyCinema, Virgin and LoveFilm. This example will use Blockbuster.

1 Type: www.blockbuster.co.uk into the address bar of Internet Explorer®.
2 You will need to register by clicking on 'Login' and then following the link for 'NEW USERS'. You will be asked for delivery details and your credit/debit card details for payment. The registration process may take a few minutes, but once registered you will be able to log in with your email address and password.
3 In common with other websites we have looked at in this book you can now either browse or search. You can browse by clicking on the links on the left, or you can search by typing what you are looking for into the search box.

4 In this case the search is for the film *The Great Gatsby*. Click on the arrow next to the search box.

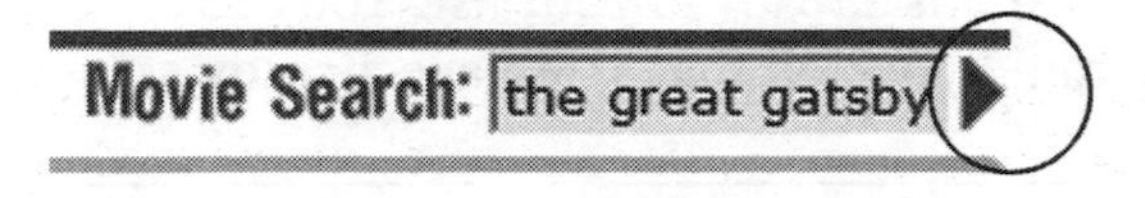

5 The results are then displayed.
6 Once you have found the film you want, you click on 'ADD TO LIST' and it is automatically added to the list of films that you want to see.

> **Hints and tips**
> The idea is to have 20 or 30 films in your wish list so that even if the film you want is out of stock, you can be sent a different one. You can adjust the priorities of the films if there are some you really want to watch sooner rather than later.

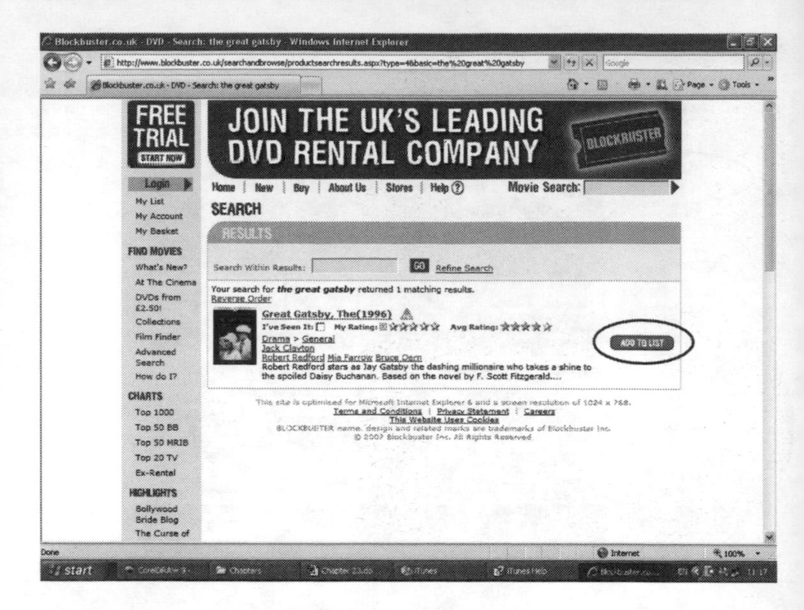

7 As time goes by you will need to add further films to your list. The 'ADD TO LIST' button changes to 'IN LIST – VIEW' if it is already in your list. You can also tick a box to remind yourself that you have already seen a film.

Summary

In this chapter we have discussed:

- Downloading and listening to music and other audio
- Downloading and listening to podcasts
- Using the Internet to buy CDs and DVDs
- Renting films over the Internet

25 dating online

In this chapter you will learn:

- how to find and register with an online dating agency
- how to search for potential dates
- how to contact potential dates
- how to set up your own profile
- how to stay safe

Aim of the chapter

This chapter will show you how to find and then join an online dating agency. You will be shown how to search the list of possible matches using different search criteria and then how to contact the people in whom you are interested. You will also need to create a fairly detailed profile about yourself. Finally, there is some advice on staying safe.

25.1 Introduction

There are literally millions of people using the Internet for dating purposes. One of the biggest in the world is www.match.com which boasts 15 million members in 240 countries. That's a lot of fish in the sea! There are many dating agencies to choose from and some of them specialize in particular interest groups or age groups. A quick **search** for "over 50s" + "dating agency" will provide you with plenty of possibilities.

They all work in a similar way:

- You register your details with the **website** and create a personal profile.
- The website stores the profiles of all the people who are registered.
- You search for the type of person you are looking for.
- The website shows you the profiles of everyone who is a possible match.
- You make contact (usually using email) with individual people.
- You establish a rapport using email, or maybe in **chat rooms**.
- You meet, you fall in love and live happily ever after.

25.2 Registering with a dating agency

Most dating websites will ask you to register your basic details with them (e.g. name and **email address**) before you can start using their site. They will usually let you search through and view members' profiles for free to see if anyone interests you. If you find someone you want to contact, you then need to subscribe to the dating agency in order to get the email address of that person.

> **Hints and tips**
> Dating agencies are commercial businesses and make their money by charging a subscription rate – usually around £12 to £20 per month.

Typically you might find that there are several people you want to contact and, once you are subscribed, you will be able to get the email addresses of any individuals in whom you are interested.

We are going to use Match.com as an example. All dating agencies will work in a similar way.

1 Type: www.match.com into the **address bar** of **Internet Explorer®**.
2 To register, click anywhere on the picture or where it says 'Make Love Happen'.

You are now asked for some basic information including the name that you want to be known by when using Match.com, an email address and **password**, and your gender and age as well as the gender and age of the person you are looking for. You are also asked for a postcode and the distance you would be prepared to travel to meet a potential date.

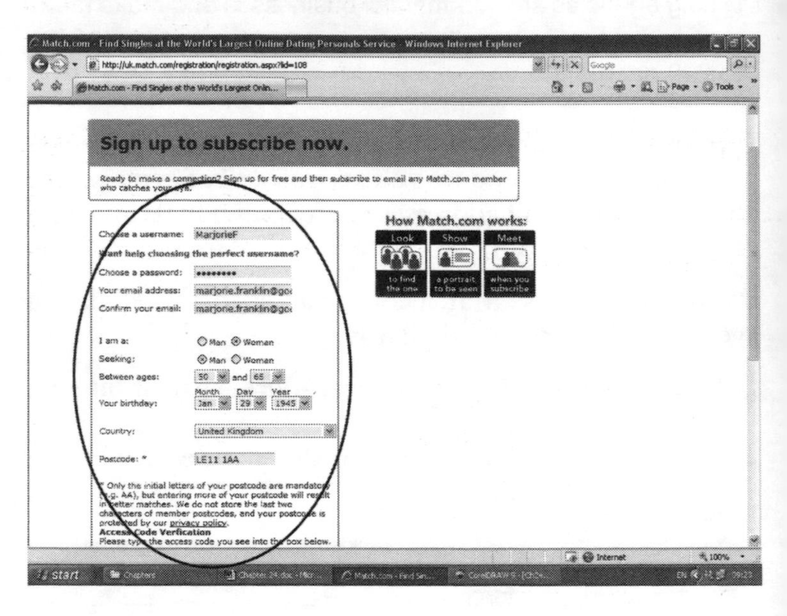

3 Complete the details and **scroll down** to the bottom to confirm.

25.3 Searching for matches and viewing their profiles

The next step is to search the dating agency site for your ideal date. You can do this in a number of ways depending on how picky you want to be. For example, you could search for all men within a 10-mile radius of where you live. Or you could be more specific and search for men aged between 55 and 60, who live within 10 miles and don't smoke, and have blond hair and are 5ft 8in exactly!

As you will see, the personal profiles are very detailed, so you can search for very particular characteristics if you want to.

1 To do a fairly simple search by age and area, click on 'My Match' at the top of the screen.
2 This will pick up the details you put in when you registered, although you can change them if you want to. In this example, the search is for men aged 50 to 65 who live within 50 miles of LE1 1AA.

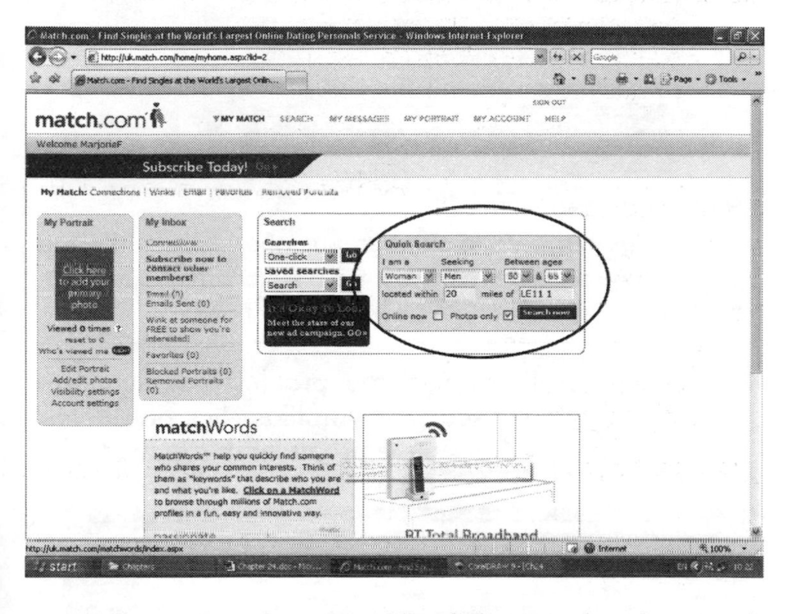

3 Click on 'Search now'. All of the people who match your criteria are now listed. This particular search has produced 17 pages of results, all of which contain 16 different profiles.

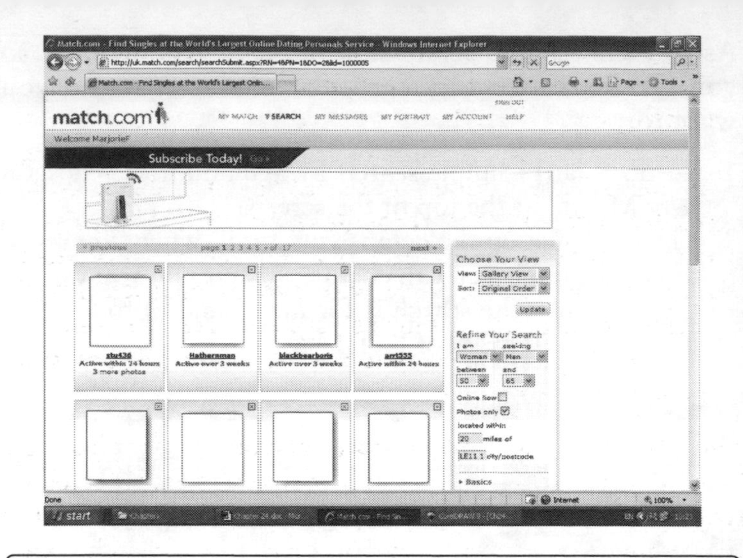

Hints and tips

You would normally see photographs of each person in the profiles here and later on. We have blanked them out in this book, because they might be married by now!

4 You can scroll through the profiles looking at the photos. If you see someone you like, click on the photograph. This will open the profile of this individual.

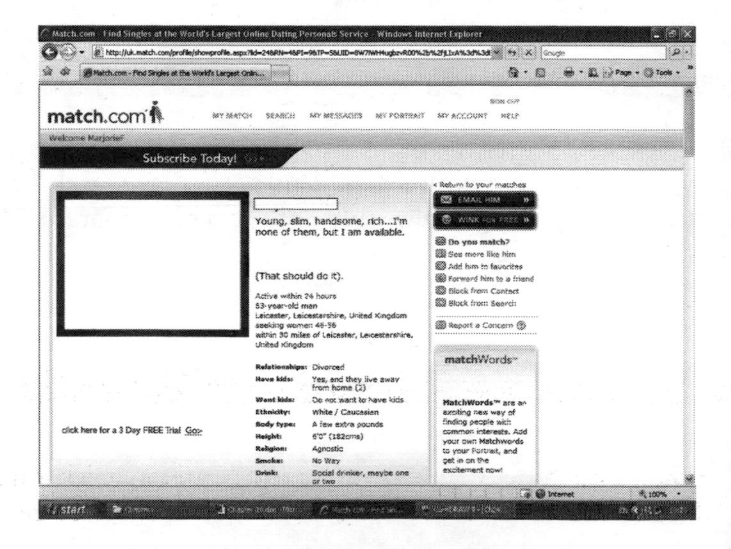

As you can see, the profile is very detailed and covers everything from physical characteristics to past relationships and lifestyle.

5 You need to take the time to read the profile, **scrolling** down, as there is quite a lot of it. You can go back to the results page and look through as many profiles as you like. Also notice that there is a **link** to 'See more like him' to find other people with similar characteristics. There is also a 'favourites' system like the one in Internet Explorer®, so that you can save profiles and come back to them later.

If you want to carry out a more specific search, click on 'Search' at the top of the screen. You will see this screen. You can now select very specific criteria to search on. In this example the search will find only people who are widowed or divorced and who don't smoke. Notice there is also a search box where you can type key words like 'fun loving'.

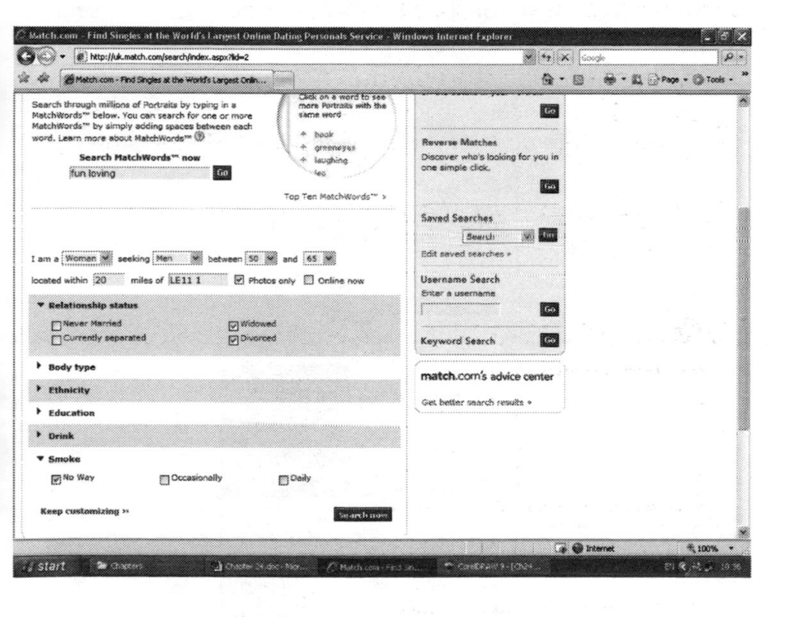

6 When you have put in your search criteria, click on 'Search now'. The results page will be shown as before,

but will show only people who match the specific criteria you have put in. Bear in mind that the more specific the search, the fewer people you will get.

7 You can now look through and view the profiles of these people as described before.

25.4 Setting up your own profile

As you have seen the profiles are quite detailed, and it does take a while to set them up. Having said that, the website does make it as easy as possible for you by prompting you with lots of questions that you then answer.

To set up your profile:

1 Click on 'My Portrait' at the top of the screen. You are now going to work through several screens completing different parts of the profile covering appearance, interests, lifestyle, background/values and a section where you can express yourself. You can also add a photograph.

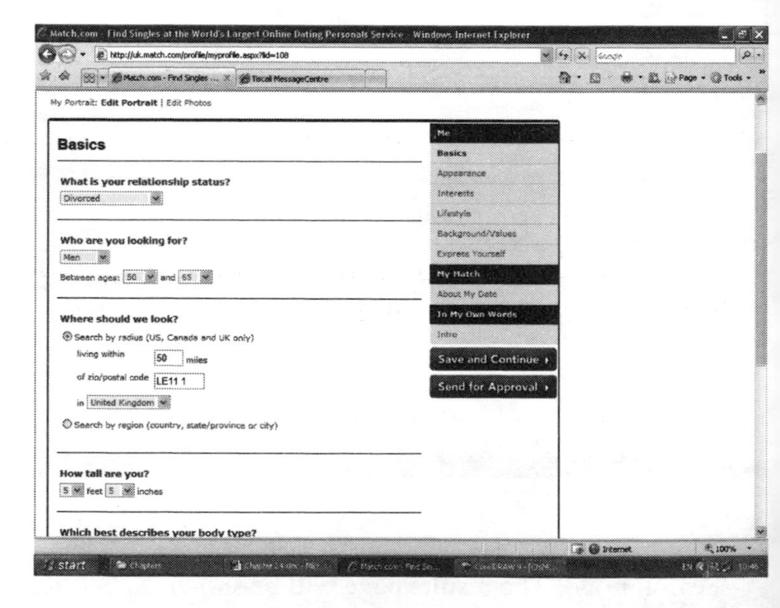

2 Complete the details on each screen (it is just like filling in a form) and click on 'Save and Continue' after each screen.
3 When you have finished with the personal profile, you will be asked for a photograph. You will need to have a photograph of yourself on your computer to do this.

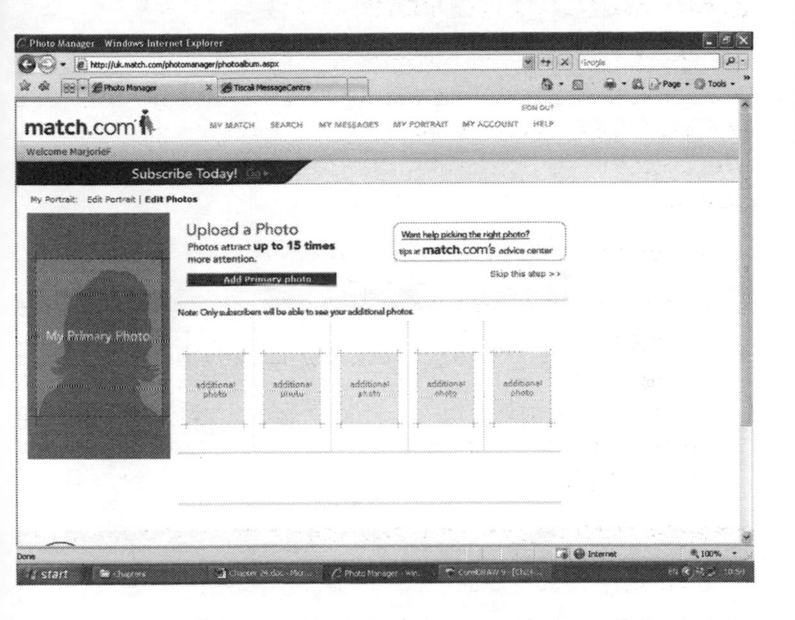

4 Click on 'Add Primary photo'.
5 Click on '**Browse**' to move to the **folder** where your photo is stored.
6 Click on the photograph and click 'Add photo'.
7 To view or edit your profile at any time, click on 'My Portrait' at the top of the page.

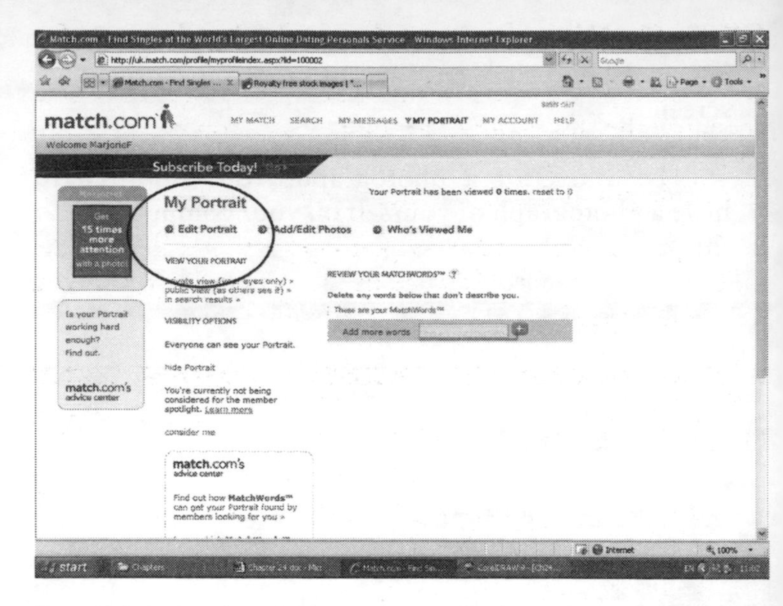

8 Click on 'Edit' if you want to change anything you have written.
9 Click on 'View' to see how your profile will be displayed.

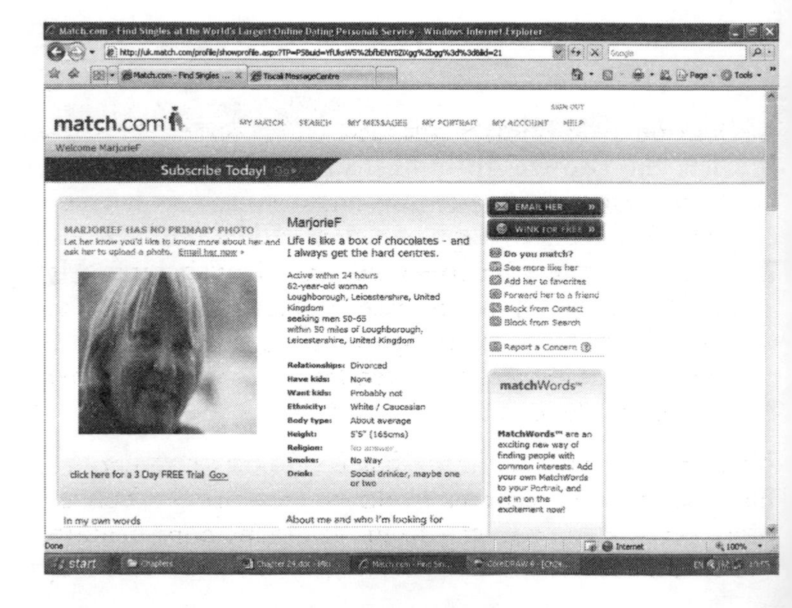

25.5 Getting in touch and staying safe

If you find people with whom you want to get in touch, then initially this is done through email. You have to subscribe at this point if you want to get the email addresses of people you want to contact.

1 To get an email address you click on the link at the bottom of the profile page of the person in whom you are interested.

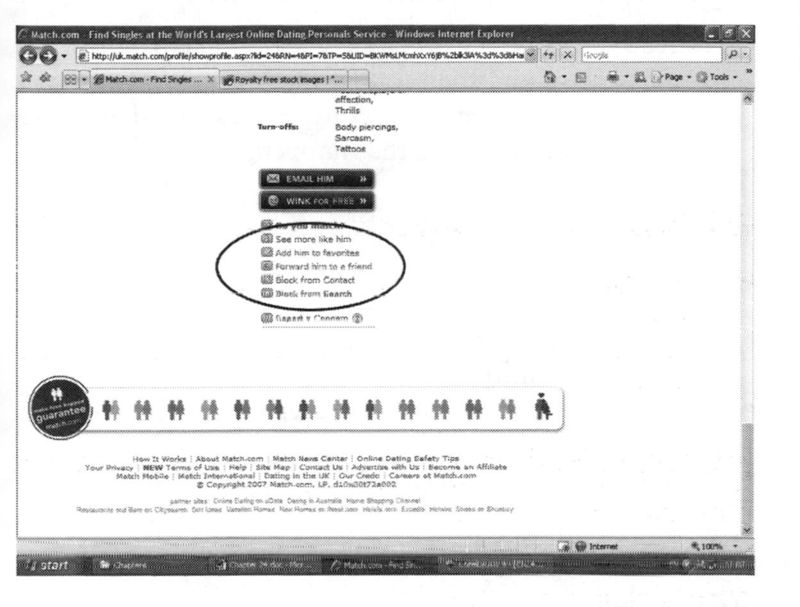

If you have not subscribed you will have to do it at this point, before you are given access to the email address.

2 People may also be contacting you having read your profile. To see if anyone has contacted you, click on 'MY MESSAGES' at the top of the page and it will show you if you have any emails yet. If you have you can then respond to these people, if you want to.

Up to this point, everything has been fairly anonymous, but once you get an email address, it starts to become more personal as you can begin an **online** conversation, which can develop in any direction you like. You may simply email each other and maintain an online relationship, or you may arrange to meet in an online chat room, or even exchange phone numbers and talk over the phone. If things go well, you may arrange to meet for real.

Obviously there is some risk attached to this as you are meeting people who you don't know and you need to exercise some caution. Most online dating services take personal security very seriously, as in this case. Match.com provides quite a lot of information on safety.

3 To read the safety information click on 'Help' at the top of the screen, and then follow the link to 'Safety tips'. There is also a 'Report a concern' feature if you are worried about anything that happens online.

The main tips for safety

When online:

- Stay anonymous until you feel confident enough to reveal your identity.
- Use sensible email names and **user names** (i.e. nothing provocative).
- Be honest in your personal profile and use a recent picture.
- Report anyone who is abusing the system.

When offline:

- Find out as much about the other person as possible before you meet.
- Arrange to meet in public.
- Tell a friend where you are going.
- Make your own travel arrangements.
- Watch your alcohol intake.
- Don't be pressured into anything.

On the whole, dating online is a fun and safe activity. Basically you just need to use your common sense as you would in any other aspect of your life. The best advice is to trust your instinct.

Summary

In this chapter we have discussed:

- Finding and registering with an online dating agency
- Searching for potential dates
- Contacting potential dates
- Setting up your own profile
- Staying safe

26 accessing websites designed for the over 50s

In this chapter you will learn:

- **how to find sites of specific interest to the over 50s**
- **how related websites are linked together**
- **how to use a portal website to link to other sites**

Aim of the chapter
So far in this book we have covered many of the typical uses of the Internet for the over 50s – everything from buying your groceries to finding your ideal partner. The purpose of this chapter is to have a look at some of the other common uses of the Internet among the over 50s. It will also explain the concept of a portal website, which acts as a link to other sites.

26.1 Introduction

The days when the Internet was for computer nerds and youngsters is well and truly over. A third of the UK population is now over 50 and more and more of the content of the Internet is now being targeted at this age group.

In this chapter we will cover everything from the arts to the zodiac. The idea of this chapter is NOT to give step-by-step guidance on how to access all of these websites but to list sites that might be of interest. Some of these sites have been designed specifically for the over 50s and some of them are designed for everyone to use, but will be of particular interest to the over 50s.

By now you will probably be quite used to searching the Internet, opening pages and following **links** and switching between pages. This chapter will be a good chance for you to put these skills to the test!

26.2 Portal websites

A **portal** is a particular kind of **website** that acts as a starting point for someone who is looking for information on the Internet. Portal sites usually have a particular theme. For example, many websites call themselves ‘portal sites for the over 50s’. This means that their website contains lots of information and lots of links to other websites that are of interest to the over 50s. If you can find a good portal site it can save you hours of Internet searching, because the portal website has already done the searching for you and listed useful sites in one place.

An example of a portal site, that we have already used in this book, is www.directgov.uk which is created by the UK government. As well as providing lots of information on public services, it also acts as a link to many other public services' websites. On its **home page**, you can see all of the links. Some of these links are to other pages on this site, but many of them will be links to pages on other websites.

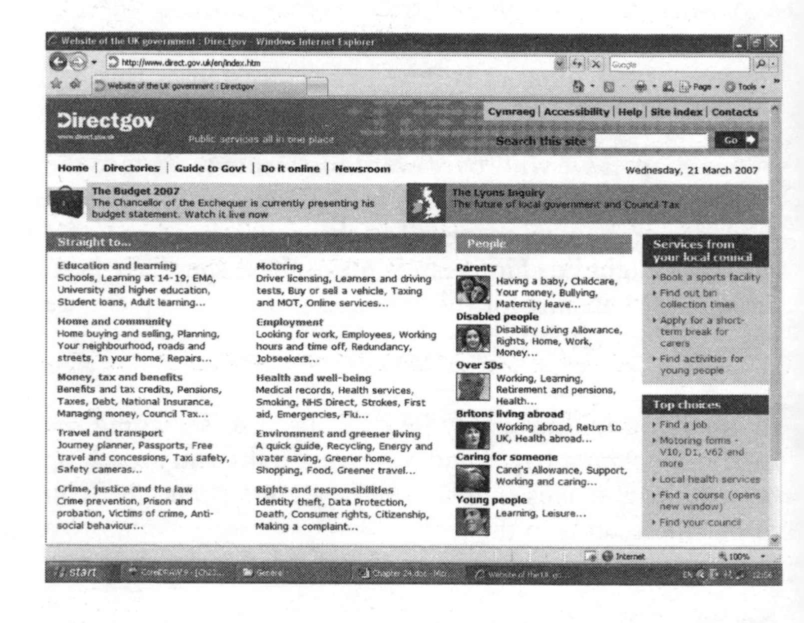

You can find over 50s portal sites by typing "over 50s" + portal into a **search engine**. Here is a typical example from www.myprime.co.uk which contains information and links specifically for the over 50s.

Follow the link to 'Directory', which in turn contains links to hundreds of other sites. These are categorized by topic, or you can click on their 'Hot Links', which will show you some of the most popular links that other people have used.

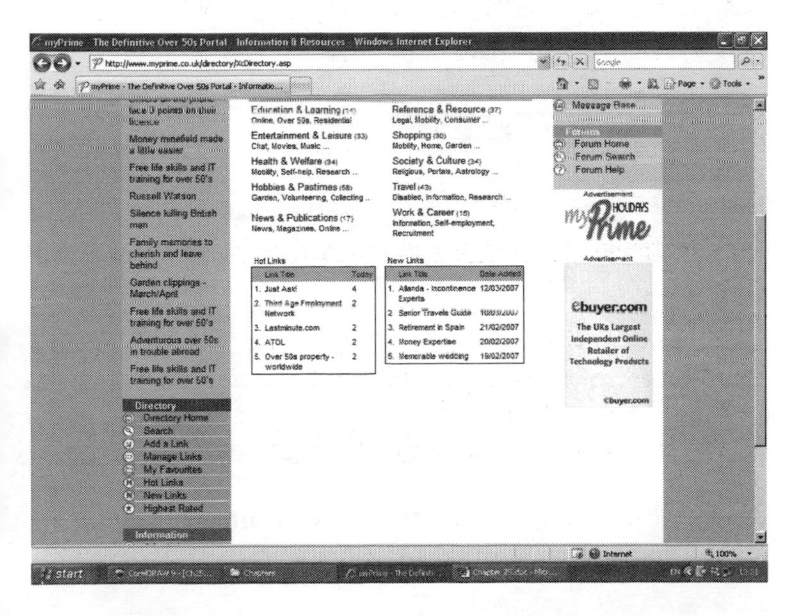

Other portal sites include:

- www.50connect.co.uk
- www.mabels.org.uk
- www.retirement-matters.co.uk
- www.seniority.co.uk

26.3 Links

You will often find that websites tend to have links to other related websites, even if they are not portal sites. For example, www.overfifitiesfriends.co.uk is an **online community** site where people can **post** profiles of themselves, join discussion **forums** and meet up locally in groups to take part in social activities. It also contains lots of links to other websites aimed at the over 50s. These links are to all sorts of sites including dating websites, other online community sites, and sites offering products and services for older people.

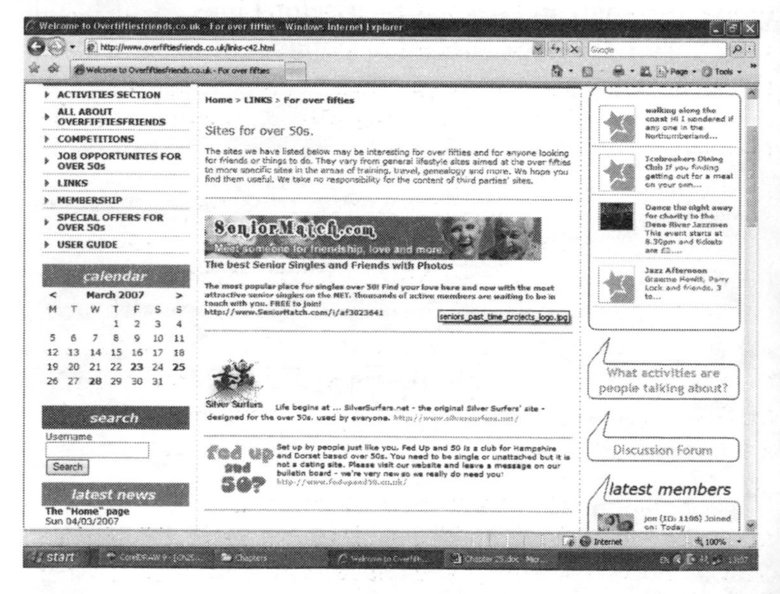

Once you find one good site, you will often find links to other good sites.

It is easy to lose track of which website you are in. Sometimes when you follow a link, it will open the **web page** in a new window. To get back to where you started you will need to click on the cross to close the new website. Sometimes the link will move you on to the new web page. You can use the 'Back' button in Internet Explorer® to move you back to where you started.

> **Hints and tips**
> Don't forget to add sites to your '**Favorites**' if you think that you will be using them regularly.

26.4 Choosing websites

There are millions of websites out there and new ones coming along all the time. Finding decent websites can be difficult. You can use a search engine to find sites, or you can ask family and friends what sites they use. Many of the national newspapers often print lists of useful websites, and it is possible to buy web directories, a bit like the yellow pages (although these can go out of date quickly). You can also get website directories on the Internet.

When you are viewing websites it is worth thinking about who owns the site and why they have it. Sometimes it's hard to tell who owns a website and why they have put it on the Internet. Many of the websites we have looked at are for government organizations or charities. Most are owned by commercial businesses and their motive is primarily to get you to buy something, so it doesn't hurt to be a bit sceptical at times.

Most websites tell you on their home page who they are and what they do. If it is not clear, try to find a link to 'About Us', which most sites have. There may be a main link to it or you may have to go to the bottom of the home page. The 'About Us' page should tell you who owns the site and what kind of organization it is.

This is the 'About FiftyOn' page for www.fiftyon.co.uk which is listed later on.

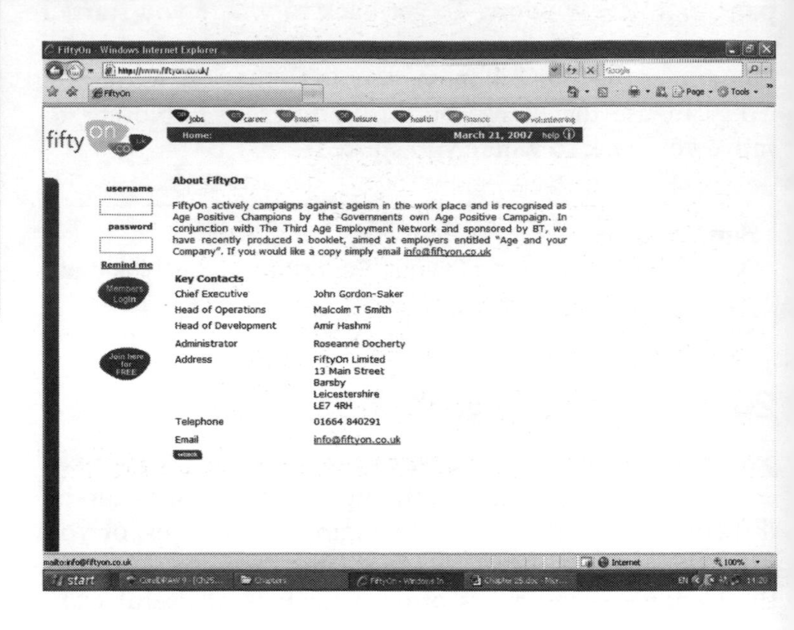

This makes it quite clear who is responsible for the site, and why they are running it.

26.5 Websites of interest to the over 50s

This section lists a small selection of websites that you might find useful, with a brief explanation of who owns the website and what it contains. We have tried to focus on general sites that in turn will contain links to more specialized interests. For example, the www.heyday.org website has links to topics such as health, money and work.

www.silversurfers.org.uk
Information relating to Silver Surfers week, which is run by Age Concern.

www.ageconcern.co.uk
The main website of the charity. Contains useful information about visual and audio aids when using computers.

www.wiseowls.co.uk
Information, advice and campaigns for the over 50s.

www.nhsdirect.nhs.uk/
Access to the services of the National Health Service.

www.saga.co.uk/
Company specializing in products and services for the over 50s.

www.dlf.org.uk/
Website of the Disabled Living Foundation.

www.heyday.org.uk/
Information on working, learning and living for older people.

www.bbc.co.uk/health/health_over_50/index.shtml
Pages from the BBC website specifically about health for the over 50s.

www.fiftyon.co.uk
Website primarily concerned with employment issues for the over 50s.

www.lifes4living.co.uk/
Online community website for the over 50s.

www.seniorconcessions.co.uk
Website that searches for discounts available for over 55s on a range of products and services.

www.theoldie.co.uk
Website of *The Oldie* magazine.

Summary

In this chapter we have discussed:

- Portal sites
- Following links
- Checking who owns a website
- Websites aimed at the over 50s

Chapters where the term is discussed are indicated by the bold numbers at the end of the definition.

address a way of identifying websites and emails (**9**)

address bar the place where you type in a web address, e.g. www.hodder.co.uk when using the Internet (**4, 9, 10, 12, 13, 14, 16**)

address book an option in email software where you can store lists of email addresses (**8**)

adware/spyware bad software that sets itself up on your computer when using the Internet (**3, 10, 16**)

attachment any file that is sent as well as an email, e.g. a photograph (**7**)

back-up a separate copy of your work usually saved onto a CD or DVD (**16**)

basket shows you what you have bought when you are shopping on the Internet (**21**)

blog a diary or journal on the Internet (**14**)

blogger someone who writes a blog (**14**)

blogging the process of writing a diary or journal on the Internet (**5**)

broadband high speed access to the Internet (**1, 11**)

browse a method of looking through information, usually by category (**3**, **9**, **13**, **19**, **24**)

browser software for looking at websites (**3**, **9**)

browsing the process of viewing web pages (**3**, **9**, **19**, **24**)

card a small plastic device inserted into a digital camera that stores the photographs (**2**)

CD-R a CD that can have information saved onto it once (**16**)

CD-RW a CD that can have information saved onto it over and over again (**16**)

chat room a place on a website where you can have online conversations with other people (**5**, **12**, **13**, **15**)

computer system the generic term for a combination of the hardware (equipment) and software (programs) (**1**, **3**, **11**)

cursor the small vertical line that flashes on the screen to show you where the text will go when you start typing (**4**, **6**)

dead link a hyperlink from a web page that does not lead to anything (**9**)

desktop the main way of using Windows® software – shows all the icons for the programs and folders on your computer. Also, a type of computer that sits on the desk (as opposed to a tower unit) (**4**, **5**, **9**)

device generic term for any piece of equipment that you can plug into a computer(**1**, **3**)

digital channels radio and TV stations that are available only in digital format, i.e. through the Internet, cable TV or Freeview, or DAB radio (**23**)

download the process of getting something from the Internet onto your computer (**1**, **3**, **5**, **9**, **11**, **15**, **23**, **24**)

DVD-R a disk that can have information saved to it once (**16**)

DVD-RW a disk that can have information saved to it over and over again (**16**)

eBay™ an online auction site (**19**)

email address a unique name that you use when emailing, e.g. marjorie.franklin@googlemail.com (**5, 6, 7, 8, 12, 13, 19, 21**)

email attachment *see* attachment (**7**)

email provider the business that provides you with access to email, e.g. Yahoo, BT, Tiscali, Microsoft (**5, 6**)

favorites (favourites) a method of storing web addresses for quick access at a later date (**10**)

file all information stored on the computer is stored in files, so a file could be a document, a slideshow, a photograph or any other kind of information (**4, 7, 8, 16**)

file-sharing websites that allow you to share files (usually music or video) with other people – often illegally (**15**)

filtering and blocking software software that prevents certain websites from being viewed (**15**)

filters devices that plug into the phone socket that allow you to access the Internet and use the phone at the same time (**1**)

firewall a method of stopping hackers getting access to your computer when you are on the Internet (**15**)

flatbed scanner a device for copying printed documents and turning them into a computerized version (**1**)

folder a place where files are stored on your computer, e.g. My Documents (**4, 6, 7, 8, 16**)

forum an online message board (**13**)

gigabytes (GB) a measurement of how much information can be stored on a computer (**1, 2**)

gigahertz (GHz) a measurement of the speed of a processor, that is, how fast the computer works (**1**)

hacking where someone gains unauthorized access to your computer – usually when you are on the Internet (**15**)

hard disk (HDD) a device inside the computer where all information is stored (**1, 2**)

hardware all the physical parts of a computer (**1**)

highlight the process of selecting text by clicking on it or dragging the mouse over it (**6, 10**)

highlighted shows when some text or an image has been selected (**6, 10, 16**)

history file a record of every website you have ever visited (**10**)

hits in a search engine, this shows the number of websites that are found when you type in some key words (**9, 14, 17, 18, 21, 22**)

home page the first page of a website that usually contains an introduction to the website and lots of hyperlinks to other parts of the site (**4, 9, 10, 11, 17, 19, 26**)

host a computer that stores websites, usually owned by big computer companies like Yahoo or Google (**13**)

Hotmail® the brand name of a web-based email service (**5, 12**)

hyperlink a link from a web page that leads to other web pages (**5, 9**)

icons small pictures used to represent different things (**4, 5, 6, 7, 8, 9, 10, 12**)

identity theft when someone pretends to be you with the intention of stealing from you (**15**)

inbox where messages are stored in email (**6, 8**)

ink cartridges	replaceable unit placed inside an inkjet printer that contains the ink (**1**)
inkjet	a type of printer that uses ink cartridges (**1**)
install	the process of adding new software or hardware to the computer (**5, 11, 12**)
instant messaging software	a program that lets you have online conversations with other people (**12**)
Internet Explorer®	software used to use the Internet. It is the brand name of Windows® Internet browser program (**3, 4, 10, 12, 13**)
IP address	the unique number that is assigned to your computer when you are on the Internet (**13, 15**)
iPod	a device for storing and playing music with headphones (**7, 24**)
Internet Service Provider (ISP)	the company that provides you with access to the Internet, e.g. Tiscali, AOL, Virgin, etc. (**1, 3, 5, 9**)
iTunes™	software used for downloading and organizing music from the Internet (**7, 24**)
jpg	a file format for photographs and other images (**7**)
keyboard	a device used to type into the computer (**1, 4**)
kilobits per second (kbps)	the unit of measurement used for Internet connection speeds (**1**)
laser	a type of printer (**1**)
link	*see* hyperlink (**5, 11, 12, 13, 14, 17, 22, 25**)
log on	the process of gaining access to a computer, or to websites. Usually involves typing in a password (**8, 18, 19, 21**)
maximize	making a window fill the whole screen (**4, 6, 8**)
media player	software for playing music and video (**3, 23**)

megabits per second (mbps)	the unit of measurement used for Internet connection speeds (**1**)
megabytes (MB)	a measurement of how big the computer's memory is (**1**, **2**)
megapixel	the unit of measurement used for digital cameras (**2**)
memory stick	a device that plugs into the computer and can be used for storing information (**2**)
menu	the words across the top of the screen in software that let you get at the various options. Menus also appear when you right click (**4**, **6**, **10**)
minimize	closing a window but leaving it available in the taskbar (**4**)
modem	a device needed for connecting your computer to the Internet (**1**)
mouse	a device used to point and click on things on the screen (**1**, **4**)
mouse pointer	the small arrow on the screen that can be controlled by moving the mouse (**7**, **9**, **10**)
multimedia	anything that combines text, graphics, sound and video (**14**, **23**)
newsgroup	a way of posting and reading messages on the Internet – organized into topics (**13**)
offline	Using your computer when it is NOT connected to the Internet (**24**)
online	using your computer when it is connected to the Internet (**8**, **11**, **12**, **13**, **15**, **21**, **25**)
online banking	doing your banking on the Internet (**18**)
online community	people with a shared interest who communicate with each other over the Internet (**14**, **26**)
online course	education or training that takes place entirely over the Internet (**21**)

online form the computer equivalent of a paper form that you need to fill in (**5**)

operating system software needed to make your computer work, e.g. Windows XP®, Vista™ (**1, 4**)

password a way of ensuring the correct person is using the computer (**5, 9, 11, 12, 15, 19, 21**)

PayPal a method of paying for something that you have bought over the Internet (**15, 19**)

peripherals any piece of equipment that can be used in conjunction with your computer, e.g. a printer or scanner (**2**)

personal chat one-to-one conversation with someone you meet in a chat room (**12**)

phishing where someone tries to get your bank account details from you via email, so that they can steal from you (**15**)

player *see* media player (**3, 23**)

playlist a collection of music (**24**)

podcast a self-contained voice, music or video broadcast delivered by subscription (**24**)

port a socket on your computer where something can be plugged in (**1, 2**)

post a comment added to a website or the act of putting a comment on a website (**13, 14**)

pop-ups windows that appear (usually advertising something) when you are using the Internet (**3, 16**)

portal a website that provides links to other websites of a similar topic (**25**)

premium dialler bad software that connects your computer to the Internet at £1.50 or more each minute (**15**)

progress bar a window that shows you how long it is going to take for something to happen (**11, 12, 16**)

random access memory (RAM)	computer chips inside your computer that store programs and data (**1**)
real-time	something that is instant or 'as it happcns' (**12, 13**)
resolution	the clarity of an image either on screen or printed (**2**)
restore	making a window bigger or smaller (**4, 6, 8**)
scanner	*see* flatbed scanner (**1**)
scroll down	moving down a page (**5, 6, 14, 17, 19**)
scrolling	the process of moving up, down or across a page (**5, 25**)
search	a method of finding specific information when using the computer (**9, 12, 17, 19**)
search engine	software for searching the Internet (**9, 10, 12, 13, 14, 17, 18, 22, 24, 26**)
secure site	a website that has extra protection for people making online purchases (**15**)
shortcut	an icon, usually on the desktop that opens a program or folder (**6**)
shut down	the process of switching off the computer (**4**)
Skype™	the brand name of a company that provides Internet telephone calls (**11**)
social networking sites	websites where people post profiles of themselves and meet other people online (**13**)
software	the programs that run on computers, e.g. Windows®, Word, etc. (**1, 3, 4, 6, 8, 11**)
spam	the email equivalent of junk mail (**3, 6, 16**)
sponsored links	links that are displayed in search engine results where the website owner has paid the search engine for the link to appear (**17**)
spyware/adware	bad software that installs itself on your computer when you are on the Internet (**3, 10, 16**)

standard email software a program stored on your computer used for sending and receiving emails (**5**)

start-up routine the process that your computer goes through when you switch it on (**4**)

surf informal term for the process of searching the Internet (**9, 17**)

tab like a tab that you might get in an address book or folder dividers in real life, a tab is used to move to another page (**7, 10, 15, 16, 19**)

taskbar the small bar at the bottom of the screen that shows which programs, folders and files are currently open (**4**)

toner powdered ink contained within a replaceable unit placed inside a laser printer (**1**)

trojan a type of virus that is hidden inside another file (**16**)

updates additions to software that provide new features (**3**)

upgrade the process of changing to the latest version of a piece of software (**3**)

URL an Internet address (**14**)

USB a method for connecting devices to your computer (**1, 2**)

USB port the socket on the front or back of the computer where you plug in a USB device (**1, 2**)

user name required for some Internet services along with a password so that you can access them (**11, 14, 15, 19, 21**)

virtual term that covers anything that happens on the Internet (as opposed to happening in real life) (**13, 21**)

virus bad software that installs itself on your computer and can cause damage to your computer (**3, 10, 16, 23**)

VOIP Voice Over Internet Protocol – allows you to make telephone calls over the Internet using your computer (**11**)

web address	the unique name used to identify a website (**9, 10, 12, 14, 22**)
web cam	a device that plugs into your computer and can be used to send moving images of yourself over the Internet (**2, 3, 11, 12**)
web page	a page of information on the Internet (**9, 10, 13, 14**)
web-based	a service that is provided over the Internet (**3, 5**)
web-based email	a service available on the Internet used for sending and receiving emails (**3, 5**)
website	several pages of information on the Internet (**9, 10, 11, 12, 14**)
wiki	a website where the visitor to the site can edit its content (**13**)
Windows® desktop	*see* desktop (**4**)
World Wide Web (www)	the collective name for all the websites and web pages on the Internet (**9**)
worm	*see* virus (**16**)

index

teach yourself

computing for the over 50s

bob reeves

- Are you unsure how to get the best out of your computer?
- Do you want to get up to speed with the IT revolution?
- Do you want to learn how your computer can help you in everyday, practical and creative ways?

Computing for the Over 50s focuses on a wide range of computer uses that are of particular relevance and interest to older computer users. Filled with clear instructions and supported with screenshots, tips, hints and a full 'jargon-busting' glossary, it assumes no prior knowledge of using a computer and takes the terror out of technology.

Bob Reeves is an ICT and Education consultant and a highly experienced writer on all areas of IT.